The Chains of the Prodigal Brother

How We All Became Slaves, and How Jesus Came To Set Us Free

by Brent Skilton

PRESS

To My Precious Rachel:

You are the frosting on my cake,

The peanut butter in my Reese's cup

The sugar in my coffee.

You are my greatest joy,

And my dearest friend.

Contents

—⁓—

Introduction

A Difficult Grace

—◦◦◦—

> One of the greatest challenges of the spiritual life
> is to receive God's forgiveness.
> Henri Nouwen/*The Return of the Prodigal Son*

W hy is it that God's grace is so difficult for us to accept?
We all know it is difficult to accept. Let's be honest
about this. We like to pretend that we actually believe we are
"saved by grace through faith," but when we are at our best
we feel like we have no need for grace, and when we are at
our worst, we cannot get ourselves to trust that God desires
to extend it. It is almost as if belief in grace has become
another religious hurdle for us to jump through, a concept
we affirm with our lips, but deny when moments later we
talk about what "God expects of us," or what "God requires
of us," or how "we have to do our part."

In fact, we often talk about grace as if it is something
dangerous. It is as if the entirety of Christian history has been
one attempt after another at arguing with Paul's bold and
unqualified proclamation of God's un-earnable esteem. We
fear that if people believe they don't have to work to earn God's
approval, they'll start sinning with abandon. Consequently,
we often find ourselves proclaiming the Doctrine of the

Asterisk. For instance, when Paul says in Ephesians that we are saved by grace and not by human effort, we feel we must place an asterisk with a footnote warning the reader that he still had better perform to some standard, or else. Still, there is no asterisk in the New Testament Gospel. And if God says in His Scriptures we are saved by grace and not by performance, then our fear of grace must point to some deficiency within ourselves, not a deficiency in God's grace.

The Bible never tells us grace is somehow deficient, or imperfect, or even dangerous. People might misinterpret grace, but that is the fault of people, not grace. If we let grace get the bad rap because of human failing, then we are letting human sin triumph over the power of God in our lives. After all, grace is the only way that sin's power over us is destroyed. When we try to substitute rule-keeping or religious performance for grace, we give up the foundation of true holiness. Paul tells us, "Sin will not rule over you, *because* you are not under law but under grace" (Rom. 6:14). Paul's statement means that to be "under law"—that is, to substitute rule-based life for grace-based life—is to empower sin. Only grace can bring true holiness, because only grace can transform us from the inside out. In fact the Bible says it is grace, not human effort, that instructs us in goodness (Titus 2:11-12):

> "For the grace of God has appeared, with salvation for all people, instructing us to deny godlessness and worldly lusts and to live in a sensible, righteous, and godly way in the present age."

Yet that brings us to another question: If it is God's grace that saves us, *and* trains us in obedience, why do we feel that we have to blunt it somehow? To rest on someone else's promise leaves one in a vulnerable position, to be sure. It means giving up our control to someone else. I wonder, is it possible that we have difficulty accepting the reality of God's unmerited love for us because it leaves Him in control instead of us? If that's the case, why are we so determined to be in control? If Someone who is infinite goodness itself offered to take care of you free of charge, and simply asked that you give up trying to take care of yourself, you'd be a fool to turn down the offer. The only reason you would turn down the offer, is if you didn't trust that Person to do right by you.

When I was growing up, I had no problem accepting and trusting my parents' grace for me. Whenever Dad took us out to eat, I never offered to foot the bill. Nor did I ever fear that, after the meal, he would suddenly spring it on me that I was expected to pay. Why would I fear something like that? Paying for the meal is what dads do, and eating the meal is what sons do. When I visited the emergency room with a broken jaw, the thought of paying the medical bill never crossed my mind. Mom and Dad would take care of it. And I never thought once of paying rent to my parents. To even try would be a perverse twisting of a loving relationship. When I went grocery shopping for Mom, I didn't pay for the items myself. I always used her debit card, and I even went so far as to add a few treats for myself, knowing she wouldn't object. All of these things speak of a child secure in the gracious love of his parents, a child who simply sees their grace for him as the basis of his life as a son. I knew that my parents desired to take care of me, and I hadn't much problem trusting their offer. In fact, until I left home, I never had a chance to live in any other way but by their provision.

But it seems so much more difficult to live by the provision my heavenly Father wants to give me freely. Why? An earthly father's grace towards his son is a natural and expected component of the father-son relationship. In fact, it is the foundation of the relationship: A father favors his child before the child is even born, long before he is old enough to earn his father's love. This all seems normal to us, and in fact if the father started out by not loving his child in this way, we would think there is something wrong with the father. Any father who will not love his child until the child does enough to earn that love, is twisted. If everything is as it should be, grace is what the father is supposed to give to his child, and the child is expected to live by the grace of his father's provision. Yet we have such a difficult time wrapping our minds around the fact that the same principle of grace applies for our relationship to our Father in heaven. Why?

Maybe a clue to the problem lies in the parable of the Prodigal Son. The older brother became incensed when his father freely welcomed the Prodigal Son back into the household. The older brother shook his fist at his father, angrily pointing to his own hard work that he thought would earn the father's love. For the father to freely accept the Prodigal Son back into the family, was an affront to the older brother's hard work to merit his father's favor. He had misconstrued the relationship as that of a slave to a master, rather than a son to a father. But the father told him, "You are always with me, and everything I have is yours" (Luke 15:31). It was not that the father was withholding anything from the older brother, but that the brother wasn't willing to receive it on the terms of grace. He would only receive what he could merit by his efforts. Why?

If we saw something like that in a son's relationship to his earthly father, we would have to conclude the son is very confused about what it means to be a son. Yet when we try to relate to our heavenly Father, we do the same thing. In fact, just as the brother had contempt for the Prodigal Son, we also sometimes chastise those who seek to relate to our heavenly Father simply as a broken recipient of His grace. We feel offended at their alleged free-loading, because we feel that *we* have done the hard work necessary to be accepted by the Father. Why?

Works are like a security blanket for the Christian who isn't comfortable getting something for free. It washes that humbling and vulnerable feeling away and replaces it with a self-deserving sentiment.[1]

Maybe like the older brother, we think of ourselves as slaves, when God wants us to be adopted as His sons and daughters. Maybe the idea of God as an eternal slave-driver has been so pounded into our thinking that we find it impossible to think of Him in any other way. In fact, it might be that we are born with that misconception, and it so infects every facet of our lives that even our loftiest sentiments are tainted by it. What if we have trouble accepting the grace God offers because we are born with the heart of a slave instead of the heart of a son? What if we don't trust Him to do right by us, apart from our control, because we have only ever looked at Him through the lens of slavery? What if we have trouble living in His embrace because we have an unwarranted fear of His lash?

It is instructive to realize that early Christians did not pray the same way we do today. We pray with our heads pointed down, our hands clasped. Tertullian described Christian prayer posture in the early third century this way:

Thither [to heaven] we lift our eyes, with hands outstretched, because free from sin; with head uncovered, for we have nothing whereof to be ashamed; finally, without a monitor, because it is from the heart we supplicate.[2]

Many archaeological discoveries, including art in the catacombs, affirm that Tertullian is not describing some exception to the rule. Rather, he is describing the common way that early Christians approached God in prayer. Our prayer posture today looks like that of a cowering slave, fearful and ashamed, waiting for his master to strike him with the rod, and pleading not to be beaten too harshly. But the posture in early Christianity was like that of a young child, holding out his hands, waiting for his daddy to scoop him up in his arms and hold him close. Tertullian said this prayer posture reflected the power of grace in the lives of early Christians: They prayed that way because they knew God held them guiltless and had taken away their shame. Have we lost something along the way, something that was central to the early Christian consciousness, but which has disappeared from modern experience? Could it be that we have lost sight of what it means to live in the grace of a divine Father who loves us deeply? Are we still living as slaves, while the early church knew what it meant to live as free children of God?

These are questions that demand answers. Everything depends on whether or not we have misconstrued the reality of grace. Grace is the one thing that separates Christianity from the world's religions, and if we misunderstand it, we misunderstand everything. If we think God wants us to be the Prodigal Brother, when He desires us instead to come to Him as the Prodigal Son, then ours is a case of mistaken identity so terribly grievous that it strikes at the very foundations of the universe. Such a misunderstanding would cause us to misinterpret who He is, why He created us, and what He wants from us. It would cause us to misunderstand the nature of the fall in Eden. It would taint our perception of Abraham and Sinai and the entire Old Testament. And worst of all, it would make us misunderstand the very nature of the death and resurrection of Jesus Christ. Such a misconception would sit like a veil over our faces, keeping us from seeing the glory of God even if He were right in front of us.

That is the point of this book, in fact: Humanity's chief problem isn't that we do bad things. Our chief problem is that, when God offers us His love freely, we find ourselves unable to accept it. And we reject His grace because we don't trust Him to do right by us. As we shall see in the chapters that follow, the problem of humanity is that we have chosen to live and think and act as slaves, when God made us for something far greater: The freedom and rest and holiness that come only by living in His grace for us. And, as we shall also see, God's solution to that problem was to come to us as an infant in a feed trough, live among us as a friend of the destitute and broken, pour out His blood for us at the hands of tyrants, and rise from His tomb to bring us into the freedom of His love.

Chapter 1

In Vino, Veritas[1]

—◦◦◦—

"Here you are, mother," said Bacchus, dipping a pitcher in the cottage well and handing it to her. But what was in it now was not water but the richest wine, red as redcurrant jelly, smooth as oil, strong as beef, warming as tea, cool as dew.

"Eh, you've done something to our well," said the old woman. "That makes a nice change, that does."

C.S. Lewis|*Prince Caspian*

The Apostle John begins his Gospel with a phrase that is scandalous to the religious world's way of thinking. The Prodigal Brother—the slave within all of us whose life is consumed with his religious observances and achievements and efforts—very much thinks that God's deepest desire is for us to conform to the right lists of rules and rituals and so on (if, like me, you often skip a book's introduction, you should look there to see whom I mean by "the Prodigal Brother"). In other words, the Prodigal Brother sees the rules, in some form, as the central point of everything. And that is why John's statement about Jesus is so difficult for the Prodigal Brother to deal with. In fact, you may live your whole life in some corners of Christendom and never

17

hear that statement mentioned in a sermon, and that statement is this (John 1:16-17):

> Indeed, we have all received grace after grace from
> His fullness,
> For although the law was given through Moses, grace
> and truth came through Jesus Christ.

Undeniably, John makes two earth-shattering assertions. First, John implies that grace is superior to the Law. That is not at all how the Prodigal Brother sees things. The Prodigal Brother will often talk about grace, but he only means God's grudging forgiveness of sins. The Prodigal Brother thinks God doesn't really, deep down, want to forgive sins, but that it is the only way He can find to give people a second chance at achieving righteousness by rule-keeping. In other words, the Prodigal Brother sees grace as secondary, or subordinate to, the rules. In his mind, grace is a mere tool God uses to get the rules to win out. But that is not at all how John sees it. He says that Jesus is better than Moses *because* of His grace: "We all have received grace after grace from His fullness."

Second, John plainly says that the Law lacked truth. Something can be true, yet not possess the fullness of truth. The rules do not fully reveal who God is, why He made man, and what He is seeking to bring about in man's life. Some people like to refer to the Decalogue as the "eternal moral law of God," even though the Bible never uses any language even remotely close to that. But John is saying that there is moral truth and goodness that is beyond the Law, beyond the Ten Commandments and the thundering of Sinai and all that. In fact, if the truth surpasses the Law itself, then it must go beyond the entire rule-based way of living that is embodied in the Law.

It is as if John was echoing Paul's sentiments in Romans 3:19-21. Paul said that in Jesus, a righteousness—God's righteousness—was revealed "apart from the Law." Paul speaks of a righteousness that is greater than religious ways of thinking, greater than rituals and lists of rules. Paul might as well have said Jesus revealed God's righteousness "apart from religion," for that is precisely what we find in the Gospels, and it is precisely the broad thrust of the entire Pauline writings. And in fact, Paul nearly did say that in Romans 3:21. In the Greek, he left out the definite article—so that it literally reads "apart from law"—not only apart from the regulations and formulas and lists of rules in the Law of Moses, but apart from that kind of thinking altogether. John and Paul are both stating there is some goodness, some beauty, some *truth*, which religion cannot touch.

The Restoration

In Hebrews 9, we find a discussion of the Old Covenant Temple services. The Temple was divided into two compartments, the *Holy Place*, and the *Holy of Holies*, or *Most Holy Place*. The priest could go into the Holy Place at any time, and would perform rites within that part of the Tabernacle or Temple every day. But he could only enter the Most Holy once a year, on Yom Kippur. Why? Because that was where God's presence would reside. The Jewish people—even the High Priest himself—did not have free access directly to God. They had to access Him through special externally-focused rules and rituals that acted as buffers between Him and them. Hebrews says of this (Hebrews 9:8-10):

> The Holy Spirit was making it clear that the way into the holy of holies had not yet been disclosed while the first tabernacle was still standing. This is a symbol for the present time, during which gifts and sacrifices are offered that cannot perfect the worshiper's conscience. They are physical regulations and only

deal with food, drink, and various washings imposed until the time of restoration.

What is this "time of restoration" that Hebrews is talking about? Context shows the "time of restoration" refers to the life, death, and resurrection of Jesus. But restoration of what? Evidently, restoration of the direct intimacy with God that we had rejected. It was because of that rejection that mankind could only approach God through the Old Covenant Temple services. But these services couldn't restore that intimacy. Man could not restore intimacy with God through religious observance, because religion only dealt with externalities and not the internal spiritual reality. Though men could not go directly into the presence of God, God Himself came directly to live with men. And that is very much the epitome of what grace is about. So it is really no mystery why John would say that grace was greater than the Law, that Jesus was greater than Moses.

Death and Freedom

I remember how surprised I was when I first really read 2 Corinthians 3. Paul referred to the Decalogue, not as "God's eternal moral law," but as "the ministry of death, chiseled in letters on stone," and "the ministry of condemnation" (2 Cor. 3:7, 9). In contrast, Paul referred to the life of the Christian as "the ministry of the Spirit" and "the ministry of righteousness." That was an earth-shattering assertion for me! If you have been raised in one of the many traditions touched by Covenant Theology's description of the Ten Commandments as the "highest standard of righteousness," then it would be earth-shattering for you as well. Paul is certainly saying that life in Christ is greater than observing lists of rules. The Prodigal Brother had me believe that the Decalogue was the point of it all, that it had been given to Adam in Eden, that

Adam had rebelled against it, and that Jesus came both to take the punishment for rule-breaking, and thus get us back on track in focusing on the rules.

But Paul indicates that the Law only demonstrated to man that he was terminally ill. It offered no cure. The curse could not be the total final truth of God. He did not make man simply so man could suffer and die generation after generation. And that must be why, in contrast, Paul calls the new ministry of Jesus, "the ministry of righteousness" (2 Cor. 3:8). Indeed, Paul's words in 2 Corinthians 3 look like a commentary on John's words in John 1:16 and 17.

Not only does Paul also call Jesus' ministry, "the ministry of the Spirit," but then he adds something quite profound: "Where the Spirit of the Lord is, there is freedom" (2 Cor. 3:8, 17). The God who brings freedom is not the god many people in Christianity are taught. They are usually taught about God as someone who demands proper and specifically-defined religious services, outward rule-keeping, and sullen seriousness. That is not at all freedom. In fact, it sounds a lot more like the "ministry of condemnation" that Jesus came to free us from.

But Paul writes of freedom or liberty throughout his epistles. In Romans 8 he speaks of the "glorious freedom of God's children." In Galatians 2 he speaks of men who "came in secretly to spy on our freedom that we have in Christ Jesus, in order to enslave us." In Galatians 5 he states that "Christ has liberated us into freedom," and then counsels us to "stand firm and don't submit again to a yoke of slavery." In fact, "Paul uses the term *eleutheria*, freedom, or one of its cognates frequently throughout his writings, some twenty-nine times in all—only a little less often than *soteria*, salvation, and its allied terms."[2]

The religious ways of thinking I had grown up with made me see freedom as akin to sin. I was taught that man desired freedom in Eden from his religious duties, and that was how sin had entered the human race. But Paul seemed to paint slavery to religious thinking as the basis of sin, and he painted freedom from those ways of thinking as the basis for true holiness.[3] When I began to realize this I began to feel like Neo in the Matrix, and I had just swallowed a pill and woken up in a cocoon to find the Matrix was all a cybernetic illusion. Or, as Paul put it (2 Cor. 3:12-18):

> Therefore having such a hope, we use great boldness—not like Moses, who used to put a veil over his face so that the sons of Israel could not look at the end of what was fading away. But their minds were closed. For to this day, at the reading of the old covenant, the same veil remains; it is not lifted, because it is set aside only in Christ. However, to this day, whenever Moses is read, a veil lies over their hearts, but whenever a person turns to the Lord, the veil is removed. Now the Lord is the Spirit; and where the Spirit of the Lord is, there is freedom. We all, with unveiled faces, are reflecting the glory of the Lord and are being transformed into the same image from glory to glory; this is from the Lord who is the Spirit.

Rediscovering Jesus

John and Paul had both seen something in Jesus that I had never noticed. To be honest, the religious Jesus I had grown up with wasn't really that appealing to me. I just thought of Him as a golden ticket into heaven. Life was a game of Monopoly, and Christianity was just a Get Out of Hell Free card, or actually a Get Out of Hell by Working card. So where did the New Testament writers find this freedom-loving Jesus whom they raved so much about? Where did

John and Paul see this Jesus of liberty, when so many can only find a Jesus of rules?

The answer is in the Gospel records themselves, writ large for all the world to see. I had merely missed it because my eyes had been trained to gloss over it and focus on only a few isolated proof-texts, rent sadly from their narrative context. But when the veil was removed, this Jesus of freedom and grace was on every page. John's Jesus is a great philosopher-king who stands against the philosophical foundations of the religious state, triumphs over it, and becomes its greatest intellectual judge. Matthew's Jesus stands up to the religious establishment of His day and declares, "I desire mercy and not sacrifice," or as we might paraphrase it today, "I desire grace, not religion." Luke's Jesus sets at liberty the captives and declares the antitypical year of Jubilee, the Jewish year of release when slaves would be set free and all work and toil and labor would cease. Mark's Jesus travels like the wind up and down the Levant, a tough-yet-tender man who takes care of the poor and sick, and gets in the face of the self-righteous and arrogant.

In the Gospels, there is an ethic of freedom for the down-trodden and hopeless and guilt-ridden, and an ethic of judgment against the proud and religious and self-righteous. The Apostle James characterized it this way: "God resists the proud, but gives grace to the humble" (James 4:6). And if you look for this principle, you can see it in action from the very start.

The Camel-Wearing, Locust-Eating Prophet

John the Baptist came as a Jewish Prophet, proclaiming the arrival of the Messiah right before Jesus began His ministry. John was not normal. He wore camel-skin clothes, and he ate locusts and honey. Locusts, you might be surprised to hear, are actually kosher for Jews, but that isn't the same as saying they are good food. Still, John thought they were, and I think that shows us something: John was a terribly fascinating individual. I wonder today if we, with our milque-toast definition of holiness, would be able to differentiate him from a raving lunatic on a street corner. He was simply one of the most interesting characters in the Bible.

John, like all Jewish Prophets, preached a call to repentance. The Greek word used in the Bible for *repenting* literally means to think differently, to change one's mind. It is not primarily a change in outward behavior. Now, in the process that obviously might cause someone to act differently, but doing a philosophical 180 is much bigger than merely trying to change behaviors. Specifically, John preached (Matt. 3:7-10):

> Brood of vipers! Who warned you to flee from the coming wrath? Therefore produce fruit consistent with repentance. And don't presume to say to yourselves, "We have Abraham as our father." For I tell you that God is able to raise up children for Abraham from these stones! Even now the ax is ready to strike the root of the trees! Therefore every tree that doesn't produce good fruit will be cut down and thrown into the fire.

Admittedly, this might sound like the same words you'd hear today from a fire-breathing fundamentalist preacher. But unlike the fundamentalist, John's call wasn't primarily to prostitutes or gays or the forlorn laity sitting in the pews, or anyone like that. Certainly they need Jesus just as badly as the modern fundamentalist does, but they weren't John's focus. John demanded repentance from religious types, Pharisees and Sadducees, the professional holy men of the day. They were widely revered for their Law-based holiness, at the same time that many Jewish people quietly despised them for their harshness and abuses of power. Imagine if someone toured the 100 most famous churches in America one Sunday at a time, stole the podium at every one and demanded that the congregation repent of its self-righteousness, judgmentalism, and rejection of grace. That was a bit like what John did in demanding repentance of those who were allegedly the most holy people in Israel. And imagine if John preached at those churches that all their supposed good works were actually terribly sinful, and instead they had better produce good fruit in the place of their religious works. Certainly those congregations would be dumbfounded. Similarly, the Pharisees must have been quite perplexed by John's call to repentance: If their assiduous Law-keeping was not good enough, what was this "good fruit" they were to produce? Clearly, God did not start off the new "ministry of righteousness" (2 Cor. 3:9) with a call to greater religiosity.

The Wild Vintner

John did not preach for long before Jesus came on the scene to surpass him. John, after all, was merely the royal bugler. Jesus began His ministry at a wedding in the town of Cana. Unfortunately the wedding feast had run out of wine. This, of course, would have been a huge embarrassment for the wedding family. I suspect they were relatives of Jesus, because His mother asked Him to do something about the wine shortage.

Jesus chose to solve the social *faux pas*, but the way He did it would have been quite scandalous. He ordered the servants to fill six jars with water, and then told them to take the water to the chief servant, the first century equivalent of a wedding coordinator. But the water had turned to wine, and evidently it was very good wine. The chief servant exclaimed, "Everybody sets out the fine wine first, then, after people have drunk freely, the inferior. But you have kept the fine wine until now."

On its face, this sounds like a kind thing to do, and indeed it was. But the greater impact of it doesn't become obvious until you realize what the jars were for: The jars were religious relics intended for "Jewish purification" (John 2:6). Jews would ceremonially wash their hands in water to symbolize purification, but Jesus had turned their holy water jars into celebratory wine barrels. It is no wonder that the Pharisees called Jesus a "winebibber"! (Matt. 11:19, KJV). As Bruxey Cavey states, "I was faced with an unexpected but undeniable fact: Through his first miracle, Jesus intentionally desecrates a religious icon."[4] In the place of dreary-hearted religious obligation, Jesus had brought "wine that makes man's heart glad" (Psalm 104:15).

But Jesus would not stop at merely putting wine into religious jars in the backwater of Palestine. John next shows Jesus going to Jerusalem for Passover, the joyous remembrance of the seminal event in Jewish history, the deliverance from slavery in Egypt. But in the Temple, He did not at all find the pure Jewish feast as it was meant to be. The Temple had been taken over by moneychangers, who would change the allegedly "defiled" Roman money into special Temple coins, no doubt at an exorbitant exchange rate. He found businessmen selling all kinds of animals for the sacrifices, turning a house that represented Israel's connection to God, into a place of religious abuse and economic exploitation.

And that is frequently what happens in religion. Too often, those who manage to climb to the top rungs of the religious ladder use their position to enrich themselves at the expense of those poor innocent souls who in all honesty just want to be accepted by God. The Prodigal Brother will dangle acceptance with God before others, telling them that if they just give enough to the Prodigal Brother, or do enough for his system, God will grant His favor towards them. The underlying ethic of human religion is that God's favor—His grace—is something to be bought or sold. Invariably, once the Prodigal Brother can convince others that he is God's chosen grace salesman, he will use religion to expropriate wealth for his own hand. The sale of indulgences in 16th century Europe was not a bizarre exception to the rule of the Prodigal Brother's world, but rather the logical destination of the path of religious thinking. What Jesus saw was most likely the same thing: the Prodigal Brother was selling the sacrificial animals, needed for the atonement of sins, at inflated prices, turning prophecy into profiteering.

What Jesus did never set well with me when I would read through the lens of religious thinking. It seemed so harsh, so wild and uncontrolled. He made a whip out of cords and began chasing the culprits across the Temple complex. In a fit of rage, He drove the animal salesmen out of the Temple and turned over the tables of the moneychangers. In disgust, He finally exclaimed, "Get these things out of here! Stop turning My Father's house into a marketplace!" (John 2:16).

If you have ever seen the Temple Mount in person or on television, you will know that it is no small place. It is, in fact, the size of a modern basketball arena. And there would have been thousands, perhaps tens of thousands, of Jews all clamoring to get in and out of the area so they could give the requisite sacrifices. This was no small act on the part of Jesus. It would be as if, during a tithe or offering call at the largest mega-church you can imagine, the speaker had begun to guilt-trip the attendees into giving more than they could afford, dangling God's grace as a reward (which is too often how it is done). Jesus stampedes into the service from out of nowhere. Twirling a whip around his head, He chases the speaker off the podium, and then takes out after the elders, the deacons, and even the pastor himself! At the end, He grabs the microphone and declares, "You will not sell My grace for profit!"

27

What of this Jesus who turns religious vessels into wine fountains, and then goes running around the Temple, cracking a whip and chasing people and turning over tables? Certainly there is a wildness to Him that was never mentioned in the religious circles I grew up in. It seems the Prodigal Brother wants his "gentle Jesus, meek and mild," because that Jesus is easy for us to control and manipulate and re-define to suit our purposes. That kind of Jesus is a Jesus whom the Prodigal Brother in us can easily dismiss, easily put back on a shelf when he is done with Him, and return to living life as a cold-hearted Pharisee. But this wild-hearted Jesus seems, not so much like the emotionless Jesus in the stained-glass pictures, but more like Bacchus, the untamed Greco-Roman god of wine and merriment, and his companion Silenus, who rides a donkey and brings joy and freedom wherever he goes. One of the earliest prophecies about Jesus sounds so very much like Bacchus and Silenus, that I cannot help but wonder if the Greeks stole that picture from the Old Testament (Gen. 49:11, 12):

> He ties his donkey to a vine,
> and the colt of his donkey to the choice vine.
> He washes his clothes in wine,
> and his robes in the blood of grapes.
> His eyes are darker than wine,
> and his teeth are whiter than milk.

But before that, we read (Gen. 49:10):

> The scepter will not depart from Judah,
> or the staff from between his feet,
> until He whose right it is comes
> and the obedience of the peoples belongs to Him.

Just as He wielded the fruit of the vine, He wielded a scepter, a rod, a whip of judgment. But Jesus did not turn His whip against the sorts of "sinners" that our religious mindset causes us to despise. He turned the whip on the Pharisees who oppress those "sinners" and hold them back from the grace of God. The Jesus taught me by the religious world was a complete contrast to John the Baptist. But the real Jesus of the gospels seems to be intellectually the same thing He was genetically: The cousin of that wild prophet.

True Goodness

This Jesus was not a Messiah who pushed people towards the trappings of religious life. Instead, He spent His time subverting the very foundations of religious thought. This, as I said, was not the kind of Jesus I had been taught about. The kind of Jesus I had been taught about was a tame, weak Jesus whose entire mission was to get humanity to conform to religious ideals, to live life as an exercise in rule-keeping, and to think of God merely in terms of the things we could offer Him to gain His favor. But in the Gospels we find a real Jesus who would chase that false Jesus out of the church with a whip. Indeed, I think He means to.

Yet this is not to say that Jesus was at all a libertine. There is a pure, primal goodness to Him that we cannot deny. It is a goodness that defies religious stereotypes of good and evil. He never comes close to true dissipation, and in fact the legalistic Pharisees were miles behind His holiness. Everywhere He goes He feeds the hungry and heals the sick. Yes, He speaks of hell fire. But like John the Baptist, His focus is not the "sinner," but the clergyman: The Pharisee and the Scribe.

Instead of directing men to live out life based on religious ways of thinking, He contrasts His new ethical teaching with the religious rules given at Sinai. In the Sermon on the

Mount, He gives a vision of a pure holiness that is intrinsic to the ideal man, instinctive and un-forced. The ideal holiness is foundational to a truly loving person, not brought about by that person's hard efforts to keep the rules. He contrasts His new commands with the ones given long ago, on Sinai. "You have heard that it was said," He declares, and He quotes a command from the Law. He adds, "But I say," and then quotes a new concept of righteousness, one that goes beyond the mere behaviorally-focused commands of religion and into the very heart of a person's identity. His new way of living is based on instinctively relating to people out of the fundamental value God has given to every individual.

His new commands seem to be founded on one over-arching principle: Grace. He describes grace as an ethical foundation in its own right, an ethic that first comes to a man from God, and that a man then lives out in his life to others. After all, He tells us to love, not only our friends, but also our enemies, because that is what God does. "He causes His sun to rise on the evil and the good, and sends rain on the righteous and the unrighteous" (Matt. 5:45). That is grace, the favor and blessing that comes to us before we have done anything to earn it, and despite everything we have done to deserve the opposite. Immediately after He describes the grace that God gives the unrighteous, Jesus commands us, "Be perfect, therefore, as your heavenly Father is perfect" (Matt. 5:48). God's grace constitutes the core of His perfection, and if we were like God, grace would be the basis of our relationships with others.

But how can a human being love his enemies? Quite frankly, it seems humanly impossible. Love must genuinely exist in a person's heart long before he acts it out in his relationships. So where on earth do you get that love for someone who hates you? You can't force yourself to love a friend, let alone an enemy. Either you have love, or you don't. Perhaps that is why Jesus said we must all be "born again." Maybe that is the key to Jesus' understanding of true goodness: "Love is from God, and everyone who loves has been born of God." (1 John 4:7).

But this whole business of love is the central problem Jesus' teachings pose to religious thinking. Religion sees good actions as a thing we do to win God's favor or secure some greater blessing from Him. Religious thinking seems to come from the idea that doing good—keeping the rules—will make you good. Jesus' teaching goes in the opposite direction: In order to be like God, you must have His love inside of you. You cannot do good in order to get His love. You must have His love in order to do good. In that sense, you must first *be good* before you can truly *do good*.

Woe to *Whom*?

After giving the Sermon on the Mount, Jesus goes on to illustrate how grace triumphs over the righteousness of human religiosity. He twice declares, "I desire mercy and not sacrifice," once in Matthew 9, and again in Matthew 12. And right in the middle, in Matthew 11, we find Him boldly pronouncing judgment (Matt. 11:21-24):

> Woe to you, Chorazin! Woe to you, Bethsaida! For if the miracles that were done in you had been done in Tyre and Sidon, they would have repented in sackcloth and ashes long ago! But I tell you, it will be more tolerable for Tyre and Sidon on the day of judgment than for you. And you, Capernaum, will you be exalted to heaven? You will go down to Hades. For if the miracles that were done in you had been done in Sodom, it would have remained until today. But I tell you, it will be more tolerable for the land of Sodom on the day of judgment than for you.

Tyre and Sidon? Sodom? To His Jewish audience, these cities were the embodiment of Gentile licentiousness and defilement. Yet Jesus was saying it would be better for those pagan cities on Judgment Day than for the highly religious, rule-keeping Jewish cities of Chorazin, Bethsaida, and Capernaum. Even today, Sodom stands as a symbol of sexual perversion. We sometimes derogatorily refer to homosexuals as "Sodomites." Jesus did not argue that Sodom was fault-less. But certainly there was something about self-righteous religiosity that was even more offensive to Jesus than the sexual corruption of Sodom.

Later in Matthew, we find Jesus again heaping scorn on the religious leaders of his day. Eight times he says, "Woe to you," and two in particular stand out (Matt. 23:25-28):

> Woe to you, scribes and Pharisees, hypocrites! You clean the outside of the cup and dish, but inside they are full of greed and self-indulgence! Blind Pharisee! First clean the inside of the cup, so the outside of it may also become clean.
>
> Woe to you, scribes and Pharisees, hypocrites! You are like whitewashed tombs, which appear beau-tiful on the outside, but inside are full of dead men's bones and every impurity. In the same way, on the outside you seem righteous to people, but inside you are full of hypocrisy and lawlessness.

Isn't that the way it is in religion? Isn't the focus so often on keeping up a good external face? Don't we try hard to clean the outside of the cup and dish, convinced that doing so will somehow make God love us more? The term *hypo-crite* doesn't mean someone who says one thing and does another. It means "stage actor," and it refers to someone who merely does things for external show without having a true internal holiness.

But what Jesus said shortly thereafter about judgment seems to really bring the house down on religious ways of thinking. He said (Matt. 23:37):

Jerusalem, Jerusalem! The city who kills the prophets and stones those who are sent to her. How often I wanted to gather your children together, as a hen gathers her chicks under her wings, yet you were not willing!

We were not willing? The Prodigal Brother had always told me that the problem was that *God* was not willing to receive us, so Jesus had to bear the brunt of His anger so that the Father could feel better about us. Jesus, the thinking goes, had to extend grace as a stop-gap solution because *we* refused to live up to our religious obligations. But the way Jesus paints it, the central problem is that *our* desire for religious obligation keeps us from receiving the grace *He* always wanted to extend.

A World of Religion

Religion isn't relegated to church buildings. When we think of religious excesses, we think of the murder and theft of the Crusades, the destructive hatred of modern Islamic radicalism, the irrational injustice of the Salem Witch trials, and even the bizarre kamikaze imperialism of Japanese Shinto in World War II. But religious thinking isn't limited to those who believe in the supernatural. Wrote Philip Yancey:

I know of no legalism more all-encompassing than that of Soviet communism, which set up a web of spies to report any false thinking, misuse of words, or disrespect for communist ideals. Solzhenitsyn, for example, spent his years in the Gulag as punishment for a careless remark he made about Stalin in a personal letter. And I know of no Inquisition more severe than that carried out by the Red Guards in China, complete with dunce caps and staged displays of public contrition.[5]

The Marxist believed that he could use the power of the state—the law or the rules, if you will—as a means to expunge evil from human nature and bring humanity into a glorious new utopian existence. Likewise, the Nazi believed that he could use the power of force to rid the world of genetic defects and thus bring about a race of supermen. In fact, if you look at Nietzsche, Hitler's intellectual inspiration, you find that his argument was that man just had the wrong set of rules: Instead of Jewish or Christian ethics, Nietzsche said we needed to abide by a set of ethics compatible with Darwinian thought. And if man did that, he would usher in a new golden age. That seems to be the universal promise of religious thinking: If we could only find the right set of rules, and work to conform our behaviors to them, all our problems would be solved.

What Do I Still Lack?

But Jesus didn't see things that way. A rich and powerful religious ruler came to Jesus one day. Some have speculated that it was actually Nicodemus, but the Bible doesn't say. He asked Jesus, "Teacher, what good must I do to have eternal life?" (Matt. 19:16).

Jesus responded with a mysterious question and a cryptic answer, "Why do you ask Me about what is good? There is only One who is good" (Matt. 19:17). The young man, it seemed, was asking entirely the wrong question. He saw goodness as something he gave to God, and in return God would grant him eternal life. Goodness was, in his mind, an economic transaction, just like his other business dealings. But Jesus stated that goodness is only found in God. Man cannot have a goodness apart from God which he can render to God in return for God's favor. But that is unfortunately how religion sees goodness: Not as a gift God gives to us from His fullness, but as a gift we give to God from ours.

Jesus continued, "If you want to enter into life, keep the commandments" (Matt. 19:17). This seems in a sense, to contradict what Jesus had just said. I think the contradiction was clearly intended, because to Jesus' statement the man responds, "Which ones?" (Matt. 19:18)

There were 613 commandments in the Law given at Sinai. To try to achieve life by keeping all of them would be a daunting task, and that seems to be the point Jesus was making. So Jesus responds by listing several members of the Decalogue with an extra command from Leviticus 18: "Do not murder; do not commit adultery; do not steal; do not bear false witness; honor your father and your mother; and love your neighbor as yourself" (Matt. 19:18, 19).

It is the young man's response to this statement that shows the point of the discussion. He says, "I have kept all these. What do I still lack?" (Matt. 19:20). Despite his careful rule-keeping, the man knew he still came up short. It is as if Jesus told Him to keep the commandments specifically because that would cause the young man to see there was something in him that he still didn't have. That something, it appears, was perfect goodness. The man could not achieve goodness by doing good things.

If we might in any way conclude that Jesus was trying to tell the man to gain acceptance before God by keeping the rules, we need only read how Mark describes Jesus' demeanor. Jesus did not look at him in judgment because he could not measure up to the religious bar. Rather, Mark says poignantly, "Then, looking at him, Jesus loved him" (10:21).

Jesus replied to the rich man, "If you want to be perfect go, sell your belongings and give to the poor, and you will have treasure in heaven. Then come, follow Me" (Matt. 19:21). Perfection is not something that can be achieved by careful commandment keeping. Jesus had already spoken of God's perfection as a perfection characterized by grace, and that is how He responded to the young ruler. He told the young ruler to give all his possessions to others, and then follow Him. The man had always trusted in his possessions, in his own efforts and works. The man's religious life merely reflected that same mercenary ethic. Jesus, in contrast, told the man to give up his trust in himself and instead rely on Jesus' provision for His needs. Jesus indicated that perfection comes, not by Law or "religion," but by a trust in His grace to provide for us what we obviously lack.

The Knowledge of Good and Evil

The young man wanted the knowledge of what good he must do in order to gain eternal life. I wonder very much if this story would have reminded Matthew's Jewish audience of another story, thousands of years earlier, in a beautiful and perfect Garden. It was a story where God offered two people eternal life, free of charge, and they instead chose to gain that same life by their "knowledge of good and evil." It almost seems as if Jesus was pushing the man toward the realization that the "knowledge of good and evil" does not actually bring life or perfection. Jesus told him to keep the commandments, in the hope that the man would attempt as much, find that he still lacks something, and then come to Jesus for what he could not gain by his efforts.

It was this realization of who Jesus was and how He reacted to religious ways of thinking, that got me to question much of what I had been told. The Prodigal Brother teaches that Adam and Eve's sin was a sin of shirking religious duties, of desiring to be free of religious obligation. That, the Prodigal Brother says, is what the Devil offers us. In contrast, the Prodigal Brother always told me that God required religious acts and behaviors of us, and that it really couldn't be any other way. God was a God who demanded gifts from us, not who gave them to us freely. In the Prodigal Brother's understanding, Adam and Eve wanted grace, but God offered only religion. Adam and Eve wanted mercy, but God required sacrifice.

And yet, God came to this earth announcing, "*I* desire mercy and not sacrifice." He was fellowshipping with "tax-collectors and sinners," (Matt 9:11), and the religious crowd heaped scorn on Him for doing so. What did He say? "I didn't come to call the righteous, but sinners" (Matt. 9:13). I had always thought God wanted those who were righteous: If you did the right things, then God would prefer you over those who did not. But Jesus said quite the opposite, and I had to wonder why. Could it be that He preferred sinners because they couldn't deny their need for grace? Is that why He said, "I desire mercy and not sacrifice"? Could our problem be that we desire sacrifice—religion—instead of God's grace?

The Prodigal Brother

Hanging in the Hermitage in St. Petersburg is a 6-by-8 foot painting by renowned artist Rembrandt van Rijn. It tells a tender story: A young man, in tattered rags, is kneeling with his back to the artist. And an older man, in the fine clothes of royalty, is bent over the younger man, embracing him with a look of serene compassion and joy on his face. The name of the painting is *The Return of the Prodigal Son*.

That painting captures the vital essence of Jesus' well-known parable. The younger son requests his inheritance early, leaves home to live a life of drunkenness and debauchery, and finds himself in the end as a pauper who wishes he could eat as well as the pigs he's tasked with feeding. So he decides to return to his father's house in hopes of being hired on as a slave. At this point, the story does not differ much from religion. Indeed, all religion has some concept that man must work to repay a debt, his squandered inheritance. Were a Pharisee to tell the story, the young man would be made a slave, and he would be required to earn back every drachma his father had given him. Sure, some tellers might have the father forgiving a tenth, or maybe even a half, of what the boy had wasted, but Jesus went much further than that.

On his way home, the young man finds his father running out to meet him. As Jesus so gently put it, "But while the son was still a long way off, his father saw him and was filled with compassion. He ran, threw his arms around his neck, and kissed him" (Luke 15:20). Rather than require him to repay his lost inheritance, his father won't even give him the chance to offer his services as a hired hand. Instead, the old man directs the servants to slaughter the fattened calf and prepare a grand celebration.

Then Jesus added something that would sound terribly out of place in the religious world. He said, "So they began to celebrate," or in the King James Version's eloquent Elizabethan prose, "And they began to be merry" (Luke 15:24). In fact, Jesus described the festivities as "music and dancing" (v. 25). Did Jesus demonstrate the same principle with the Prodigal Son that He showed at the wedding in Cana? Did He see the point of His mission as one of joy and freedom, where the religious water of our attempts to be accepted as slaves was to be replaced with the rich red wine of reconciliation and merry-making?

Certainly that version of Jesus, the Jesus who brings celebration and freedom and the wine of reconciliation, is not the Jesus many of us have known. So perhaps we've missed the entire point of the parable of the Prodigal Son.

Perhaps we have forgotten that the parable doesn't end with a party, but with another, older son.

That son was not laying about or cavorting with prostitutes. He was out dutifully working in the field when the news of his brother's return came to him. He was trying to earn his place in his father's house. The servants told him that his father was planning a great party to celebrate his brother's return. Perhaps the audience expected the brother to be just as overjoyed as the father, so perhaps what Jesus said next would have surprised them: "Then he became angry and didn't want to go in" (Luke 15:28).

He was angry? Why? The son was angry because of the absurd nature of his father's grace. He said to his dad, "Look, I have been slaving many years for you, and I have never disobeyed your orders, yet you never gave me a young goat so I could celebrate with my friends. But when this son of yours came, who has devoured your assets with prostitutes, you slaughtered the fattened calf for him" (Luke 15:29-30).

He "didn't want to go in." The older brother was incensed by his father's grace. He couldn't accept grace, and therefore *he*, the older brother, didn't want to go in to the celebration. The Prodigal Son had returned, and now the older brother had become a Prodigal himself, leaving his father's house and letting a party of grace go to waste because of his pride. This Prodigal Brother seems a bit like Jerusalem, the city who killed the prophets and would not come to God so He could protect them like a hen protects her little chicks.

In his own words, he had "been slaving" his entire life. He thought he was a slave, not a son. He was working himself to death in order to earn his father's approval. The older son had been hoping that his father would throw him a party, even killing merely a young goat, to celebrate his perfect obedience and hard work. He saw his father's love as something he could earn by always obeying his father's orders and slaving in his fields. His entire life, he had misconstrued his father's desire for him.

The father replies to the older son, "You are always with me, and everything I have is yours. But we had to celebrate and rejoice, because this brother of yours was dead and is alive again; he was lost and is found" (Luke 15:31-32). If the older son had wanted a young goat, or in fact even the fattened calf, all he really had to do was ask. The father said, "Everything I have is yours." The reason the Prodigal Brother didn't receive a party was that he sought it by means of his own slaving works, rather than by trusting in his father's grace. In place of the feast of grace, he wished to substitute his own cheap efforts. The parable doesn't so much tie up with a nice ending, as hang with an open question: Will the Prodigal Brother repent of his pride and come back home like his younger brother? Or will he stay away from grace and go off like his brother to live in "a distant country"? Will we?

The Sons of Effort and Promise

The Parable of the Prodigal Son makes me think of another two brothers whom Paul references in his epistle to the Galatians. He writes (Gal. 4:21-26, 28-30):

> Tell me, you who want to be under the law, don't you hear the law? For it is written that Abraham had two sons, one by a slave and the other by a free woman. But the one by the slave was born according to the flesh, while the one by the free woman was born as the result of a promise. These things are illustrations, for the women represent the two covenants. One is from Mount Sinai and bears children into slavery—this is Hagar. Now Hagar is Mount Sinai in Arabia and corresponds to the present Jerusalem, for

she is in slavery with her children. But the Jerusalem above is free, and she is our mother.

Now you, brothers, like Isaac, are children of promise. But just as then the child born according to the flesh persecuted the one born according to the Spirit, so also now. But what does the Scripture say?

"Throw out the slave and her son, for the son of the slave will never inherit with the son of the free woman."

Paul represents the Law as Hagar, the slave mother of Abraham's son Ishmael. Ishmael, the son of a slave woman, was born by Abraham's human efforts to bring about what God intended to give to him freely. And Paul says that those who are under the Law are under slavery, when God intended men to be free of a life lived to religious ways of seeing the world. Ishmael was not the free child God intended for the promise. Ishmael was a slave whom Abraham tried to substitute for God's promise. It seems Paul is saying that the slavery of religious obligation wasn't really what God wanted, but what man chose as his own substitute for God's grace. And so Paul exhorts the New Covenant churches of Galatia to "throw out the slave and her son."

Getting Our Wires Crossed

But all of this has to make us sit back and take notice. To hear the Prodigal Brother tell the story, the problem was that Adam and Eve chose freedom when God demanded religion. Allegedly, the problem was that we had chosen the wine of merriment and joy when God had offered the water of religious duty. The problem was that we had chosen to live freely in grace, when God wanted us to have a knowledge of good and evil, and seek life by those commandments like the rich young ruler. The problem was that we had chosen celebration—killing the fattened calf—when God wanted us to be out slaving in the fields. The problem, as we had all been taught, is that we wanted to live freely like Isaac, when God wanted us to live like Hagar and Ishmael, as slaves to human effort.

A man is known, not only by the company he keeps, but by the enemies he makes. When Jesus came, His greatest enemies were not the down-and-outers. They seemed to know that the only chance they had of real life was His mercy. His enemies were those who wanted to foist religious obligation, moral debt, guilt, and condemnation on themselves and others. The Prodigal Brother's traditional way of looking at this cosmic slugfest becomes quite problematic in light of the revelation of God in Jesus Christ. We are to believe that in Eden God came demanding religious duty as the means of living in His love, and Satan came offering freedom from that religious duty. Then, half-way through the dispute, God and Satan suddenly switch sides, and God is offering grace and freedom, while Satan, in the form of the scribes and Pharisees, is offering bondage and religious condemnation.

Simply put, the Prodigal Brother's interpretation is silliness. It does not hold together. God does not switch sides in the middle of a battle. He is not a traitor to Himself. Something else must be going on, and to find out what it is, we must go back in time to the beginning of time itself.

Chapter 2

The Genesis of Grace

—◦◦◦—

God is most glorified in us when we are most satisfied in Him.

John Piper|*Desiring God*

There is something wonderful about the creation story,
something that its original recipients would have
rejoiced in, but which doesn't exactly impact us the same way
today. I learned it while watching one of those "Mysteries
of the Bible" documentaries on the History Channel. The
scholars spoke of how the Jewish creation account differed
markedly from the creation accounts of other religions of the
time. Other religions had the gods creating man in order to
be their slave, to build their buildings and work their fields
and generally do back-breaking work their whole lives, in
order to please the gods and thus win a special reward.

That is not at all how the creation account begins. The
creation account begins with a God who makes everything.
But then, perhaps inexplicably to the readers of the time,
God freely gives everything He made to man. Yes, man was
instructed to take care of the Garden, but he was to do so
for his benefits. He reaped the rewards of his care-taking. In

Athens, Paul described it to the pagan Greeks this way (Acts 17:24-29):

> The God who made the world and everything in it—He is Lord of heaven and earth and does not live in shrines made by hands. Neither is He served by human hands, as though He needed anything, since He Himself gives everyone life and breath and all things. From one man He has made every nation of men to live all over the earth and has determined their appointed times and the boundaries of where they live, so that they might seek God, and perhaps they might reach out and find Him, though He is not far from each one of us. For in Him we live and move and exist, as even some of your own poets have said, "For we are also His offspring." Being God's offspring, then, we shouldn't think that the divine nature is like gold or silver or stone, an image fashioned by human art and imagination.

Worlds Apart

The difference between the Jewish and pagan creation accounts is quite profound. The pagans, like the Athenians, viewed man as a slave created to give the gods everything they needed and required. Man was created to toil away for the gods, to offer them special services, special offerings, and so forth. If man was good at this, he received a special blessing from the gods. In other words, the pagan view was of gods who created man to live in religious obligation.

But the Jewish view was entirely different. God created everything and, before man had any chance at all of earning it, God gave it completely over to man. He declared man to have dominion over everything, and gave man everything in creation for man's enjoyment. God had favor on man before man had merited it at all. Christianity has often defined grace as "unmerited favor," and it is precisely this unmerited favor that we find in the beginning of the creation account. We find a God who created man to live by His grace.

The triune God said to Himself, "Let us make man in our image, in our likeness" (Gen. 1:26: Notice He didn't say "images" or "likenesses"—God is one Being, one essence in three persons). What God said is precisely the opposite of what the pagans thought. As Paul preached in Athens, the pagans thought the gods created us to make a shrine to them for them to dwell in, or idols for them to represent themselves to us. Then, we were to serve that idol or shrine in a temple. But, in contrast, the Biblical account has *God* making *man* in His image.

This implies many things. Most of all, it implies that man is primarily a spiritual being, because, as Jesus said, "God is spirit" (John 4:24). Now, bread and water can feed the body, and ultimately the mind insomuch as our gray matter uses food too, but who can feed the spirit? "Man does not live on bread alone but on every word that comes from the mouth of the LORD" (Deut. 8:3). Man, made in God's image, requires God's revelation of Himself in order to truly live. We don't mean merely pulse and breath and thought, but joy and love and peace! Man was made to live in the grace of God, to live in His love, as God reveals His love to man:

> God designed the human machine to run on Himself. He Himself is the fuel our spirits were designed to burn, or the food our spirits were designed to feed on. There is no other.[1]

Six Days of Grace

In the first chapters of Genesis, the Bible relates the story of God creating man and his world. It is a very fascinating

45

story. The point of the story isn't merely that God made things. This He did indeed do, but the *how* of the matter shows a much deeper point that we often fail to recognize. The point of the Bible isn't just the physical world, but the broader spiritual realities it represents.

The creation story starts with God, of course, but it starts by assuming something was there that had been made before, the earth, but only in a basic rock form that wasn't much to look at (Gen. 1:1-2):

> In the beginning God created the heavens and the earth.
> Now the earth was formless and empty, darkness covered the surface of the watery depths, and the Spirit of God was hovering over the surface of the waters.

On the first day, God created light and darkness, and called the light "day" and the darkness "night." On the second day, God created the sea and sky by separating water from air (what this means I don't fully understand). On the third day, God created the land by collecting the waters into bodies apart from the land. He also made plants, which He later pointed out (vs. 28-30), were primarily meant for food.

Then, on day four, we find Him creating the Sun, the Moon, and the stars. If you are a bit confused at this point, you are paying more attention than most usually do. God created light and darkness before the Sun and Moon. In this, modern scientific man finds a contradiction. This alleged contradiction isn't really meant to be a contradiction at all. Rather, it is meant to show us the broader point of what God did. Moses wasn't so stupid as to not realize that light came from the Sun. The ancient Egyptians, who gave him the best education available in the world at that time, knew that light came from the Sun. You can see that fact depicted in their artwork. The Bible argues that the actual mechanism of God's act of creation is in a sense incomprehensible to us. That, for instance, was one of God's statements to Job. The point isn't to figure out the mechanics of creation, but to understand how God used it to get a bigger idea across.

This isn't to say God used some form of "theistic evolution." It is to say that God is an artist, and when He does something literally, He is also being symbolic about it. In the words of the band Jars of Clay, He is begging us to "see the art in Me." We cannot fully understand God's work of creation. It really is too big and awesome to comprehend. We are merely meant to be awed by it. But to be awed by the bigger picture, we must consider the next two days.

On day five God created the fish and the birds, and on day six He created the land-based life-forms, and man. There is a pattern in all this that is often missed. It is this pattern that shows why the Old Testament is such delightful literature. I have included it in the table below:

First Three Days	**Last Three Days**
Day One – Light and dark, day and night	Day Four – Sun, Moon, and stars to have dominion over day and night.
Day Two – Sea and sky	Day Five – Aquatic animals and birds
Day Three – Land and vegetation to eat	Day Six – Land-based animals and man

If we ask too many silly questions that are beside the point, we won't actually get the point. This is what too many do when they read this. The question about the Sun, Moon, and stars is one of these silly questions. But it is the most important silly question, because in it we see the beauty of what God is trying to explain, the beauty that goes beyond the exact form.

In each of the first three days, God creates a reality, and in the next set of three days, he creates a thing to live in that reality. The story of creation, above all else, is the story of God's grace. He graciously gives us everything we need to live, and this is what He wants us to understand above all else in this story. So the problem with the Sun, Moon, and stars is dealt with by seeing that He is trying to explain how He provides something in which all things live, by His grace. The Sun, Moon, and stars are created for a purpose, and that purpose is to have dominion over day and night, to mark them off.

The Purpose of the Ages

To understand Scripture, you must ask yourself to whom it was first written, and why. Once you see what it meant to them, you see what it means to us. The book of Genesis was first written by Moses to the children of Israel after they were freed from bondage to the Egyptians and given the Law at Sinai.[2] The primary point was to show the Israelites their special place in God's design. These Israelites were given several feasts, like Passover, Shavuot, Yom Kippur, the Feast of Tabernacles, etc. When Moses records the creation of the Sun, Moon, and stars, he says, "They will serve as signs for festivals and for days and years" (Gen. 1:14). Now, even though Moses refers to the festivals, no one, especially not Moses, is proposing that people kept Passover or Shavuot from the beginning of creation onwards. That would be silly. Moses himself records that the feasts weren't given until the Israelites were freed from bondage to the Egyptians.

Passover, especially, makes this clear. It is a recollection of the time when God caused the Angel of Death to visit the Egyptians and kill their first-born sons, finally propelling them to let the Israelites go (you must remember these were cruel slave masters to whom He had already given nine previous warnings). This simply would have made no sense to Adam and Eve. They were never in bondage to the Egyptians. They had nothing to commemorate in this. In fact, they didn't even know at that time what death was, as the second and third chapters of Genesis explain.

Rather, Moses is showing that even at creation God was thinking forward and creating a purpose and history for Israel, and then for all humanity. In fact, if you read carefully, you will find a number of similar themes throughout the early chapters of Genesis, for instance in the discussion of Noah's son Shem and Noah's grandson Canaan. I won't go into them, because it is more fun to find them on your own.

Man was made for a purpose. That is what the fourth day tells us. God provides a means to mark days and years, implying history. Man needs a purpose. And that ultimate purpose is to seek God throughout history. That was what the Sun, Moon, and Stars were for, to mark history. Or as Paul put it, God has "determined their appointed times... so that they might seek God."

But what, exactly, is the over-arching purpose of God? Scholars consider Ephesians the most transcendent and overpowering of Paul's epistles. In this I have to agree. It is truly beautiful. While Paul's epistle to the Roman Christians contains a highly detailed systematic theology of redemption, Ephesians goes beyond this, putting redemption within the context of God's "purpose of the ages." In Ephesians 3, Paul discusses his apostolic ministry, interpreting it through the definition of God's eternal purpose for us (Eph. 3:8-15):

> This grace was given to me—the least of all the saints!—to proclaim to the Gentiles the incalculable riches of the Messiah, and to shed light for all about

the administration of the mystery hidden for ages in God who created all things. This is so that God's multi-faceted wisdom may now be made known through the church to the rulers and authorities in the heavens. This is according to the purpose of the ages, which He made in the Messiah, Jesus our Lord, in whom we have boldness, access, and confidence through faith in Him. So then I ask you not to be discouraged over my afflictions on your behalf, for they are your glory.

For this reason I bow my knees before the Father from whom every family in heaven and on earth is named.

Paul defines his ministry as piece of God's "purpose of the ages," or "eternal purpose" as some translations have it. He says that He prays for the churches in Ephesus "for this reason," the reason of God's eternal purpose. In the next few sentences, Paul defines God's eternal purpose by stating what he prays for (vs. 16-17a):

I pray that He may grant you, according to the riches of His glory, to be strengthened with power through His Spirit in the inner man, and that the Messiah may dwell in your hearts through faith.

God's eternal purpose is for us "to be strengthened with the power of His Spirit in the inner man, that the Messiah may dwell in your hearts through faith." God's eternal purpose is to dwell within us. This is possibly what Genesis meant when it said God made man in His image. God desired man to be a living shrine to Himself, a living Temple in which He Himself would dwell and thus His image would be all over creation. He intended this as part of His desire for an intimate relationship with humanity. Paul explains how the fullness of this reality is accomplished by God in His grace (vs. 17b-19):

> I pray that you, being rooted and firmly established
> in love, may be able to comprehend with all the
> saints what is the length and width, height and depth
> of God's love, and to know the Messiah's love that
> surpasses knowledge, so you may be filled with all
> the fullness of God.

To be filled with the fullness of God—to come to the full measure of living in and by God's indwelling—we must come to comprehend the incredible, majestic, and over-whelming power of God's love. We don't come to the fullness of what God desires by seeking to know external principles of right and wrong, or external scientific facts, or anything of the sort. Through one of his usual linguistic puns, Paul says that we are filled with the fullness of God when we come "to *know* the Messiah's love that surpasses *knowledge*." We don't come to the fullness of God's purpose by knowing or doing the right things, but by living in His love.

God's eternal purpose for man is not primarily ethical or intellectual, but existential. To "know" the love of God that surpasses "knowledge," means to know it, not by the derivation of principles and concepts, but to experience it, to comprehend it, not primarily via our minds, but in our spirits by relationship with God. The work of the mind, and by extension the body, then flows from the spiritual foundation of faith. To exist is more than to know. To exist in God's reality, His love, is far more than mere "knowing" can ever be. It is the basis out of which our "knowing" develops. Frank Viola explains God's eternal purpose like this:

> It is the heart of the biblical story, the meta-narrative
> (overarching story) of holy writ. The Father obtains a

bride for His Son by the Spirit. He then builds a house in which He, the Son, and the bride dwell together in the Spirit. The Father, the Son, and the bride live in that house as an extended household and they have offspring by the Spirit. The offspring constitutes a family, a new humanity called "the body of Christ."[3]

The Bible uses the three metaphors of bride, house, and offspring, to describe God's eternal purpose for us. We were created to be the bride of Jesus Christ, His one true love. We were created to be the house in which Jesus dwells. We were created to be His offspring, born again by the Spirit of God. God does not want slaves. God desires a family.

That part about offspring is particularly meaningful to me: Man was meant to live every moment in God's love, like a toddler living every moment under the gentle loving care of its mother. In fact, God wants this so much that He wants to live, not next to us, but *within* us, communing every moment with us. The best way to understand how God intends us to live, was shown me by Wayne Jacobsen. If you picture yourself a two-year-old, being held in the great strong arms of a loving Daddy, and resting your head on His chest, completely contented and safe from all harm, then you are beginning to understand what God's eternal purpose is for you. In fact, Paul says that because of Christ, we are brought to refer to God, not simply as "Father," but as "Daddy" or "Papa" (Rom. 8:15, Gal. 4:6).

A Comprehensible Picture of the Incomprehensible

We must completely settle this in our heads. Until we accept that God's eternal purpose is for us to receive His love as His bride and His children and His home, then none of the rest of this book will make sense to us. Nor will the Scriptures, or even life itself. No matter what else we have been taught about God, the Spirit Himself says this is why He made us. We see this when God first talks to man in the Garden (vs. 28):

> God blessed them, and God said to them, "Be fruitful and multiply; fill the earth and subdue it; have dominion over the fish of the sea, over the birds of the air, and over every living thing that moves on the earth."

Note something important here. Before giving them any commands, God first blesses them. To bless, in this sense, is to demonstrate and declare your favor to someone. This is what God does. We find this when we find Him later looking over His creation and declaring that "it was very good" (Gen. 1:31). On each of the days before He made Adam and Eve, He only saw that it was good. It wasn't until He made Adam and Eve that God saw that it was *very* good.

As we said, Adam and Eve had done nothing to earn God's favor. This is central to understanding the entire Bible. God simply chose, separate from their ability to merit it and in a way we cannot fathom, to find favor in them. This is what we mean by grace. So when God blessed Adam and Eve, He was explaining to them His grace.

When I was young, I used to build airplanes out of Legos. I would make them very detailed, as close as childly possible to the actual proportions and structures I observed in planes on TV. They were never color-coordinated because my blocks were all different colors, but still I liked my planes very much. I would look at them and find them favorable to me.

The thing is, these planes did nothing to earn my favor. They couldn't. Because I made them, there was nothing in them that I couldn't fulfill in myself. In a strict sense, I didn't need them. They were simply an act of my creative abilities. So when I looked at them and found them favorable, I was actually enjoying *myself*, enjoying being me, in a very simple way that I didn't really think about. I didn't think about it as enjoying myself, because my focus was on the planes. This, I think is a little bit of how God's grace works. God's grace, in its most basic form, is God enjoying *Himself*, and thus finding favor in us by extension.

If you find this just a little bit hard to comprehend, that's because it is. It *is* incomprehensible. As Karl Barth said, "Grace is the incomprehensible fact that God is pleased with a man, and that man can rejoice in God. Only when grace is recognized to be incomprehensible is it grace."[4] If you think you have a handle on the majestic, overwhelming awesomeness of God's grace, then you haven't even begun to grasp it.

Now, grace is an odd thing. In fact, as was said, it is incomprehensible. Somehow, by God declaring His pleasure in man, and man trusting in that declaration of His pleasure, man somehow then becomes the very thing that is pleasurable to God. This is confusing because God is simply different than us. We cannot really understand Him.

God's eternal purpose is for man to live in His love, by Him dwelling within us. This can only happen if man trusts that God finds pleasure in him, that God actually *likes* man and *wants* to live inside of him. In so accepting this, man exercises what is called "faith." Faith means, in a sort of way, trusting in God and His grace. Once God is allowed to dwell in man, by man accepting God's grace, then God's eternal purpose for man will be fulfilled. We will talk about this story called "grace" and "faith" more when we get to Abraham.

The Divine Attributes

It's important not to think too hard about *why* God takes pleasure in us. We cannot fully grasp that. The Bible calls it a mystery, something that God reveals to us, but even when He reveals it to us, we still can never absolutely get it. A baby girl may not know exactly *why* her daddy seems so enthralled with her, but nonetheless, she knows, or should know, that he is.

Similarly, God does indeed take pleasure in us. This isn't something He has to work hard to convince Himself to do. It is simply Him being Himself. Grace isn't just something God does or thinks. Grace is who God is. Theologians say grace is an "attribute" of God. His attributes are different from traits in me. A trait is some component of my nature. But a divine attribute is simply who God is when He is being Himself. He is all His attributes at the same time. This is probably what He meant when He told Moses His name is I AM. A.W. Tozer explains it quite well in his book *The Knowledge of the Holy*:

> Love, for instance, is not something God has and which may grow or diminish or cease to be. His love is the way God is, and when He loves He is simply being Himself. And so with the other attributes.

On the Sixth Day, God Created Sex (And Some Other Things)

Once God had communicated His favor by "blessing" Adam and Eve, He then invited them to enjoy all the great things He had made for them. He told Adam and Eve to be fruitful and multiply. I think we know what this command is all about. God has a very high opinion of sex. He has much higher a view of it than our modern humanists think they have. In fact, He wrote an entire book of the Bible about it, called the *Song of Solomon*. I challenge you to read it without blushing.

But the Bible's understanding about sex goes beyond merely the act. God sees the act as both physical and spiritual, something that occurs within space and time but also transcends it. You can see now why the Bible sees sex, true sex as God intended it, to be so very good. God sees the commitment to love that surrounds the act as the thing that makes it so truly wonderful. Without that, sex just isn't what it should be. In fact, without that, sex is the opposite of what it should be: It becomes a selfish, meaningless act.

God tells them to multiply because God is very fond of children. In fact, He seems to like them more than adults, and to be honest I don't really blame Him. When God came to earth in the person of the Son, He said to those who tried to keep little children from Him (Luke 18:16-17):

> Let the little children come to Me, and don't stop them, because the kingdom of God belongs to such as these. I assure you: Whoever does not welcome the kingdom of God like a little child will never enter it.

In God's "command" to be fruitful and multiply, we don't find a "do this or else incur My wrath" sort of thing. After all, I seriously doubt that Adam and Eve ever had to struggle to keep this particular command. Instead, in this command we find God explaining the wonderful things He has given us and inviting us to enjoy them.

God then commanded Adam and Eve to "fill the earth." God enjoys mountains and rivers and valleys and deserts and oceans and prairies and trees and flowers and grass and animals and so forth. Perhaps this is why, when He came into the world in the person of the Son, God chose fishermen as His chief comrades-in-arms. So God is telling Adam and Eve to see the beauty He had made for them. He is telling them to enjoy His physical creation to its fullest.

He told them to "subdue" the earth. God is a gardener. That is why He made a garden in the beginning. Much later, we find one of Adam and Eve's sons, Cain, killing one of their other sons, Abel. Cain was a farmer, and after killing Abel he went on to found the first city. The Bible does not at all consider this transition from farming to city life a positive thing. It is not that God doesn't like cities. It is actually not a problem with cities themselves, but a means by which God communicates something that has gone horribly wrong with humanity: Man was made to be part of nature, to be in that sense "wild." But because of his sin, he became apart from nature in some way. He became "civilized," and not in the good way that we sometimes mean it.

"Subduing" the earth wasn't like modern farming. It wasn't back-breaking, sweat-producing labor. The Bible says that came later, when Adam and Eve decided not to live in God's grace anymore. The Bible refers to this "subduing" the earth as cultivating and keeping the Garden (Gen. 2:15, NASB). It was more like a leisurely, cool, sunny spring afternoon spent in the garden trimming plants and planting seeds and watering. I think this is sort of what God meant. He is telling man and woman to enjoy the Garden together. He made the Garden for their pleasure.

He then tells them to rule over the fish and birds and land animals. When God tells them to rule, He means for them to rule as He rules. He doesn't mean exploiting others to fulfill our selfish desires. He means providing for the animals, taking care of them, and enjoying their company. Again we see that God did not make this world for Himself directly, but only indirectly. He made the world for *us*, and He made *us* for Himself. He did not make us to be slaves in His plantation, but to own the plantation for ourselves.

After God made the animals, He "brought each of them to the man to see what he would call it" (Gen. 2:19). If you have ever given a pet to your child, you know exactly what is going on here. Children give pets the funniest names. There have been many dogs named "Happy" or "Stinky," or something like that. In naming that animal, the child begins to take "ownership" of it, to become responsible for its welfare. All the animals in the world were originally meant to be Adam and Eve's pets. They were created for Adam and Eve's enjoyment, and they probably enjoyed their human masters. In telling Adam and Eve to rule the animals, God is ultimately telling them to enjoy the animals as His gifts to them.

In God's instruction to be fruitful and multiply, and to fill the earth and subdue it, and to take care of the animals, we do not find command of religious works, a list of things Adam had to perform to gain God's approval. As we saw in the discussion of the blessing, Adam and Eve already had God's approval. Rather, all of this points to one overwhelming and unavoidable conclusion: God made us in order to love us. He made us to be recipients of His love, and in so receiving His love, we would inevitably and naturally return it to Him. He made us to enjoy everything that is ultimately His, so that He could share in our life and we in His. God made us to be His children, not His slaves. He did not make us for toil, but for enjoyment. God did not make us for religion. He made us for intimacy.

The Odd Words of Grace

We see this foundational reality of grace in God's next words to Adam and Eve. What He says is one of those things that we often gloss over quickly when we read the Bible. When we read it slowly, we find something unique. That something is very important, and a little odd (vs. 29-30):

> Look, I have given you every seed-bearing plant on the surface of the entire earth, and every tree whose fruit contains seed. This food will be for you, for all

the wildlife of the earth, for every bird of the sky, and for every creature that crawls on the earth—everything having the breath of life in it. I have given every green plant for food.

What is odd about this isn't that God gave Adam and Eve plants to eat. That is obvious and sensible. We know plants are healthy, and if they are prepared right—for instance as red pasta sauce or a plate of cookies—they are very delicious. What is odd about all this is that He specifically tells Adam and Eve to "Look," to see that He has given the plants to them for food. He wanted them to see that the whole point of this is His grace, His provision for their needs out of His enduring love. God always intended us to live in His grace. And the only way to actually live in grace is to realize you already live there. Jesus said God causes the rain to fall on the righteous and the unrighteous alike. Since we can only be justified by faith, the reason some are counted righteous and others unrighteous is that the righteous accept that it is God who causes the rain to fall on them, while the unrighteous do not. God always intended us to realize that fact, to look and see that He has made us for His love. Only when we accept grace as the foundation of our relationship with God, can we actually be right with Him. In fact, without grace, there is no such thing as relationship.

As long as we see religious works, and not grace, as central to God's relation to man, we will be denying what Paul said was God's eternal purpose. We will be like the ancient pagans, thinking the gods created man to be their slave. Neither the rest of the Old Testament, or the cross, or the development of the church in the New Testament after that, will ever make an iota of sense until we see that God's un-earnable love, not our religious works, is the foundation of God's relationship to us.

God is completely fulfilled in Himself. He is a Trinity. He has perfect relationship within Himself, so there isn't anything He truly *needs* that we can provide. So to say that in order to be pleased with us, He needs us to do all the right things, and none of the wrong things, we are saying there is some deficiency He has that we must fulfill. The early Protestant theologians called this trying to add to the righteousness of God. They labeled it blasphemy. I think their strong language is entirely appropriate.

The other reason we shouldn't think that God needs or, in the strictest sense, requires religious or moral performance to gain His favor, is simply that God is a spiritual Being. Jesus said, "God is spirit, and those who worship Him must worship in spirit and truth" (John 4:24). I cannot suppose, in the truest meaning, that my act of doing this physical ceremony, or that physical ritual, gives God something physical that He needs, but can't fulfill in Himself. I cannot suppose that simply keeping some rule in the outward behavioral sense can give Him something that He desires.

To use a metaphor, if I were to "walk up to" God and offer Him an apple, truly meaning in my spirit that it was an expression of my deep love for Him, He would be quite happy with that. But not because of the apple. As "spirit," He has no use for the physical apple. He makes clear in Genesis 1 that He made apples for us, not for Him. What He very much enjoys, rather, is the Gift behind the gift. He very much enjoys it when a person comes to Him, knowing His infinite love, and from that reality, loves God completely from the depths of his spirit. Or, in other words, God enjoys it when people "worship [Him] in spirit and in truth." He enjoys it because He loves us. Every loving father delights in the love of his children.

The Rest of God

But He doesn't need us, in the strictest sense. This is humbling and liberating at the same time. God's love goes outward, and then back. John wrote, "We love *because* He first loved us" (1 John 4:19). God loves us, and by grace, He causes that love to return to Him from us, in a great circle of relationship. He also causes His love in us to spread out to others. Seeing His goodness in our love for them, they return it to Him. Being loved and loving in return, is the essence of what God created man for. It is living in God's grace. It is the greatest gift of all. Nothing else compares.

The Bible refers to this life in God's grace in an interesting way. It speaks of rest. Every single day of the creation story ended with "and the evening and the morning were the nth day." Every day but the seventh. On the seventh day, God rested, enjoying what He had made. It was not followed by an "evening and morning" statement.

This shows us something we must remember about the Bible: The ancient Jewish writers would sometimes tell you as much by what they left out, as by what they put in. Rabbis, for centuries before Christ, noticed something about the absence of "the evening and the morning was the seventh day." The Hebrew structure implies that, though the seventh day certainly came to an end, the conditions that characterized it—God's rest—continued on thereafter. In fact, the book of Hebrews uses such an interpretation in its third and fourth chapters, pointing to God's "My Rest" as something that continued on unceasing from the seventh day forward. Hebrews says of it, "His works have been finished since the foundation of the world" (Heb. 4:3). The writer of Hebrews also points out that God wants us to enter into that "My Rest" with Him, by believing. He writes, "We who have believed enter the rest [God's 'My Rest']" (Heb. 4:3). Contrastingly, he says of ancient Israelites, "They were unable to enter [God's 'My Rest'] because of unbelief" (Heb. 3:19).

God's "My Rest" isn't something mankind enters into simply by taking a day off or napping. Any pagan can do that. Most pagans today do it twice a week. God is a spiritual being, not a physical one, so when He describes it as "My Rest," rather than "your rest," He is talking about something spiritual in nature. God's "My Rest" is something man enters into by believing, having faith in God, trusting in His grace. It is "the peace of God, which surpasses every thought," (Phil. 4:7). It is like a child who can live free of worry because she knows her daddy will always take care of her needs, always read her a story at night, always tuck her in with a kiss on her cheek, always tell her, "I love you." That is God's "My Rest." It is the rest of the Spirit that we may have when we come to know Him as a loving Father.

The fourth chapter of Hebrews characterizes God's "My Rest" by "a certain day — 'today,'" meaning the invitation to enter God's Rest by trusting in His grace is available to us 24/7/365. Hebrews exhorts the audience to stay in that "My Rest," because Hebrews was written to former Jews who were giving up on the whole grace thing and returning to Judaism.

Many centuries after creation, God brought the Jewish people out of exile. He chose to have them remember the Garden by giving them a special religious day, the Jewish Sabbath. He gave them two seemingly different reasons for that day. In one version, He said in the Decalogue, "For the Lord made the heavens and the earth, the sea, and everything in them in six days; then He rested on the seventh day" (Ex. 20:11). Then in a different version of the Ten Commandments, He told the Israelites, "Remember that you were a slave in the land of Egypt, and the Lord your God brought you out of there with a strong hand and an outstretched arm. That is why the Lord your God has commanded you to keep the Sabbath day" (Deut. 5:15).

Now, this dual basis serves two related purposes. First, it shows that the literal seventh-day Sabbath was only given to the Israelites who were saved from Egypt (and to their descendants), but not to anyone else. That's why, before reciting the Ten Commandments—the "Tables of the Covenant," as the Bible often refers to them—Moses told the Israelites, "The Lord our God made a covenant with us at Horeb [Sinai]. He did not make this covenant with our fathers, but with all of us who are alive here today" (Deut. 5:2-3). This is very important, because the fact that it was given only to those who were saved from slavery in Egypt helps to explain its greater purpose.

And that greater purpose is the second point: The Egyptians had exploited the Israelites as slaves. No doubt they used their view of the gods as divine slave-masters to excuse their exploitation of Israel. Their creation accounts, like the other pagans, probably had the gods creating people as their slaves to give them what they wanted, in return for which people would merit a happy place in the Egyptian afterlife. God, on the other hand, was reminding the children of Israel that He had created the world for us, that He had originally given us everything we needed so that we wouldn't have to toil for our daily bread. He had created us to live in His grace.

And He was reminding the Israelites that humanity had rejected living in His grace many years before in the Garden. He was reminding them that *they* had sought life by toil, the kind of life the Egyptians forced on the Israelites. God's "My Rest" of grace was offered freely to man, and man had chosen instead to live outside of grace, by his own efforts in toil and hardship. Man had decided to be the Prodigal Brother, relating to God by slaving in the fields. Every seven days they would be reminded why they had to toil and sweat the other six.

God's "My Rest" was first available to Adam and Eve. It was a rest that meant they didn't have to toil and scrape by, always worried about where their next meal would come from or whether they would live to see another day. They could rest in God's grace, sit contented on His mighty lap knowing that He would provide everything they needed and they could live life enjoying how wonderful He is. When Adam and Eve fell, they rejected God's "My Rest" of grace. The Israelites were to be continually reminded of that rejection, and of all the pain that came from it. They were to be continually reminded, that is, until One would come who would restore that "My Rest." It is to the rejection of the "My Rest" that we will next turn, and it is the restoration of that "My Rest," that we will find in time.

Chapter 3

Leaving Home

—◦◦◦—

Leaving home is, then, much more than an historical event bound to time and place. It is a denial of the spiritual reality that I belong to God with every part of my being, that God holds me safe in an eternal embrace, that I am indeed carved in the palms of God's hands and hidden in their shadows... Leaving home is living as though I do not yet have a home and must look far and wide to find one.

Henri Nouwen/The Return of the Prodigal Son

During Adam and Eve's life in the Garden, they didn't have any sin. Note I didn't say "sins," even though that's true as well. I said "sin." We will talk more later about the difference. Anyway, the Bible has a unique way of describing this: "Both the man and his wife were naked, yet felt no shame" (Gen. 2:25). The Bible indicates sin didn't exist by saying this thing called shame didn't exist.

If you've ever done something really stupid or wrong, and felt that the entire universe, or at least your part of it, was looking on you in disgust, that was shame. Shame, at its core, is the knowledge that there is something wrong in us. It isn't just the realization that we did something wrong, but that we *are* not as we were meant to be. This something wrong with us is not merely that we did the wrong things, or that one of our legs is a half inch longer than the other. It is the feeling that within us there is something truly vile.

Shame makes it impossible for us to enjoy God's presence. We see this, for instance, with the Prophet Isaiah. He was brought into God's presence, and, when he saw how truly good and holy and beautiful God is, he said (Isa. 6:1-8):

> Woe is me, for I am ruined,
> Because I am a man of unclean lips
> And live among a people of unclean lips,
> And because my eyes have seen the King,
> The LORD of Hosts.

Then one of the seraphim flew to me, and in his hand was a glowing coal that he had taken from the altar with tongs. He touched my mouth with it and said:

> Now that this has touched your lips,
> Your wickedness is removed,
> And your sin is atoned for.

Then I heard the voice of the Lord saying:

> Who should I send?
> Who will go for Us?

I said:

> Here I am. Send me.

Because Isaiah knew shame, he couldn't stand being in God's presence. God is truly good. If everything were as it should be, if we really loved God, and He in His goodness dwelled within us, there wouldn't be anywhere else we would rather be than in His presence. But because we aren't in ourselves very good, God's presence only heightens our sense of our own evil, tormenting us. God does not want it this way. But it is this way because of who we chose to be long ago in Eden.

When our conscience is focused on shame, being in God's presence is, in a sense, like throwing an ice cube on a hot griddle. The ice cube will spit and crack and pieces might even fly off. Eventually, it will melt and evaporate into nothing. But on the other hand, if we were truly as we were meant to be, then it would be like pouring pancake batter onto a hot griddle. The heat only serves to form the batter into beautiful, plump, golden pancakes. In the first case, what is exposed to the powerful heat is destroyed. In the second, what is exposed to the powerful heat is perfected into something delicious.

God may use shame to help us realize there is something wrong with us, so that we might be saved. But He doesn't intend for us to live in shame once we have been saved. Adam and Eve never had shame until they stopped living in God's grace. In fact, it is impossible to truly live in grace when we are focused on shame. Shame is not part of how God wants us to live in Him as His children, but merely a tool, a result of sin that He bends back against sin to free us from sin's power so that we can be adopted as His. Shame only lasts until He has us in His arms. There, it is destroyed. But so long as we cling to shame, we push ourselves from His embrace.

We need God to provide for us what He provided for Isaiah, a glowing coal to make us clean, to rid us of our shame. Then we would not be tormented by His presence anymore, and thus would be able to live in His grace. Thus, like Isaiah, we would once again enjoy and love God from the depths of our hearts, and be willing to do His bidding out of love. We would become the pancakes He wants us to be. It is the atonement, or cross, that removes that cancer in Isaiah called sin and shame. But to understand the cross, we must understand how shame entered our world.

The Tree of Life

The garden had two special trees. I had often thought of these two trees as if one was the Tree of Knowledge of Good, and the other was the Tree of Knowledge of Evil. But that isn't what the text says. Rather, one was called the Tree of Life. The other was called the Tree of Knowledge of Good and Evil. These two phrases are not what we think of as opposite. In the strict sense of the language, mankind was given a choice between life on one hand, and the knowledge of good and evil on the other. He wasn't given a choice between knowing good on one hand, and knowing evil on the other.

Life is intrinsic only to God. God is "the only One who has immortality" (1 Tim. 6:16). Jesus said, "The Father has life in Himself" (John 5:26). John says of Jesus, "Life was in Him" (John 1:4). Peter refers to Jesus as "the source of life" (Acts 3:15). And Paul says of God, "He Himself gives everyone life and breath and all things" (Acts 17:25).

This last statement by Paul is indicative: The Tree of Life obviously implies something about grace. If life is intrinsic only to God, then man has life only by receiving it as God gives it freely to man. Man cannot earn life, because life must be given to him before he can do anything at all. Paul, in Romans 5, says that grace brings life, while sin "reigns in death." Further, Jesus said, "This is eternal life: That they may know You, the only true God, and the One You have sent—Jesus Christ" (John 17:3). So the Tree of Life implies an idea of reliance on God's grace for our life. It speaks of life as something that comes to us only from a healthy intimacy with God.

When Moses describes the manna given to the Israelites, he says (Deut. 8:3):

> He humbled you by letting you go hungry; then He gave you manna to eat, which you and your fathers had not known, so that you might learn that man does not live on bread alone but on every word that comes from the mouth of the Lord.

Life comes to us only by God's provision of grace, and especially by His word. Jesus, in the New Testament, says of the manna (John 6:32-33, 35):

> I assure you: Moses didn't give you the bread from heaven, but My Father gives you the real bread from heaven. For the bread of God is the One who comes down from heaven and gives life to the world… I am the bread of life.

Just like the fruit of the Tree of Life, Jesus tells us to eat His body so that we might have life. He tells us eating His body means believing in Him: "No one who comes to Me will ever be hungry, and no one who believes in Me will ever be thirsty again" (John 6:35). And He says, "For this is the will of My Father: That everyone who sees the Son and believes in Him may have eternal life, and I will raise him up on the last day" (John 6:40). Jesus reiterates and clarifies His earlier statement by adding (John 6:47-51):

> I assure you: Anyone who believes has eternal life. I am the bread of life. Your fathers ate the manna in the wilderness, and they died. This is the bread that comes down from heaven so that anyone may eat of

it and not die. I am the living bread that came down from heaven. If anyone eats of this bread he will live forever. The bread that I will give for the life of the world is My flesh.

We find true life by knowing God in intimacy. It comes to us by trusting in Him, believing in His Son. Jesus further states (John 6:54-56):

Anyone who eats My flesh and drinks My blood has eternal life, and I will raise him up on the last day, because My flesh is real food and My blood is real drink. The one who eats My flesh and drinks My blood lives in Me, and I in him.

It should be obvious that when Jesus speaks of eating His flesh and drinking His blood, He is referring to something more than physically partaking of the Lord's Supper. He is referring to a trust relationship, belief in Him. Those who believe in Jesus partake of Him as the bread of life, and He lives in them, imparting to them the life that is intrinsic to God the Son. The Tree of Life speaks of the indwelling of God, received by trust in God and lived out in faith. It speaks of a relationship of trusting in God's grace to provide, and believing in Him as the source of true life. It means having the true eternal life that comes only by letting Him be our Father, and letting ourselves be His children.

The Accuser

Genesis says more about the Tree of Knowledge than the Tree of Life, so to understand that tree, we must follow the narrative closely (Gen. 2:16-17):

And the LORD God commanded the man, "You are free to eat from any tree of the garden, but you must not eat from the tree of the knowledge of good and evil, for on the day you eat from it, you will certainly die."

On this Tree of Knowledge of Good and Evil was a serpent. Of this serpent, the Bible says, "The serpent was the most cunning of all the wild animals that the LORD God had made" (Gen. 3:1). This particular Serpent in the Tree was deceitful and dishonest, and also very shrewd and manipulative.

The Bible doesn't tell us much about how Satan came to be, because he isn't the point of the story. We can glean that he was an angel who decided in that spiritual realm before and beyond and above time and the material universe that He didn't like who God is. He wanted to run the show himself because he thought he had a better way. That way, we find, is called "the Knowledge of Good and Evil," and we will have much to say about it in this book.

Satan is a Hebrew word that means "accuser." This is why the New Testament refers to him as the "accuser of our brothers... who accuses them before our God day and night" (Rev. 12:10). Satan doesn't like grace. He wants to run the universe like a tyrant, always pushing people around to do his bidding and using them to build things and make things for him, and to smack people around really badly when they don't do everything just right. In other words, Satan wants a god like the pagan gods, a god who sees men as his slaves.

Jesus said, "I assure you: Everyone who commits sin is a slave of sin" (John 8:34). It is the Devil, not God, who wants to make slaves of us. The Prodigal Brother in us sees this and thinks Jesus is only talking about drug addiction, or alcoholism, or something like that, so we pat ourselves on the back because we don't have these kinds of addictions.

We do this all the while not realizing that our biggest addiction is to the drug of our own pride, self-righteousness, and religiosity, compared to which heroin addiction is the lesser vice. Arrogance is the biggest addiction in all of us.

The Two Ways

This is the showdown: God calls His way of running things "Life," and the Devil calls his way, "the Knowledge of Good and Evil." These two ways are at war. God's eternal purpose isn't to be some tyrant, smacking us around when we don't do just the right thing, but rather to live in us, to live out His goodness and love and beauty through us.

God wants us to be like two-year-olds, sitting on His lap, contented and safe and free, as His strong, gentle arms surround and protect us. He wants us to enter His "My Rest." God calls this way "Life," and I think we see why. It is true freedom. No one is as free and alive as a child is around a mother[1] whom he knows loves him very much. He is free to be himself; free to say silly things and laugh and giggle and play with his toys; free to ask the silly kinds of questions children ask, without being embarrassed; free to take part in whatever his mom is doing, in whatever child-like way he can; free to learn from his parent just by watching her; etc. He is free in this because he thoroughly trusts his mom to do right by him and provide for him and respond to him lovingly, and as long as he is living in this kind of freedom, he doesn't actually do anything truly bad. He is too focused on his mother and on living in her love. It is only when he stops focusing on his mother's life that he might begin to do bad things.

In contrast, the Devil calls his way "the knowledge of good and evil." The problem with "the knowledge of good and evil," is that it sounds a bit like trying to get something by knowing all the right rules. In fact, it seems that is exactly what it is, as we shall see.

The Devil in the Details

Adam and Eve wandered by the Tree of Knowledge of Good and Evil, and somehow the Serpent caught Eve's attention. Why he caught Eve's attention primarily, and not Adam's, is something we don't know for sure. Perhaps she had an affinity for reptiles.

Nonetheless, the Serpent said to Eve, "Did God really say, 'You can't eat from any tree in the garden'?" (Gen. 3:1). What the Serpent said here is really quite tricky. In fact, many Prodigal Brothers have been tricked by reading it, exactly the same way Eve was tricked by hearing it. To be honest, I was tricked by reading it for much of my life. The Prodigal Brother reads this and sees the Serpent saying, essentially, "Did God really say, 'You *can* eat from any tree?'" This isn't what the Serpent said. The Serpent said *"can't."*

The Serpent was trying to make Eve think that God was somehow denying her need for sustenance, denying her things that are good for her to have. He wanted her to think God was denying her *all* the fruit in the garden. The Devil wanted to come as one offering freedom, and make Eve think God was offering slavery. But God commanded Adam (and by implication, Eve) to be *free* to eat of any tree, but one. The Serpent was not attacking the rules, but grace. He wasn't saying "can," but "can't."

The Serpent was framing the conversation in terms of God not actually favorably providing for Eve. He wanted Eve to think of provision for her greatest needs — especially her spiritual needs as we will see later — not as something that came from God, but as something she had to secure by her own striving. He wanted to stop her from trusting in God, to crawl off His lap.

Once you understand sin and shame, you will find the Serpent is always doing this. Getting us to do harmful things is not his main end. That is a means to his main end. He wants us to get away from grace. He knows that if he can get us to make mistakes, he can excite shame in us, and then use that shame to convince us that God couldn't *truly* have favor for us, that God couldn't truly have grace for someone as bad as us. Grace is the antidote to his shackles of slavery over us, so if the Devil can get us to distrust grace, he can get us to be his slave. He can then work more and more to get us to live by trying to do the right things and failing, and thus he can use our shame and guilt to push us around and get us to do his bidding. He may be pure evil, but he is still very clever.

Eve replied to the Serpent, "We may eat the fruit from the trees in the garden. But about the fruit of the tree in the middle of the garden, God said, 'You must not eat it or touch it, or you will die'" (Gen. 2:2-3). In Eve's reply, there is a subtlety the Prodigal Brother always overlooks. He overlooks it because it so reflects the false way that he views reality, that when he reads Eve say it, he thinks it's just the correct way to look at things. Winston Churchill once said, "Men occasionally stumble over the truth, but most of them pick themselves up and hurry off as if nothing ever happened." To see this subtlety, compare what God said to what Eve said that God said:

God's Version (Gen. 2:16-17)	Eve's Version (Gen. 3:2-3)
"And the LORD God commanded the man, 'You are free to eat from any tree of the garden, ...	"The woman said to the serpent, 'We may eat the fruit from the trees in the garden.

'but you must not eat from the tree of the knowledge of good and evil, for on the day you eat from it, you will certainly die.'"	'But about the fruit of the tree in the middle of the garden, God said, 'You must not eat it or touch it, or you will die.'"

Eve never referred to God's command until she got to the part about not eating from the Tree of Knowledge of Good and Evil. She simply took it for granted that they "may" eat from the trees. But the Bible tells us, "God *commanded* man, 'You are free to eat...'" She denied that grace is fundamental to how God designed us to live, and instead she took God's grace for granted, thinking of it as something apart from Him. In effect, she prayed what Bart Simpson once prayed: "Dear God, we paid for all this food ourselves, so thanks for nothing."

Second, she made no mention of freedom. God commanded man, "You are free..." His grace brings true freedom. Freedom was the what God desired for humanity. They didn't have to sit and worry that God will strike them down. They didn't have to worry that God wanted them as slaves. By commanding man to be free, God was inviting Adam to be His son and His friend, someone who could commune with Him and enjoy relationship. Eve, by leaving out God's *command* of freedom to enjoy His provision, started to fall into the Devil's trap of doubting God's grace.

There is a difference between a primary and a subordinate command. God's command to be free to eat of any tree was a primary command. He added the conjunction "but" before telling them not to eat of the Tree of Knowledge, making it a subordinate command. What I mean is this: Because He gave them freedom, He had to then explain that there is a right and a wrong use of freedom. We are freed by God's love, and if we use our freedom to lessen our trust in God's grace, or in some way push ourselves out of His presence, we are actually using freedom to curtail freedom, and thus committing an act of spiritual self-contradiction. We would be, as it were, using freedom to put ourselves in chains. Paul discusses this in Romans 6.

The Prodigal Brother, on the other hand, does the same thing Eve did. He skips the fact that it was a command of God to be free to enjoy His love, and instead thinks the only command was not to eat the fruit of the Tree of Knowledge. When you read the Prodigal Brother's discussion of this story, you will find that he takes the subordinate command, makes it the primary command, and does away with the *actual* primary command entirely. We must watch the Prodigal Brother closely with both eyes, because, like the Serpent, he is a cunning little devil.

Humanity is meant to run, not by avoiding partaking of wrong things, but by partaking of the Right Thing, God. We live, not just by bread and water, but by every word that comes from God's mouth, by His revelation of Himself to us. We run on God's love. We run on His indwelling. We run on relationship with Him.

There is no inherent goodness apart from God. If God had made us to run on something other than Himself, we would be running on a fuel that was less than the best. As such, we would be sure to die. If you put diesel in a gas engine, you will eventually blow a piston or crack the engine block. This is why, when God warned that the Tree of Knowledge of Good and Evil resulted in death, He quite literally meant it. God gave man freedom in the garden, and part of that freedom is the freedom to not choose God. You can't really love someone if they force you to. He wanted to always live inside Adam and Eve, but He wasn't going to force the issue.

Eve also added something God *didn't* say. God didn't say of the fruit, "You must not touch it." But Eve claimed He did. If you eat fruit, it becomes a part of you. That is why Jesus says that if we eat His flesh and drink His blood, He lives in us. But if you merely touch something, that isn't the case. God, you must understand, was giving Adam and Eve a chance to choose an aspect of their core nature. If they ate from the Tree of Life, they would become that fruit, in a sense. God would live inside them for eternity, and live out His life in them, resulting in relational intimacy. If they ate from the Tree of Knowledge of Good and Evil, they would become that fruit. God would not live inside them. Life, true life, is intrinsic only to God, so that if you reject His grace and His indwelling, you reject life as well. Their relationship with God would be severed.

By saying God's command also extended to touching the fruit, Eve injected arbitrariness into His instruction. Rather than seeing it as a statement about the nature of this reality God created, she in a sense cast it as an arbitrary religious hoop that she and Adam had to jump through in order to win God's favor or be like Him. The Prodigal Brother also sees the Tree of Knowledge this way. He says that God created a "covenant of works" with Adam, so that if Adam jumped through the right religious hoop (not eating the bad fruit), he would win God's favor and be granted something special (what exactly, the Prodigal Brother cannot say—Adam already had everything he could ever want or need). But Adam and Eve already had God's favor, and His pleasure. He blessed them, showing His favor, and He pronounced them "very good," showing His pleasure in them.

Knowing God, or Knowing Good and Evil?

Once Eve saw God's warning as an arbitrary hurdle, the Serpent's trap was set and all he had to do was spring it on Eve. And spring it he did. The Serpent replied, "No! You will not die. In fact, God knows that when you eat it your eyes will be opened and you will be like God, knowing good and evil" (Gen. 3:4, 5).

By telling Eve, "You will not die," he was trying to convince her that God isn't being forthright about this whole matter. In fact, Eve's twisting of God's statement set the table for this, because it cast God as an arbitrary tyrant. So the Serpent added, "In fact, God knows that when you eat it your eyes will be opened and you will be like God, knowing good and evil." The Serpent implied that this alleged rule from God (it was in fact more a description of reality), was His means of scaring Adam and Eve so they wouldn't eat the fruit, know good and evil, and then become like God.

The Devil has a touch of truth in his statement. God does indeed know good and evil. God knows good by knowing Himself. He has relationship intrinsic to Himself, so that for eternity He has known the goodness of that loving relationship. By extension, anything that isn't in keeping with His nature must not be good at all, but evil.

The problem comes when I try to be truly good like God by knowing what is good and what is evil. God is good, and thus knows what good is, and thus knows that what isn't that goodness is evil. It is unbeneficial. The Devil was proposing the reverse of that. He proposed that by figuring out what good and evil are, Adam and Eve could make themselves like God.

Between God and me, only One of us has good intrinsically in Him, and that One of us isn't me. God starts off as good, and knows good by knowing Himself. I start off as not intrinsically good, and then presume that by knowing good and evil, I can become good like God. These are two different realities.

The Devil's idea doesn't work because it requires me to have something I don't. What I don't have is the part the Devil intentionally leaves out, but that God demonstrates when He gives the Law later on. To be like God in His goodness, it isn't enough to simply know what is good and what is evil. If I could actually know what is good and what is evil, but did the evil instead of the good, then I would be nothing like God. In order to be like God in His goodness, I have to both know what is good and what isn't, and actually *perform* the thing that is good.

This creates two problems for me. First, I can't fully know good and evil like He does. I am not omniscient. But pretend I figured it all out. Since I don't have goodness intrinsic to me, I have nothing in me out of which I can actually do what is good. Paul talks about what this was like for him (Rom. 7:18-23):

> For the desire to do what is good is with me, but there is no ability to do it. For I do not do the good that I want to do, but I practice the evil that I do not want to do. Now if I do what I do not want, I am no longer the one doing it, but it is the sin that lives in me. So I discover this principle: when I want to do good, evil is with me. For in my inner self I joyfully agree with God's law. But I see a different law in the parts of my body, waging war against the law of my mind and taking me prisoner to the law of sin in the parts of my body.

Similarly, Jesus showed a wrinkle in this whole philosophy of trying to do good in order to be good. He said, "A good man produces good out of the good storeroom of his heart. An evil man produces evil out of the evil storeroom, for his mouth speaks from the overflow of the heart" (Luke 6:45). We can never be good enough to be like God, because we don't have the good in us that God has in Him. There is no use trying to be good enough to convince God to find favor in us, because if He has infinite perfect goodness in Himself, He certainly doesn't need our finite imperfect pseudo-goodness. In fact, the only way it would be possible to be good, is if somehow God were, by His grace, to choose us even when we weren't good, and then live in us, and in so doing live out His goodness through us.

But the Devil's idea makes good and evil purely an external concept, sort of separate from who God is, and above Him. Good, in the Devil's view, isn't some internal attribute that, when it intersects with my actions and thoughts and words, makes them good by extension. He says knowledge of good and evil is an external achievement to strive for, rather than an internal reality to strive out of. The Devil tells us the ultimate good for us is something we can achieve by eating a piece of fruit, not something we can only experience by being at peace with God.

A What, or a Whom?

So this is the point: The Devil was essentially implying that good and evil are rules or thought patterns or laws or performances that, if I do one of them and not the other, can bring me up to being like God. In other words, by knowing, apart from relationship with God, the proper definitions of good behaviors and evil behaviors, we can bring ourselves up to some better status. If that isn't the message of human religion, it is so close to it as makes no difference.

Religion, at its core, teaches the same central ethic as the Serpent: By knowing what is good and evil, and doing the good, man can perform his way up to a higher spiritual status. That status may be a status of approval by "God," or a state of Nirvana, or the realization of a socialist utopia on earth, or even a glorious thousand year *reich*. It is all in its essence the same.

God's definition makes good primarily a spiritual reality that expresses itself in the material world. Satan's definition makes good primarily a material reality (proper thoughts, actions, and words) that one can use to manipulate the spiritual world. God's idea of good is centered in the spiritual reality, and thus foundational, while the Devil's idea is centered in material reality, and thus becomes arbitrary. The Devil's definition of good is primarily a "what" while God's definition is primarily a "Whom." Perhaps that is why, when Paul details what went wrong with all of us, he says, "Because they did not think it worthwhile to have God in their knowledge, God delivered them over to a worthless mind to do what is morally wrong" (Rom. 1:28). Our problem is not primarily that we don't want to retain some understanding of what is right or wrong, but that we don't want to retain God *Himself* in our knowledge, so inevitably our understanding of right and wrong ends up skewed—"worthless." We reject the "Whom" that is good, and consequently end up with a false view of "what" is good.

Being like God—if we have a correct concept of God—is good, because God is good. But if you believe the Serpent's lie, and the Prodigal Brother in each of us does, then the "God" it implies is not really good. He is a God who withholds what is good from us, and lies to us. By eating the fruit, Adam and Eve would be accepting this concept of God into who they were. They would be distrusting God. They would be denying faith. They would deny the "Whom" that is good.

The Domain of Shame

Unfortunately, that is exactly what Adam and Eve did. Eve foolishly believed the Serpent, and ate. Adam, who was with her, just took it from her and ate as well. One of the first effects of sin in man is that fools follow after fools unquestioningly. Fools only ever question the truly wise. Why did so much of Germany follow after the foolish Nazis?

Specifically because they were foolish. Had they been truly wise, no one would have followed them.

Immediately after they ate the fruit, we read: "Then the eyes of both of them were opened, and they knew they were naked; so they sewed fig leaves together and made loincloths for themselves" (Gen. 3:7). These loincloths were the first attempt by mankind to hide his shame. Humanity has figured out more and more complicated ways to cover up his shame, but all the ways we deal with shame are essentially externally focused. This is because there is nothing we can do about the internal problem. In Jesus' day, He told the Prodigal Brother (Matt. 23:25, 27):

> Woe to you, scribes and Pharisees, hypocrites! You clean the outside of the cup and dish, but inside they are full of greed and self-indulgence! ... You are like whitewashed tombs, which appear beautiful on the outside, but inside are full of dead men's bones and every impurity.

Shame doesn't let us live truly free. It doesn't let us live as the care-free child on our Father's lap. It taunts us and jeers us and bullies us constantly. It forces us to always try to get rid of it, to cover it up so no one — especially not ourselves — can see it. We do all kinds of things to silence shame: Things like doing charity work to make ourselves feel better (the wrong reason to do charity), or praying special memorized prayers we really don't mean, or working really hard for our religious institutions, or trying to make a lot of money to increase how good and powerful we look to others, or engaging in pleasure as a sedative to "medicate" our shame, or trying to have the "correct" political ideas that make others think we are truly wise and compassionate, or.... etc. All of these things in some way are attempts to convince ourselves and others that we aren't really as broken as we feel deep down inside. These things we do to cover up our shame are religion at its very core. Some of them aren't, in themselves, bad, but when they are used to cover up shame, they become so. Sin causes shame, and shame causes more sin. Humanity has become one great obsessive-compulsive race, constantly washing and re-washing our hands like Lady Macbeth, trying to rid ourselves of the "damned spot" of shame. Shame is our realization of what Aslan said to young Digory: "The fruit is good, but they loathe it ever after. All get what they want; they do not always like it."[2]

By eating the fruit of the Tree of Knowledge of Good and Evil, Adam and Eve accepted into themselves a portion of the Devil's DNA, if you will. They chose their nature. That portion of DNA is something black and cancerous and vile, and as such it causes us to feel, in a spiritual sense, icky. That is shame, and there really isn't anything we can do to get rid of it until God rids us of it. We have it in our spiritual nature because our parents had it in their spiritual DNA.

If you're objecting to this idea that we have this sin thing just because Adam and Eve had it, you're not alone. This idea—called "original sin"—that Adam and Eve could pass along a sinful nature to their progeny, is not always popular. But think of it this way: If the Prodigal Son had fathered children while he was away from his father's estate, they would have been born divorced from their heritage, their identity, and their true grandfather. They would be born in "a distant country" (Luke 15:13), or as Paul puts it, in "the domain of darkness" (Col. 1:13). There is no way they could be born on the father's estate, where they truly belonged.

Moreover, the Prodigal Son left the estate because he hated his father. By demanding his inheritance before his father died, he was telling his father that he wished the man were dead. What if, then, he always told his children that their grandfather was a mean and cruel tyrant whose ultimate desire was to douse them with gasoline, throw matches at them, and enjoy watching them burn? What if, even before learning such an idea from the Prodigal Son, his children somehow were just born with his distrust for the father who lives far away on the estate?

Like the sons and daughters of immigrants, the "distant country" would be all they had ever known, and its ways of looking at things would be intrinsic to their nature as children of that country. They would have no desire to return to the far off estate of their grandfather, whom they were told was a malevolent despot. Perhaps the only reason they would try to live right, is that they were told that someday the cruel grandfather would come looking for them, and if they were not doing the right things, he would destroy them in his anger. So it is not at all a stretch to understand what "original sin" means. If we are born to those in "a distant country," we ourselves will, from birth, live in "a distant country," or as Paul calls it, "the domain of darkness."

Instead of desiring our grandfather to come looking for us, we would be afraid of him. We would believe, as we were told, that he was coming someday only to see if we look and act exactly as he demands, and if we don't, he would toast us like marshmallows. We would have to clothe ourselves in as much fig leaves of religious works as possible, in order to fool our grandfather if he ever came for us. Like our parents, and their parents, and their parents, we are born into the domain of shame.

God did indeed come looking for Adam and Eve. He found them hiding from Him. But it wasn't God who couldn't stand to be around Adam. Rather, Adam was afraid of God's presence. The Bible says God was "walking in the garden at the time of the evening breeze," (Gen. 3:8) implying this was just something He did regularly, even before Adam and Eve ate the fruit. He was just out for a stroll, in a manner of speaking, desiring to be with His children. That is why He asked, "Where are you?" Normally, Adam and Eve would be with Him, so their absence indicated something was out of sorts.

Adam and Eve heard Him coming, and hid, because they were ashamed. Like Isaiah, their shame made it impossible for them to truly bear God's presence. It made them, and us, doubt grace. If Adam and Eve hadn't sinned, they certainly wouldn't have hid from God when He came to be with them.

When God asked Adam where He was, Adam gave an interesting reply: "I heard You in the garden, and I was afraid because I was naked, so I hid" (v. 10).

So God asks, "Who told you that you were naked? Did you eat from the tree that I had commanded you not to eat from?" (v. 11)

Implicit in the first question—"Who *told you* that you were naked?"— is the fact that Adam was just as naked before he ate the fruit as after. Note the Biblical record: First, "Both the man and his wife were naked, yet felt no shame," and afterward, "Then the eyes of both of them were opened, and they knew they were naked." Nothing at all changed in terms of clothing. They were naked the whole time. What changed was internal to them: All of a sudden they felt shameful about it. They knew shame, that crawling, oily, naked feeling you have when you realize that who you are is somehow very wrong, and you are sure the whole world can somehow see it on your skin.

The second question—"Did you eat from the tree that I had commanded you not to eat from?"—is not so much a question as an answer. It answers the first question by showing Adam that it was the fruit that had changed something deep within him, something he couldn't really cover by scratchy fig leaves.

Some Hebrew scholars translate the "tree of knowledge of good and evil" as "the tree of the conscience." When Adam and Eve sought to live by their "knowledge of good and evil," they displaced God from their conscience and replaced Him with their own efforts, their own performance, and their own attempts to achieve greatness by knowing right from wrong. In their conscience, harsh and unforgiving rules replaced the God of love and grace. The result was that they could only feel naked and ashamed.

Adam replies to the two questions, "The woman You gave to be with me—she gave me some fruit from the tree, and I ate" (v. 12).

One of the ways the Prodigal Brother tries to hide his shame is by shifting blame to someone else. Adam first shifts blame to Eve, and then to God. He says in essence, "The woman *You* gave me made me do it." What is more interesting, though, isn't so much the blame shifting, as the fact that it shows Adam had already lost trust in God. He had come to believe that God doesn't actually give good gifts, but bad. This is what our sinful religious nature has done to us. It has made it impossible for us to see God as anything other than a conniving and tyrannical adversary whom we must somehow appease by praying the proper prayers or doing the proper ceremonies, or in this case trying to divert His anger to someone else. Because of Adam and Eve's foolish choice, we have come to view God as a mercenary whom we keep at bay by giving Him whatever He wants. We view Him as a Viking pillager, and so long as we pay Him from the wealth of our religious monasteries, He will not burn down our village.

Eve, for her part, is at least more straightforward. She admits her fault: "It was the Serpent. He deceived me, and I ate" (v. 13). In this she is mostly right. It *was* the Serpent, but it wasn't *just* the Serpent. She played her role too. However, she is very right to point out that the Serpent deceived her. That is exactly what happened, and this is something that we must always understand: The Prodigal Brother in us is the way he is because he has been utterly deceived. To be sure, he played his part in the drama of deception, but we should understand we are criminals *because* we were first victims.

The Seed

God eventually gives Adam and Eve animal skins in place of the fig leaves. Animal skins are of course much more suitable for clothing, but it implies something more: God, not man, would provide the means to take away humanity's shame. Religion cannot do it. Religion only hides and exploits shame. But God would take it away—from us as well as from Adam. Just as God gave Adam and Eve animal skins to cover them, so He gives His Prodigal Sons and Daughters His royal robe to cover their tattered clothing and filthy bodies. God promised Adam and Eve that the wrong they did would be made right by Him (v. 15):

> I will put hostility between you [the Serpent] and the
> woman,
> And between your seed and her seed.
> He will strike your head,
> And you will strike his heel.

In dealing with a similar passage in Genesis regarding Abraham's seed, Paul points out that the fact that the term is "seed" and not "seeds," is meaningful. The "Seed"— singular—is Jesus Christ (Gal. 3:16). God promises Adam and Eve that the evil they did will someday be undone, that the Messiah would come and put everything to rights and restore the joy humanity once knew. God gave them a hope, and in so doing showed them His favor, grace, which they had done everything to *not* deserve.

But before the promised Seed could come, God explains to Adam and Eve the results of their choice. He tells Eve (Genesis 3:16):

I will intensify your labor pains;
You will bear children in anguish.

This is another odd thing to say. What does childbirth have to do with any of this? I am not sure, but I think it is something along the lines of what Paul wrote in Romans 8:20-25:

> For I consider that the sufferings of this present time are not worth comparing with the glory that is going to be revealed to us. For the creation eagerly waits with anticipation for God's sons to be revealed. For the creation was subjected to futility—not willingly, but because of Him who subjected it—in the hope that the creation itself will also be set free from the bondage of corruption into the glorious freedom of God's children. For we know that the whole creation has been groaning together with labor pains until now. And not only that, but we ourselves who have the Spirit as the firstfruits—we also groan within ourselves, eagerly waiting for adoption, the redemption of our bodies. Now in this hope we were saved, yet hope that is seen is not hope, because who hopes for what he sees? But if we hope for what we do not see, we eagerly wait for it with patience.

The fact that women are willing to go through such horrible pain in order to bear children, and that they are often eager to do so, tells me that whatever pain they have in bearing a child is "not worthy to be compared with the glory" of holding a newborn baby in their arms. They hope for the child when they cannot see it, and when it is about to come, it brings great pain, but once the pain is gone they have nothing but immense joy. God's statement to Eve was a promise to all humanity that, though the pain brought by sin would be intense, it would not last forever, and once it was gone, the joy of being reconciled to Him would be well worth the pain.

And to Adam, God says,

> The ground is cursed because of you.
> You will eat from it by means of painful labor
> All the days of your life.
> It will produce thorns and thistles for you,
> And you will eat the plants of the field.
> You will eat bread by the sweat of your brow
> Until you return to the ground,
> Since you were taken from it.
> For you are dust,
> And you will return to dust.

Adam and Eve's life in the Garden was characterized by enjoying God's "My Rest," resting in His loving care and enjoying Him as He lovingly provided for all of their needs. They didn't know true toil like we know it today. They didn't know sweaty, harsh, cruel labor to get what they needed to survive. They rested in the great gracious arms of their Father, their "Abba" or "Papa." But it seems that God viewed their choice as rejecting His "My Rest": Evidently, despite what the Prodigal Brother tells us today, God doesn't see the problem merely as Adam and Eve—and us—violating an arbitrary standard that He put in place. He saw the problem as us rejecting His love. He seems to see things as if we have decided to leave His great estate where we are always cared-for and loved. Like Prodigal Sons and Daughters, we have left the safety of our home with our Father, demanding the inheritance of this world in order to live by our own efforts. By seeking their inheritance apart from Him, Adam and Eve declared to their Father that they wanted Him dead. If that is indeed how our "Papa" sees it, then that is heartbreaking indeed.

Chapter 4

God Flushes the Toilet

—⟨∂∕∂⟩—

> It's not a question of God 'sending' us to Hell. In each of us there is something growing up which will of itself *be Hell* unless it is nipped in the bud.
>
> *C.S. Lewis/God in the Dock*

*C*orrupt is an interesting word. For something to become corrupted, it must first have been uncorrupted—pure, good, wonderful, beautiful, etc. In the words of Genesis 1, it must first have been "very good." When we say something is corrupt, we really mean that it was meant to be something good, but instead has become twisted and corroded and mangled into something not at all good.

Several hundred years after Adam and Eve's choice, we find this interesting word—*corrupt*—used by the Bible to describe Noah's world: "Now the earth was corrupt in God's sight, and the earth was filled with violence. God saw how corrupt the earth was, for all flesh had corrupted its way on the earth" (Gen. 6:11, 12). To borrow from William Butler Yeats' poem "The Second Coming," because man had rejected a relationship with his only Father, the "the falcon cannot hear the falconer," and consequently:

Mere anarchy is loosed upon the world,
The blood-dimmed tide is loosed, and everywhere
The ceremony of innocence is drowned.
The best lack all conviction, while the worst
Are full of passionate intensity.[1]

Rules, or Reality?

To really understand why God found the world so
corrupt, we must understand how God sees good and evil,
versus how the Prodigal Brother in all of us sees good and
evil. The Prodigal Brother categorizes good and evil in terms
of rules. The problem with living to a set of moral rules is
that the set of rules is outside of you, not part of your core
nature, but rather against your nature. Consequently, the set
of rules enters the conscience as an external concept that the
person tries to keep. But it is never actually real to us in
terms of our core nature. It isn't *who* the person is, just *what*
the person tries (and usually fails) to do. Good and evil thus
become more like pure mental abstractions, dueling intellectual paradigms, rather than realities we experience and
know.

To see how God categorizes good and evil, we must
discuss what we mean by *good*. In the English language,
there are two meanings for the word *good*. We might say that
a wedding celebration was very *good*, by which we mean
that everyone was joyful and happy and love overflowed. Or
we might say that we had a *good* time relaxing with friends
and family, by which we mean that we enjoyed the love we
had for each other and the joy and peace that came from it.

On the other hand, we might use *good* in the sense of
the exercise of moral rules. We might say that feeding a
homeless person, rather than insulting him, is "good." Or we
might say that telling the truth, rather than a lie, is "good."
But in this ethical sense of *good*, we immediately must ask

ourselves *why* we characterize one act, and not another, as "good." To simply say it is *good* because the rules say so, is circular reasoning. Why do the rules say it is good?

When God looked down at His creation, He saw that it was "very good" (Gen. 1:31). The Hebrew word employed here is *towb*, and it connotes not the second "ethical" sense of *good*, but the first.[2] *Towb* means, in essence, that something is joyous, pleasant, lovely, peaceful, or even pleasurable. In the King James Version, *towb* is often translated as "beautiful," or "bountiful," or "cheerful," or "at ease," or "loving" or "merry", or (my favorite) "joyful."[3] These are not words we use to describe ethics, but words we use to describe weddings.

In other words, when God saw that creation was "very good," He meant that it was full of joy and beauty and cheerfulness and pleasure and love. He did not mean it was good in the sense of moral rules, as if everyone did the right "ethical" things. It isn't that people did bad things before the fall, but that this concept of "ethics" was not a concept intrinsic to God's uncorrupted reality. What I mean is, God sees things as either truly good, or corrupted. He does not see things as simply "allowed" or "not allowed." Adam and Eve avoided bad things because they had not yet become corrupted, not because they had the rules in their consciences always telling them what they should or should not do. Good was *who* they were, not simply *what* they tried to do.

When the Bible mentions the Tree of Knowledge of Good and Evil, it uses the word *ra'* for evil. The word *ra'* is derived from the Hebrew word *ra'a'*. In its literal use, *ra'a'* means, "to spoil (literally, by breaking to pieces)," or "to make (or be) good for nothing."[4] I suspect God uses the term *ra'* because He sees something as evil if it spoils or destroys that which He sees as good. Or, we might say, evil is bad because it *corrupts* those things that bring true joy and peace and love, and the greatest "thing" that brings joy and peace and love to man is intimacy with God Himself. Ultimately, God made man to enjoy Him, and that is good: It is pleasant and beautiful and loving. Everything that interferes with that intimacy is evil, *because* what is good is simply so "very good."

In God's eyes, good *is* what was meant to be most pleasant to us, if we were in our right minds (sadly, because of sin we aren't, so our understanding of good is skewed). Once we have come to see reality as God sees it, we see that evil is not merely "breaking the rules," but actually the twisting and corruption of something that was made to be "very good." Good can exist on its own, but evil cannot exist without twisting what was once good. Thus, what is good is indeed a *true* description of what God meant for reality, and evil is a *false* state or description of reality that is inherently unworkable and doomed to self-destruction. Good and evil are not just alternate behaviors to choose from. They are not mere rules or commands or laws. Instead they are in some way concepts like truth and falsehood. One is real and foundational, and the other is a twisting of what is real and foundational.

If we see the rules as the point, then we miss the bigger picture. We miss the forest for the proverbial trees. If good and evil are simply constructs of the rules, then the rules are arbitrary themselves. There is nothing above the rules that gives them meaning. Living by the rules denies the greater reality beyond the rules.

Consequently, when we try to live by rules, we see the rules as withholding something good from us, because the rules don't want us to have pleasure. But God sees things as evil because in some way they destroy true happiness. Sin becomes desirable to us because we have settled for a rules-derived definition of goodness. We have become children of a lesser good, disconnecting true goodness from the ideas of joy and love and happiness and peace and intimate relationships. In other words, we define good and evil simply in terms of "what is or is not allowed on pain of punishment," and thus we have no idea of what is truly good.

Not Delighting in Good

That is why man was made to live in the love of God: The love of God is a holiness greater than the rules, just like John said that the grace that came in Jesus is greater than the Law that came through Moses. To see the difference between living in intimacy with God, and living entirely to a set of moral rules, consider a father holding his baby daughter on his lap. He bounces her up and down and laughs with her and talks to her, and she giggles and smiles and shakes her little hands in enjoyment. God looks on this, and, seeing the utter beauty of such a moment, describes it as "very good."

When God sees a father and daughter behaving this way, He declares it to be "very good" because He sees in it a reflection of the love that is within Himself. It is of highest consequence first and only because He is of highest consequence. Any true and pure expression of love is an expression of something intrinsic to Him, so that really nothing can be more consequential than something like a father and his baby daughter loving each other. The great feats of battle or the great struggles for political or social justice are not greater than a daddy holding his daughter on his lap. Instead, they are merely lesser things people do in order to remove those things that impede the greater good of intimacy between daddy and daughter. Daddy and daughter cannot hold each other close in joy and peace if one of them has been sold into slavery, or if the Nazis are bombing their town.

When God sees the joy and beauty of the father and his child, He sees the father and daughter enjoying a gift of His grace to humanity. As such, He would not simply call the father and daughter "good," in a "rules" sense, but actually truly *holy*.

But say instead the father decides to behave like the Prodigal Brother. The Prodigal Brother thinks the way to the Father's heart is by doing all the right things on his Father's estate like a slave, rather than by living as a son in the Father's love and affection. So he scours the Bible, or some other document he considers authoritative, and finds what he thinks is a rule that he is to spend time with his daughter. He believes that, by keeping this command, he will receive some special blessing or status or avoid some punishment. So he goes to his daughter and says to her, "The rules say I must hold you, I must play with you, and I must act like I am enjoying it. Moreover, they say you must as well, so let's both be obedient and get this whole 'daddy-daughter' thing out of the way so we can do whatever we'd rather be doing."

When the Prodigal Brother takes what is truly good, and turns it into a mere rule or religious obligation, he robs that act of its beauty and true goodness. The relationship between father and daughter goes from being something wonderful, merry, and lovely, to being something stilted, formulaic, and rather sickening. In fact, we might say the relationship became corrupted.

Similarly, when Adam and Eve ate the fruit, they chose to replace God in their consciences with the knowledge of good and evil. Paul writes of fallen humanity, "Because they did not think it worthwhile to have God in their knowledge, God delivered them over to a worthless mind to do what is morally wrong" (Rom. 1:28). Humanity's problem isn't that we refuse to retain rules in our knowledge. Rather, we refuse to retain God Himself in our knowledge. If God alone is intrinsically good, then the only way to actually have any true knowledge of good, is to seek first the knowledge of God Himself. That is only possible through intimacy with Him. When the rules displace God as the focus of the conscience, then the "good" in the rules becomes corrupted, just like the relationship between the daddy and daughter became corrupted. It is not a stretch to see that a focus on "the knowledge of good and evil" would have, by Noah's time, created a world so devoid of the knowledge of the true goodness of God that only evil was left.

The Requirements of the Law

The Prodigal Brother simply cannot see what is truly holy about a father and daughter enjoying time together, or a mother baking cookies for her son, or a talented artist painting a beautiful landscape. Because none of these things speak to his narrow rule-based framework, the Prodigal Brother in us doesn't know them to be truly good. In other words, to the Prodigal Brother, good is not a true and present reality. Good is nothing other than performance to a set of religious obligations.

Now, most Prodigal Brothers will be able to see what is wrong with the father in the above illustration, but all of us do the same thing in many other relationships without even realizing it. The reason is that the Prodigal Brother in us cannot see love as truly good on its own merits. Instead, he views love's goodness as derived from its ability to motivate someone to keep the right rules.

On the other hand, the Bible says rules are good only in so much as they are derived from, and always subordinate to, the underlying reality of love. Jesus said the entire Law, and indeed the entire Old Testament ("the Law and the Prophets") hangs on the two commands to love God and love others. Similarly, in the book of Romans, Paul speaks of Gentiles who had no knowledge of the Torah, but still fulfilled the "Law's requirements" (Rom. 2:26-27):

Therefore if an uncircumcised man keeps the law's requirements, will his uncircumcision not be counted as circumcision? A man who is physically uncircumcised, but who fulfills the law, will judge you who are a lawbreaker in spite of having the letter of the law and circumcision.

An uncircumcised man who doesn't know the Law, but "keeps the Law's requirements," is a person who "fulfills the Law." Now, one of the commandments of the Law is to be circumcised on the eighth day after birth, so evidently an uncircumcised person can break that rule, and yet still "fulfill the Law." In fact, because Paul is talking about something Gentiles might do in his day, we would have to negate most of the 613 rules in the Torah. Most of those were contextualized for the Jewish people in Israel, and were not done by Gentiles. Hundreds of the Torah's commands deal with the sacrificial system that the Gentiles did not have and were not allowed by the Torah to take part in. Biblically, Gentile is not simply an ethnic term. It is also a religious term. Paul knew that by definition, a Gentile was someone who ate pigs; didn't pay tithes; didn't keep the Jewish Sabbath, New Moons, or Feasts; didn't have tassels on the edges of his garment; and did not study the Torah (because most did not even know what a Torah was, and the vast majority were illiterate anyway). So in God's eyes fulfilling the Law must be entirely different than keeping the rules. Through Paul, God later tells us what it means to "fulfill the Law" (Rom. 13:8-10):

Do not owe anyone anything, except to love one another, for the one who loves another has fulfilled the law. The commandments: "You shall not commit adultery, you shall not murder, you shall not steal, you shall not covet," and if there is any other commandment—all are summed up by this: "You shall love your neighbor as yourself." Love does no wrong to a neighbor. Love, therefore, is the fulfillment of the law.

Instead of telling the Roman Christians to focus on keeping the rules in the Law, Paul just tells them to love others and not worry about the rules specifically. The reason, as Paul saw it, was that the rules were derived from the greater principle of love. Love is good on its own, so love really is the point, not the rules. The rules may tell us what love will not do, but they don't really express the depth of the beauty of what love does between individuals. The rules do not explain the Mother Theresa's of this world. Rules cannot do that.

Further, the problem with love is that you cannot fake it. You can externally keep the rules Paul listed, or at least try very hard, but you cannot treat someone in a truly loving way, from the core of your being, unless you love them in the first place. Love comes first as an internal, spiritual reality that then expresses itself in action. Again we see that true goodness is foundational to who someone is in their inner person. Goodness is not simply external rules or principles that someone keeps to get something else.

If we think about love's version of the father and daughter, versus the Prodigal Brother's version, we see the difference between living by the love of God, and living by a set of rules. The first is truly real, truly foundational, truly natural. The holiness expressed in the relationship of the father and daughter was just who they were. It was unforced and instinctive because of the love they had in them. The second is a horrible *corruption* of what is truly good. It may fool some, but it would not for a moment fool an all-knowing God who can see into the depths of the heart. On top of that, when push comes to shove, what is to keep the father from treating his daughter horribly if he thinks there is some greater rule that can be kept in doing so? On the other hand, what power do the rules have to actually cause him to willingly lay down his life to protect his daughter? What power do the rules have to move him to desire her well-being as his deepest yearning? If we think of good only as a set of rules, and not as the actual heart of a loving God, there is nothing to keep us from eventually becoming violent like Noah's contemporaries. We merely have to convince ourselves that the rules either warrant it, or at least allow it in certain cases.

The Parable of the Buddhist and the Businessman

Up to this point we've mostly dealt with the "knowledge of good and evil" in terms of what we call religion. Or more precisely, what most people call religion. But the same underlying ideology of human religion is also present in pretty much everything else we see in human nature. In fact, it all comes under the umbrella of trust in one's own knowledge and abilities, rather than trust in God.

Suppose we have two men. One is not particularly wealthy. He is not concerned with being rich. In fact, he lives in a sort of religious commune. He has a shaven head and wears a long orange robe. He is a very devout Buddhist monk. He meditates for several hours a day. He dutifully studies the implications of the Four Noble Truths, and he has dedicated himself to perfectly following the Eight-Fold Path, all by focusing on the Middle Way. He punctiliously follows the Five Precepts, avoiding violence, theft, sexual immorality, dishonesty, and intoxication. He goes even further, seeking perfect observance of the 227 Patimokkha rules specifically designed for monks. He puts himself through all of this in hopes that someday, whether in this life or the next, he will achieve enlightenment, find true inner peace, and break the cycle of reincarnation. He seeks the knowledge that will bring to him the peace that he lacks.

In contrast, the second man is well-off. He lives in a 4,000 square foot house, has a beautiful BMW, and a nice little ski boat. He is a businessman. He studies business ideas and financial books, dedicating himself to mastering the art of business. He tries to find the best ideas regarding the art of negotiation, and he has learned everything there is to know about how to close the big deal. He is a master at analyzing cash flows and financial statements. He works 70 hours a week, and spends his off-time rolling around business ideas and financial strategies in his head. His greatest hope is to retire early a famous multi-millionaire, with a Ferrari and an even bigger house in Park City, Utah. He believes that if he could have those, he would truly have the peace he has always wanted. So he seeks the knowledge of business necessary to achieve that goal.

Really these two men are one and the same. They both hope, by their knowledge and their own efforts and abilities, to bring themselves some higher existence or state of peace or happiness or what have you. The first is what we might call "religious," and if you look at a lot of what he does, it isn't bad in itself. To be unconcerned with wealth would be a nice change for all of us. The Five Precepts are pretty much universal to all faiths, not just Buddhism, and it would be good for society if everyone obeyed them. The idea of following a "Middle Way"—avoiding the pitfalls of extremism—is generally a helpful life principle.

But the monk is always seeking something that he can never bring himself. His abstinence from violence, theft, sexual immorality, dishonesty, and intoxication is not rooted in a love for the people in his life. Rather, he avoids these bad things in order to achieve some greater blessing. But there is no greater blessing than love. There is no greater peace than to receive the love of God, to return that love, and to pass that love on to others. No reality is more wonderful. I do not mean to single out Buddhism. It is the same in every human religious system. The monk is like every compulsively religious person, so dedicated to his religious "goodness" that he has forgotten the true goodness inherent in relationship. Consequently, he is a slave to his religious ideas.

Similarly, there is nothing inherently wrong with a lot of things the second man does. Work is not a bad thing at all, if for no other reason than that sitting around doing nothing gets dull very quickly. Wanting to do a good job is not bad, in itself, either. Certainly being retired in Park City would be quite nice, and really there is nothing inherently wrong with that either. In fact, I might like to retire there someday myself. In addition, I admit it might be nice to have a ski boat to use with family and friends, and BMWs are excellent automobiles. But the businessman is so dedicated to his business practice that he doesn't have time to enjoy any of this, and loving relationships with others go by the way side. He is not seeking fulfillment by being God's child, living in God's love, and enjoying that love as it expresses itself to others. Instead, he is seeking fulfillment via physical toys, and he sees everything else in life as a means to that end. He is, like the monk, a slave to his business dreams.

Both of these men are trying to take things that might be good, and use them to achieve something else. They do not appreciate goodness for its own sake. Even worse, they do not appreciate loving relationships, which are the highest form of good available. They are ignoring what is truly good, and instead embracing lesser things, to achieve something they want. Both of them are so busy trusting in themselves, in their "knowledge of good and evil," that they cannot "be still, and know that I am God" (Ps. 46:10). They are not willing to trust in the only One who loves them perfectly and wishes to supply to them everything that is truly good. Instead, they only want what they think is good. So they want to be slaves on the Father's estate, working like dogs in the hopes that maybe, someday, they will have earned the right to kill and eat a mere goat.

We might say that trying to achieve what is good by knowing and performing the right list of rules or business principles is akin to "the knowledge of good and evil." The problem with trying to become like God through the "knowledge of good and evil," is that it sees *good* as only a means to some greater end, not as the ultimate end Himself. God did not intend humanity to do good in order to become something else. He intended us to actually *be* good in the true "wedding" sense, to be joyful and in love with Him and peaceful and contented and merry. And He made us that way to begin with. That goodness—love—is not a means to an end, but the beginning and the end of what God meant for us to be. And the only way for us to truly be good, is intimacy with God, Who alone is good.

Man became evil when he tried to live by his own rules or schemes or whatever you want to call them, instead of living by God's grace. He became evil when he set "good and evil" up as a means to achieve some other end. This isn't to say that rules are all bad. Certainly in an imperfect world, with imperfect people, they can be quite useful for limited purposes, for instance restraining violence.

Indeed, the Bible even gives rules for born-again believers, although these rules do not come with the threat of eternal destruction. The Bible gives such rules because the believer still has traces of the Prodigal Brother within him. Those traces—the flesh—need rules for restraint. As we saw with the discussion of the "law's requirements," the point for regenerate Christians is to allow God in His grace to cleanse our hearts more and more of the traces of the flesh, so that eventually the rules will be unnecessary for us. The point of a Christian's life is not to seek the knowledge of the rules, but to seek the knowledge of the God behind the rules.

The more we know Him, the less we need rules: We begin to love instinctively.

That demonstrates the problem: Rules can restrain certain impulses, but in terms of dealing with the core problem of evil within us, rules just don't work. Only grace offers a true solution to evil. In order to perfectly keep the rules, one has to be perfectly good in the first place. And if one is perfectly good in the first place, rules are superfluous.

Corrupted

The point of how this fits in to the story of Noah is that it explains how corruption came about. The Prodigal Brother—fallen man—has *corrupted* what is truly good into some means to either get something he wants—power, wealth, or pleasure—or to avoid some kind of punishment. He does not see it as good in its own right, but only insomuch as it brings something else. Put another way, the Prodigal Brother believes that knowing good and evil can get him something better. He thinks he is a slave, so he only does what he thinks is good so that he can eat the young goat or avoid being whipped. What this means is that the Prodigal Brother, no matter how dedicated he is to the rules, does not truly love what is good. And he doesn't truly love the One who alone is intrinsically good. He might say he loves God, but he only says it because he thinks the rules require him to say it.

So we have an entire world of people who do not love good for its own sake. Like the monk and the businessman, they love what they can get for themselves through knowing good and evil. It should be obvious that they thus believe their own desires or utopian visions—divorced from relationship with God or others—are the greatest objective. If good and evil are things one respectively performs or abstains from in order to attain a higher goal, then ultimately they become subordinate to whatever the Prodigal Brother perceives that goal to be. Good and evil become poorly marked paths to a goal. Consequently, it is no problem to bend the rules if you think it can get you the greater objective. This becomes very easy to do if the rules come from your own narrow "knowledge of good and evil." In fact, it often happens without us even realizing it.

Believing that he has always been a dutiful rule-keeping slave on the Father's estate, the Prodigal Brother in us wants to see the rules, and not people, as the thing that life is truly about. Thus, he feels free to mistreat and abuse and exploit others if it somehow causes the rules to triumph. After all, he thinks it is the rules, not love, that will bring him and others to some wonderful goal. So the rules must win out even at the expense of love. There is no value to mercy in such a worldview. This is why the Pharisees treated people so harshly in Jesus' day.

In his book *The Lotus and the Cross*, Ravi Zacharias creates a fictionalized conversation between Jesus, Buddha, and a former prostitute named Priya who was dying of AIDS. Jesus told Priya of the woman who had come to wash his feet with perfume:

> **Jesus:** ... She had lived a life of prostitution. She once came into a room full of self-righteous people, and they were horrified that I would even let her near me, let alone touch me. You see, that's what legalism does. What do you think would happen to you, Priya, if you hugged that [Buddhist] monk, or even put your hand on his shoulder?
> **Priya:** "Oh my! That would be the end of me... and, for that matter, of him!"[5]

The rules would not allow the Buddhist monk we discussed earlier to touch a broken former prostitute who was suffering from AIDS. He could not express kindness to her, because the rules said it would keep him from achieving his greatest hope of Nirvana. In fact, she would be punished if she sought to express kindness by hugging him. The rules had made love subordinate to the monk's greater purpose, and thus love could not truly win out.

I do not mean here to insult Buddhism above other religions. I mean instead that the religious Prodigal Brother in us is like the monk. He makes good subordinate to something else, and seeks that something else by the knowledge of the rules or principles. Thus, he rejects love—specifically God's love for us and in us—as the very ultimate good for which he should yearn. Thus, the end result is an unloving corruption. Eventually, as in Noah's day, that unloving corruption leads man to a violent abuse of others to get what he wants.

Scheming Evil

After looking at the corruption of man, God said, "I will wipe off the face of the earth man, whom I created, together with the animals, creatures that crawl, and birds of the sky—for I regret that I made them" (Gen. 6:7). Directly before this verse, we find that God was "grieved in His heart." If we see good and evil as He does, then we might be grieved as well: The world was made for love. Man was meant to live in the unending perfect experience of God's love, as he himself would be a vessel through whom God's love overflows to others. It would have been a true bliss next to which our happiest moments today would be pathetic forgeries. God was grieved because that reality had been corrupted into the evil before Him. It was because this world could have been so very good, that its violent corruption was so hurtful to God. God does not hate evil for evil's sake. He hates evil for goodness' sake.

The text says that "every scheme [man's] mind thought of was nothing but evil all the time." The text doesn't say simply that man's mind thought evil, which is bad enough. It says the mind of every man was creating evil schemes every moment. A scheme is much more than a mere thought. It is a plan, a strategy to bring about some end. Both the Buddhist and the businessman had their schemes to get some greater blessing. So do each of us.

Seeking life by schemes causes us to devalue others, because it treats them only as tools we can exploit for our purposes. Love, on the other hand, does not treat people according to selfish schemes. The further and further we push ourselves away from knowing God's love, the more and more evil our thoughts and schemes become. We can only have a godly love for others if we first freely receive the love God freely offers us.

But cut loose from intimacy with God, man could live to things apart from God, to his own "knowledge of good and evil," which he could twist and manipulate to fit his schemes.

Because Adam and Eve shut humanity off from God, they were not subject to His love. Instead, they could seek their own distorted "knowledge of good and evil." As we discussed before, since man had no good within him, the evil that was there could simply twist or concoct whatever rules it wanted, until eventually "every scheme his mind thought of was nothing but evil all the time." If asked to describe what man concocted of evil schemes continuously, and evil schemes that resulted in widespread violence, we would have to answer Hitler, or maybe Stalin.

The sad state of humanity—divorced from God's goodness, rejecting His grace and by nature unable to trust Him—is that every person has the potential to be something like Hitler. By choosing a nature categorized by their attempts to be good by their own power and efforts, divorced from God's love, Adam and Eve really chose the opposite of God. Mark Andrew Ritchie, a highly successful businessman, records that the moment of his salvation came with the realization of the little Hitler within him:

> I tried to pull myself together and ask myself what the big deal was... I'm not Hitler, after all, I reassured myself. And it *was* reassuring, at this low point, to know that I was at least better than someone. But I couldn't convince myself. I knew history too well. Wasn't it Hitler's conviction of his racial superiority that caused him to do what he did? He was just like me except that he had the power to deal with the "undesirables." I was, in fact, a Hitler who was merely out of power. [6]

Ritchie saw in his own pride and selfishness a little bit of Adolf Hitler, and it is this little bit of Hitler that is in all of us. Perhaps not a big Hitler, perhaps not to the degree of Hitler, but in this consolation we find only a consolation of *degree* and not of *kind*. In Noah's day, this consolation of degree had grown so minute that the Hitler-ism of humanity was rampant. If you reject the only truly good Being, you will have no other chance but to end up evil, just like if you do not continue to re-fill a bath tub with hot water, eventually the water in it will get cold.

Christians often say about Jesus that He is True God and True Man. In this, we primarily mean that He, though truly God, is also truly human, not merely divinity masquerading in an elaborate human-like costume. But I think there is something more to His status as True Man. Paul, in Romans 5, discusses how Jesus, in essence, takes the place of Adam. Adam, because he sinned, fell in nature from what humanity was meant to be, taking all of his progeny with him. Jesus, because He is sinless, is exactly what God sees as essential, uncorrupted humanity: He exemplifies in His humanity what mankind was always meant to be, but isn't. Someone once said, "There is a difference between 'normal' and 'average.' Jesus is normal. The rest of us are only average."

If the world was filled almost entirely with little Hitler's, then it would have been a dire situation indeed. If we look at Jesus as the epitome of what true humanity actually is, then we cannot see Hitler as human at all. Rather, we would see him, and those like him, as wild, brutish, and unthinking animals.

Jesus brings life, but Hitler only brought death. In fact, it does not seem at all unlikely that, had God not done something to wipe out this race of little Hitler's, mankind would have rendered itself extinct. From the Bible's description of mankind in Noah's day—corrupt, spoiled from what it was meant to be, horribly twisted and mangled—we find that whatever this race called "man" was, it was not truly human in God's sense of the word. It was a race of diseased spiritual mutants, a race of wrecks, a people that weren't so much human, as they were the remains of what was once human. In a sense, God saw that this toilet called earth was full of useless filth, so He flushed it.

Whatever God finally destroyed, it wasn't what humanity was made to be. It was something that had so twisted itself that it didn't, in His eyes, appear human at all. And, what's more, inside each of us is something that is growing more and more to destroy our true humanity, made in God's image. It is as if, because of the nature Adam and Eve chose, we have a great cancerous tumor within us. That cancer does not love what is good. It cannot love what is good, no matter how hard it tries. Instead, it is only able to see goodness as subordinate to its selfish desires. It devalues others because it devalues goodness. It devalues Love Himself, so it has no love in it.

A New Commandment

But God saved humanity from self-destruction by condemning Hitlerism in man. He chose Noah and his family to carry on the line. And after the flood God provided the world again to Noah just as He had to Adam (Gen. 9:1-5):

God blessed Noah and his sons and said to them, "Be fruitful and multiply and fill the earth. The fear and terror of you will be in every living creature on the earth, every bird of the sky, every creature that crawls on the ground, and all the fish of the sea. They are placed under your authority. Every living creature will be food for you; as I gave the green plants, I have given you everything. However, you must not eat meat with its lifeblood in it. I will require the life of every animal and every man for your life and your blood. I will require the life of each man's brother for a man's life."

Just as God blessed Adam and Eve and told them to multiply and fill the earth, so He blessed Noah and his sons and told them to multiply and fill the earth. God not only blessed them in words: Just as God offered Adam and Eve every plant for food (except one), so He commanded Noah and his sons to partake also of meat. I, for one, am glad He did. Fried chicken is a gift of God.

But notice the stark differences between what God told Adam and Eve, and what He later told Noah and his sons. Man is no longer commanded to subdue the earth. Why? Perhaps man, seeking to live by his own strength, would misconstrue this command as a command of dominance and power, a command to victimize and destroy. Perhaps this was how man was living before the flood. After all, people were subduing one another with rampant violence.

In place of this command to subdue the earth, God placed in animals a fear of man, indicating that in some sense man had become a threat to them. Man was no longer fit to subdue, to have dominion over the earth. Certainly a wild animal's fear of man will often keep him from attacking us, but it also keeps him from submitting to us. Men needed protection from wild animals, to be sure, but the text can also be interpreted to mean that wild animals needed protection from men. Indeed, Rabbinical scholars have for centuries interpreted it this way. In place of the command to rule over the wildlife, Noah and his sons were given the much weaker nod to their mere "authority" over the wildlife. It has been said that a king rules while a President governs, and perhaps in these contrasts we see the same principle. Fallen man, no longer fit to truly rule, could now merely govern.

God's declaration in Eden contains no indication that He would require either an animal's blood or man's blood for killing man. It contains no statement that He would put fear into anyone or anything, animal or human. But in the new command to Noah this is precisely what we find.

In Eden (Gen. 1:28-30)	After the Flood (Gen. 9:1-7)
"God blessed them [male and female – vs. 27], and God said to them..."	"God blessed Noah and his sons and said to them..."
'Be fruitful, multiply, fill the earth...'	'Be fruitful and multiply and fill the earth...'[Reiterated in vs. 7]

'and subdue it...'	'The fear and terror of you will be in every living creature on the earth, every bird of the sky, every creature that crawls on the ground, and all the fish of the sea...'
'Rule the fish of the sea, the birds of the sky, and every creature that crawls on the earth...'	'They are placed under your authority...'
"God also said, 'Look, I have given you every seed-bearing plant on the surface of the entire earth, and every tree whose fruit contains seed. This food will be for you, for all the wildlife of the earth, for every bird of the sky, and for every creature that crawls on the earth— everything having the breath of life in it. I have given every green plant for food.'"	'Every living creature will be food for you; as I gave the green plants, I have given you everything. However, you must not eat meat with its lifeblood in it.'

Nothing	'I will require the life of every animal and every man for your life and your blood. I will require the life of each man's brother for a man's life. 'Whoever sheds man's blood, his blood will be shed by man, for God made man in His image.'"

Why did the command to Noah contain a fear-based warning, but the command to Adam and Eve did not? We see the answer by understanding the fall. Man chose, as part of his nature, to live to external rules rather than relationship with God. Fallen man does not have God's love in Him. He does not submit to love, so he requires an external power to control him. Fallen man can only understand the rules, so he can only be governed by fear-based commands. Like the monk and the businessman, the Prodigal Brother in us seeks life by rules and head knowledge. It is not because he truly wants to live that way, but because that is simply who he is. Unless he is born again, he can be no other way. God's fear-based command was meant to control the Prodigal Brother in us, so that mankind would not destroy itself completely.

This is partly why we see Paul write, in his epistle to the Galatians, "Why the law then? It was added because of transgressions" (Gal. 3:19). The best way to understand this is to think of what heaven would be like. Is it possible that in heaven, we will be walking around thinking, "I really would like to punch that angel over there in the face, but God said 'No,' so I had better not"? This is absurd on its face! In this situation, evil still clearly exists within such a person, as a desire or hope in his heart. This would not be heaven, as the Bible speaks of it, because evil would still be around. In heaven, the perfected man would not even consider punching an angel in the face, precisely *because* he would be perfected.

Another way to think about why God gave a threat-based command to Noah, but not to sinless Adam and Eve, is to think about why we have laws in the first place. If man had no tendency to do rotten things, we would have no need for laws with built-in punishments. The punishments are only in place to deter the evil in men by promising some pain if the law were broken. But if man was of a sort that didn't have the cancer of sin within him, there would be no need to threaten punishment, since by nature man wouldn't do bad things in the first place. This is why James Madison, a central player in the debate concerning the adoption of the U.S. Constitution, famously wrote, "If men were angels, no government would be necessary."[7]

But since man did not seek the indwelling of God, he now has no ability within himself to truly do good and not evil. There is, in place of God, a dark emptiness that can only be restrained by the threat of severe punishment. Because sinful man needs this threat in order to control himself, he can never be truly free and at the same time truly good. He must always and everywhere be a slave living in fear. That is the lot Adam and Eve chose when they attempted to find goodness apart from God. And it is this lot that is overcome at the cross, when life by relationship with God is made available once again.

Babylon Is Fallen

Many years after Noah, we find the first discussion of Babylon, or Shinar. In the Bible, God uses many metaphors for human evil, but the most central and common one is that of Babylon. It appears in a literal and historical way in Genesis, again in the histories of Israel, and then in the Old Testament prophecies and symbolically in the New Testament book of Revelation. If Jesus brought us the Kingdom of God, then the kingdom He invaded to do so would have to be called the Kingdom of Babylon.

Many Biblical scholars will tell us about the "Law of First Mention." This isn't a law in the traditional sense. It is more like an interpretative tool. It says that the first time a concept is mentioned in the Bible usually sets the stage for the discussion of that concept from then on. The "first mention" of something is in some way foundational. So the first mention of Babylon should tell us what this other kingdom is all about. The story is short, so we will read it in full (Gen. 11:1-9):

> At one time the whole earth had the same language and vocabulary. As people migrated from the east, they found a valley in the land of Shinar and settled there. They said to each other, "Come, let us make oven-fired bricks." They had brick for stone and asphalt for mortar. And they said, "Come, let us build ourselves a city and a tower with its top in the sky. Let us make a name for ourselves; otherwise, we will be scattered over the face of the whole earth."
>
> Then the Lord came down to look over the city and the tower that the men were building. The Lord said, "If, as one people all having the same language, they have begun to do this, then nothing they plan to do will be impossible for them. Come, let Us go down there and confuse their language so that they will not understand one another's speech." So the Lord scattered them from there over the face of the whole earth, and they stopped building the city. Therefore its name is called Babylon, for there the Lord confused the language of the whole earth, and

from there the Lord scattered them over the face of the whole earth.

The book of Genesis is not favorable towards cities. In fact, almost everywhere that it speaks of cities, it speaks negatively of them in some respect. The first city, it says, was built by Cain after he murdered his brother Abel. He had to build a city in order to live because he could no longer live by farming. The city became a locus of evil, a place where people did not live off the land as God had always intended, but by their own means in some sort of wicked way. This is not to say that it is sinful to live in a city. But it is to say that the idea the city represents in the book of Genesis is worrisome, and we see that idea in the story of the tower.

The people wanted to build "a city and a tower" in order to "make a name for ourselves" so that they would not be "scattered over the face of the whole earth." God had previously told Noah and his sons to go out over the face of the whole earth. He had once again given them the entire earth as theirs. The Babylonians, in contrast, wanted to build up a reality for themselves by their own efforts. They wanted to reject the reality freely offered by God, and to substitute something else in its place by their own works. They did this hoping to make a name for themselves, to bring themselves up to some greater reality or status and bring a great blessing to themselves. In other words, they were quite "religious." They were a lot like both the monk and the businessman. They sought some greater reality by means of their human efforts.

God didn't think highly of this. He says, "If, as one people all having the same language, they have begun to do this, then nothing they plan to do will be impossible for them." God had already seen, in Noah's day, what happens when sinful men start planning and scheming. Evil results and the world becomes nothing but violence. God had already promised not to flood the earth again, so He instead nipped the problem in the bud by confusing their languages. "The Lord scattered them from there over the face of the whole earth, and they stopped building the city."

The Hebrew word *Babylon* means confusion, and that is why we read, "Therefore its name is called Babylon, for there the Lord confused the language of the whole earth, and from there the Lord scattered them over the face of the whole earth." There is something fascinating about the wording of the text. It implies that God effectively called both the city, and the whole earth, Babylon. It says the place in question is called Babylon because "the Lord confused the language of the whole earth, and from there [the city of Babylon] the Lord scattered them over the face of the whole earth." In other words, the confusion that started at Babylon spread to the entire world.

Babylon, in some sense, represents the entirety of human religious thinking. Not just religion proper, but the underlying spirit of bondage that comes from reliance on ourselves, on our own knowledge, and on our own power. Babylon is the slavery of the monk and the businessman, the bondage to our own rules and schemes and efforts, completely divorced from the joy and freedom of godly love. It represents the chasing after more, better, best. It represents our attempts to become "like gods" as some translations render the Serpent's promise in the garden.[8] Babylon is, at its heart, a rejection of God's provision and an attempt to procure something else by our own means. In the metaphor of the Prodigal Son, it is leaving home and "living as though I do not yet have a home and must look far and wide to find one."[9] It speaks of a boastfulness in our own power that comes by rejection of grace. That, in a nutshell, is what humanity doomed itself to in Eden.

The Third Man

But what if, in addition to the monk and the businessman, there was a third kind of man? What if there was a kind of man whose life was founded on trusting a God whom he knew loved him? What if that man's hope was not in what he could bring about on his own, but on the true good that God had promised to him? What if his life was centered in his relationships with others, and especially with his God? That kind of man might look very different from the two others, and it is to such a man that we will next turn.

Chapter 5

The Faithful, of the Father

—∞—

Abraham believed and did not doubt. He believed
the preposterous.

Soren Kierkegaard/*Fear and Trembling*

If you were to ask Christians who was the greatest man
ever to live, they would all obviously say Jesus Christ.
If you were to ask them who was the second greatest man
ever to live, you might get more diversity of opinion. Some
might say King David. Others might say Moses or Elijah.
A few might even say Paul of Tarsus. But if you were to
ask Jesus and His Apostles, they might have said Abraham.
Jesus rebuked the Pharisees for not believing as Abraham
did (John 8:39-41, 56-58). When Peter preached to the
Israelites in Solomon's Colonnade, he identified Jesus as the
Seed promised to Abraham (Acts 3:25). When James wanted
to contrast real faith with a forgery thereof, he referred to
Abraham (James 2:20-23). When the author of Hebrews
sought to show the power of faith, he dwelt on the examples
of Abraham and Sarah.

Yet none of the Apostles seems to go so far in adula-
tion as Paul. Paul's view of salvation centers on the right-
ness with God that comes only by faith. So when Paul wants

to illustrate what it means to be "justified by faith," (Rom. 3:28, 5:1; Gal. 2:16, 3:24) he twice nods to Abraham (Rom. 4, Gal. 3-4). He writes an entire chapter about Abraham in his epistle to the Romans, and two chapters about him in the epistle to the Galatians. All this for good reason.

To be sure, Abraham had his share of embarrassing failures. He fathered a child by Hagar instead of trusting God's promise to bring a child by Sarah. He lied to Pharaoh about his marriage to Sarah, allowing her to be taken into Pharaoh's harem. And if that wasn't enough, he did the same thing by lying to Abimelech. If we were to be honest about his life, Abraham is not what the world would call a "good" man. But if we were to see him as God does, we would have to agree that Abraham was a great man.

Abraham's greatness came because of his simple trust in the God of grace. Abraham did not seem to live to a list of rules. He often showed a deep understanding of what is right and what is wrong, such as when he bargained with God to prevent the destruction of the righteous at Sodom and Gomorrah. But that instance demonstrates that his understanding of right and wrong was derived, not from rules, but from his belief in the intrinsic value of every human being. His life was not so much a life focused on "ethicality" or "morality," as one of a deep and magnificent trust in a God who values His human creations.

The Justifying God of Abraham

To weaken the example of Abraham's justifying faith, the Prodigal Brother will often quote God's declaration that "Abraham listened to My voice and kept My mandate, My commands, My statutes, and My instructions" (Gen. 26:5). The idea is that Abraham's rightness with God came because Abraham followed the right rules. But if the Prodigal Brother were to be consistent, he would have to demand a re-trial from God in light of the aforementioned embarrassments regarding Pharaoh, Abimelech, and Hagar. God, it seems, just glosses right over these moral lapses. In fact, He doesn't so much gloss over them, as act like they never even happened. We rarely find the rest of the Bible ever referring to Abraham's failures. For instance, the Bible doesn't again bring up the Hagar incident in any depth until the New Testament, specifically Galatians 4. And Paul only uses it so that he might illustrate what it means to cease living to the slavery of religious performance and obligation (Gal. 4:21-31). In this, Paul implicitly praises Abraham for throwing out Hagar, rather than castigating him for sleeping with her in the first place.

Why does the Bible seems to simply "write off" Abraham's moral deficiencies as if they never occurred? For the Apostles, the answer centered around a single verse: "Abram believed the LORD, and He credited it to him as righteousness" (Gen. 15:6). Scholars tell us the Hebrew verb tenses do not point to the verse as something that happened in Genesis 15, but something that occurred beforehand, with its effects continuing through Genesis 15.[1] As such, Genesis 15:6 seems to serve as an explanation, not merely of the events in that chapter, but of the entire relationship between God and Abraham: This strange God simply declared, or accounted, or "credited" Abraham as righteous, based not on Abraham's moral efforts or religious feats, but simply on Abraham's trust in God's promise.

This is simply not the Prodigal Brother's god. His god would never do such a dangerous thing as to grant someone right standing simply because of that person's trust in a promise. In the eyes of the Prodigal Brother, to do so is to give someone a license to sin. The Prodigal Brother thinks that we only do good and abstain from evil, in order to get a greater prize. So if God gave Abraham the greatest prize of all, a right relationship to Himself, simply because

Abraham believed His promises, then the Prodigal Brother thinks God would be taking away the only true motivation for doing good. This is why Luther wrote, "Jealous for its own religious views, the world ... charges the Gospel with being a subversive and licentious doctrine, offensive to God and man, a doctrine to be persecuted as the worst plague on earth."[2]

The Unreasonable Calling

Genesis 15:6 said faith was credited to Abraham as righteousness. But that fact never led Abraham into rampant and unrepentant sinning. In fact, we find in Abraham's life that the only times he did unrighteous things, were when he stopped trusting in God and instead tried to bring about God's purposes by his own efforts. He slept with Hagar to father Ishmael because he did not trust God to bring about a son by Sarah. He lied to Pharaoh about Sarah because he did not trust God to protect him and his family. Similarly, he deceived Abimelech because he did not trust God to watch out for him. We must understand the power of faith in Abraham's life in order to fully grasp Genesis 15:6. In so doing, we will see why "[God] credited [Abraham's faith] to him as righteousness." We will see that faith is intrinsically justifying.

God called Abraham when he had done nothing to deserve it. God said to him: "Go out from your land, your relatives, and your father's house to the land that I will show you" (Gen. 12:1). Bizarrely enough, Abraham went. I say it is bizarre because it is not something a "normal" person would do. God was not merely calling Abraham to walk down the street to the grocery store and pick up a gallon of milk. He wasn't even calling Abraham to move to a new city. He was calling Abraham to walk out the front door of his home and go—quite literally—to God knows where. He was called to be a homeless nomad. The author of Hebrews states (Hebrews 11:8, 9):

By faith Abraham, when he was called, obeyed and went out to a place he was going to receive as an inheritance; he went out, **not knowing where he was going.** By faith he stayed as a foreigner in the land of promise, living in tents with Isaac and Jacob, co-heirs of the same promise.

Abraham wasn't reasonable. He was faithful. Faith isn't reasonable. Faith will cause someone to do the most unreasonable things of all. Faith caused Moses to give up life in the royal court of the most powerful king in the world, in order to lead a bunch of uneducated, whining slaves out into a desert, where they walked around aimlessly for forty years. Faith caused Peter to give up a perfectly good fishing business in order to spread the Gospel, suffer terrible hardship and persecution, and eventually die by crucifixion. Faith caused Paul to give up a life as one of the most respected religious leaders of his day. He not only gave up a life destined for the Sanhedrin, but referred to that life as "filth" (Phil. 3:8). Faith led a 16th century monk to give up a promising and prosperous career as a Catholic clergyman in order to nail 95 theses to the door of a church in Wittenberg, making himself a hunted criminal and the scourge of the European political order. Faith just doesn't do reasonable things.

The author of Hebrews said Noah's faith "condemned the world" (Heb. 11:7). This is what faith does when it comes time to act. Faith runs counter to the very nature of the world of the Prodigal Brother. It raises its fist against the world as it is, and against the religious lies upon which it is built, and says, "I do not accept a thing about you!" This is why the author of Hebrews tells us Abraham forsook the city and went to live in tents: "He was looking forward to the city that has foundations, whose architect and builder is God" (Heb. 11:10). In Chapter 4 we discussed how, in Genesis up to this point, cities had come to symbolize human efforts, human boasting, and human rejection of God's grace. So when the author of Hebrews says that Abraham "was looking forward to the city that has foundations, whose architect and builder is God," we shouldn't at all take this lightly. By leaving the city of Haran, Abraham was rejecting human efforts to achieve greatness. He was instead trusting in God's grace. He was hoping in faith for the day when God would, by His might and not by our abilities, overcome the problem of sin and create a new world founded entirely on His love. Abraham, like Noah, was condemning the world of the Prodigal Brother by trusting in the God of grace. Rather than following those who sought to "make a name for ourselves," Abraham chose to trust the God who promised to "make your name great." He was choosing to return to his Father's great estate, rather than slave away on the filthy pig farms of human religion.

Loving Lot

When Abraham had originally left Haran, his nephew Lot had decided to tag along. The Bible never really tells us why, but paints Lot as a *schlemiel*, to borrow a Yiddish term. He was a well-intentioned bungler. Peter referred to him as "righteous Lot," (2 Pet. 2:7) so his problem wasn't that he was unrighteous before God. His problem was simply that he wasn't very clever. In that sense, he is easy for all of us to identify with.

By Genesis 13, Abraham had become quite wealthy, so that his herdsmen and Lot's were getting into fights about watering holes. The Bible implies that Abraham loved Lot. In fact, he seemed to treat Lot as his clumsy kid brother who needed his protection. So Abraham said to Lot, "Please, let's not have quarreling between you and me, or between your herdsmen and my herdsmen, since we are relatives. Isn't the whole land before you? Separate from me: if you go to the left, I will go to the right; if you go to the right, I will go to the left" (Gen. 13:8-9).

Lot chose to live in the plain southwest of the Dead Sea, specifically in the very evil city of Sodom. He did this because it looked nice. Poisoned berries often look more delicious than edible ones. An axis of ancient kings also agreed with Lot that the plain looked inviting. So around the time that Abraham and Lot parted ways, this axis decided to attack the cities of the plain. This led to rebellions and more battles, until the king of Sodom and some other kings decided to stand up to the invaders. This didn't do any good. The ancient axis merely sacked Sodom and Gomorrah, and carried off the cities' wealth, along with Lot himself.

Because of his love for his nephew, Abraham wasn't about to let Lot live in slavery (or worse). So Abraham did what any decent man with his own private security force would do: "When Abram heard that his relative had been taken prisoner, he assembled his 318 trained men, born in his household, and they went in pursuit as far as Dan" (Gen. 14:14). The region of Dan was in northern Israel and Syria, so Abraham pursued Lot's captors for quite a while. Abraham attacked the axis at night and freed both Lot and all the possessions of Sodom and Gomorrah.

The Order of Melchizedek

As Abraham made his way back, the king of Sodom came out to meet him. This is entirely logical. Abraham was carrying Sodom's goods, as well as several of her citizens. But what happened next was unexpected: Right after the king of Sodom came out to meet Abraham, Melchizedek, king of Salem, came out as well. Salem, or modern-day Jerusalem, was not among the cities of the plain that had been sacked.

So there is no earthly reason for Melchizedek to come out to meet Abraham. I say "no earthly reason," because we shall see that Melchizedek's reason was heavenly. Unlike the King of Sodom, Melchizedek did not come looking for something from Abraham. He came to give Abraham something.

The Old Testament has very little to say about Melchizedek. He is mentioned only here and tangentially in Psalms 110:4. The New Testament book of Hebrews, in contrast, dwells on the subject of Melchizedek for three entire chapters (5-7). The author applies Psalm 110:4 to Jesus, saying He is "a priest forever in the order of Melchizedek" (Heb. 5:6, quoting Ps. 110:4). In fact, the author re-iterates this Psalm twice more, in Hebrews 5:10 and 6:2. The author then explains more of Melchizedek:

> For this Melchizedek—King of Salem, priest of the Most High God, who met Abraham and blessed him as he returned from defeating the kings, and Abraham gave him a tenth of everything; first, his name means "king of righteousness," then also, "king of Salem," meaning "king of peace"; without father, mother, or genealogy, having neither beginning of days nor end of life, but resembling the Son of God—remains a priest forever.

As I have said before, often the Bible indicates as much by what it leaves out, as it does by what it puts in. The Law of Moses came 430 years after the events in Genesis 14 and 15, as Paul says (Gal. 3:17). That Law had a priest who was determined by descent. Specifically, he was to descend directly from Aaron, Moses' brother. Consequently, his genealogy would determine his status as priest.

In contrast, the Bible records no birth for Melchizedek. It doesn't even record a genealogy. The reason the Old Testament is so full of "begats" is that genealogy is vitally important to the Near Eastern mindset. Where a person comes from determined much of what that person would be. It determines where that person fit in history, and in a sense, where that person fit in God's purposes. But all we know of Melchizedek is that his name meant "king of righteousness," and he was "king of Salem," which when translated to English, means "king of peace."

So to be described as "priest to God Most High," and yet have no recorded genealogy, would put Melchizedek noticeably out of place in an ancient Jewish worldview. His priesthood was superior to Aaron's because it had no recorded beginning, nor recorded end, and the Bible does not record that Melchizedek received the priesthood by inheritance from his father. Or, as Hebrews puts it, his priesthood was symbolically greater because Melchizedek exemplifies a greater High Priest, a Priest of righteousness and peace who "doesn't become a priest based on a legal command concerning physical descent but based on the power of an indestructible life" (Heb. 7:16).

Melchizedek's priesthood was above Aaron's because Abraham gave one tenth of the booty of war to Melchizedek. Had Abraham not given a tenth to Melchizedek, then Abraham would have retained his rights to it. Thus, by inheritance, Aaron and his priesthood might have retained their rights to it. But since Abraham gave it to Melchizedek, Aaron in a sense did so as well. In the Jewish way of thinking, this made Aaron's priesthood, which came by the Law, below and subordinate to Melchizedek's (Heb. 7:4-10).

This is central to understanding Melchizedek. Hebrews speaks of Melchizedek as "resembling the Son of God" (Heb. 7:3). Christ, like Melchizedek, has neither beginning nor end. His priesthood is the priesthood of Melchizedek: It continues infinitely because He lives eternally. What this all means is that Christ's ministry pre-dated the Law given at Sinai, and would continue long after that Law was fulfilled at the cross. It is not that Christ, His cross, and His redemption were based on Moses, Aaron, and the Law, but the other way around.

The book of Revelation describes Jesus as "the Lamb slain from the foundation of the world" (Rev 13:8, NKJV). Similarly, Peter refers to Jesus as "a lamb without defect or blemish" who "was destined before the foundation of the world" (1 Pet. 1:19-20). When God created the world, He knew what would happen in Eden, and He was fully prepared. Christ knew that, in creating the world, He would someday die to redeem it. As such, His cross arches across time, in a sense. It's affects transcend time, going backwards and forwards so that Abraham could be saved by the cross just like you and I can. Truly, the cross is the foundation of all human reality, destined from before we were even created. As Ignatius of Antioch wrote in an epistle to the Christians of Magnesia, "Christianity did not base its faith on Judaism, but Judaism on Christianity." The grace of Calvary came before the rules of Sinai, and it will continue long after. That is what we see in the story of Abraham and Melchizedek.

The First Supper

The thing about Abraham's story, is what he brings with himself, and what Melchizedek brings with *himself.* Abraham is carrying with himself the booty of war, treasures gained from the greatness of his own efforts. Melchizedek, in contrast, brings something utterly different. He brings bread and wine. If we know that Melchizedek was the perfect type of Christ, and he offered to Abraham bread and wine, then the metaphor jumps out at us all at once: Jesus, in His priesthood, left His believers with a meal of bread and wine to symbolize the redemption He had won for them at Calvary.

God was, through Melchizedek, communicating the Gospel in type to Abraham. Abraham could not truly be sustained by the trophies of conquest. The feats of his own sinew could not bring life to him, but the blood and body of the promised Messiah could. And this blood and body were freely offered to Abraham. He did not win the sustaining bread and wine by giving Melchizedek his riches. Rather, Melchizedek gave Abraham bread and wine, and then blessed Abraham, mediating God's gracious favor to him. And it was only after the declaration of God's favor that Abraham gave a tenth of his trophies to Melchizedek. Unlike the Prodigal Brother, Abraham did not come to Melchizedek claiming his rights to the things he had supposedly earned by slaving for God. Rather, he came to Melchizedek to freely receive something far greater.

Showdown in the Desert

But God was seeking a showdown. The king of Sodom came out first to meet Abraham, but Melchizedek intercepted him. Melchizedek gave Abraham the symbols of the Gospel, and declared God's grace to him. After that, we find why the king of Sodom had come out. He told Abraham, "Give me the people, but take the possessions for yourself" (Gen. 14:21).

Gifts from politicians always come with strings attached. After invading England from Normandy, William the Conqueror granted land and title to several of his loyal supporters. Because they received their wealth from William, he in turn expected their fealty. Abraham detected a similar goal behind the offer of the king of Sodom. So he replied (Gen. 14:22-24):

I have raised my hand in an oath to the Lord, God Most High, Creator of heaven and earth, that I will not take a thread or sandal strap or anything that belongs to you, so you can never say, "I made Abram rich." I will take nothing except what the servants have eaten.

Abraham had chosen to trust in God's grace. That was his oath. Had he instead accepted the wealth from the king of Sodom, he would owe his well-being, not to the God he trusted, but to the unrighteous king of an unrighteous city. Certainly he had secured the booty by his own extraordinary efforts. He had done what even the king of Sodom could not. But Melchizedek had first declared God's grace to Abraham by saying:

Abram is blessed by God Most High,
Creator of heaven and earth,
And give praise to God Most High
Who has handed over your enemies to you.

By returning the wealth to the king of Sodom, Abraham was rejecting the idea that his own might could truly fulfill his greatest needs. He was accepting the declaration of Melchizedek that he, Abraham, was blessed by God, a recipient of God's love. Instead of trusting in himself, he agreed with Melchizedek that it was truly God who had "handed over your enemies to you." Because of his trust in God, he gave back to Sodom what he gained in battle. He would not live by bread alone. Not earthly bread, anyway.

Abraham did not take credit for God's grace. He did not attempt to make God's grace secondary to his own power. He did give in to the temptation of the king of Sodom, who sought to bring him under political bondage by convincing him to reject the gracious blessing of God and trust in himself. Melchizedek offered the free, infinite grace of the omnipotent God. The king of Sodom offered mere gold and rubies and, with them, slavery.

In this, the king of Sodom was a bit like the Serpent in the Garden. Abraham was wealthy in his own right by that time, but the king of Sodom offered him the possessions of an entire city! This would have made him one of the richest men in the world. Adam and Eve, similarly, had all the fruit they could eat, but the Serpent was promising them that, by trusting in their own "knowledge of good and evil"—in their own efforts, rather than in God's grace—they could receive a greatness that they had not even imagined.

Adam and Eve did not see that they would become slaves to the Serpent, to circumstance, and to themselves. Abraham, however, perceived the small print that Adam and Eve had ignored: He knew that God's grace was far better than the tripe offered by the king of Sodom. The grace of God promised a freedom and joy and greatness that neither his own efforts, nor the power of Sodom, could grant. But accepting the offer of the king of Sodom would bring Abraham under Sodom's jurisdiction and power.

Abraham's Loving Reward

Abraham was troubled after his meeting with Melchizedek and the King of Sodom. Though he had trusted God's promise and rejected the great wealth of Sodom, it seems he could see no way for God's promise to come to fruition. He was plagued by doubt. I suspect that he wondered whether he had misunderstood the entire situation, and was meant to accept what the king of Sodom offered.

In one of the tenderest moments in the Old Testament, God came like a Father to gently allay the worries of his troubled child. God said, "Do not be afraid, Abram. I am your shield, your exceedingly great reward" (Gen. 15:1). God was Abraham's protection. And what's more, He told Abraham that his reward was more than the gold and silver of Sodom, or of the whole world. Abraham's reward went beyond simply the land of Israel. God Himself was Abraham's "exceedingly great reward." God was, in that sense, the bread and wine offered by Melchizedek.

This is the reality that Jesus Christ came to give us. It is the reality of God as a loving Father who gives freely of Himself to His children. Abraham, in type, had faith in the promise of Jesus Christ. He had faith in the Son of God. Abraham knew in the promise what the followers of Jesus know in the fulfillment: "To all who did receive Him, He gave them the right to be children of God" (John 1:12). Christ didn't come merely to save people from hell. He came so they could know the sweet, long embrace of His Father. To those who partake of the flesh and blood of Jesus Christ, God Himself is their exceedingly great reward, and Abraham is their grandfather by faith.

God next repeated His great promise to Abraham, and it is then that we read those words of Genesis 15:6, mentioned so often by Paul and the other Apostles. Long before the Law, long before Sinai, long before Aaron and Moses and the Ten Commandments and all the rules of Judaism, we find in type the simple gospel of Jesus Christ. Abraham partook of the blood and body of the crucified Lord. He rejected the Tree of Knowledge and trusted in Him who is the Tree of Life. He was reconciled to God and received the love that Adam had rejected. By the grace of God in Jesus Christ, we read, "[Abraham] believed in the Lord, and He accounted it to him for righteousness."

Faith Not Lived

Abraham's faith was before and beyond and above mere head knowledge. He didn't know how God's promise would come about, but he trusted in God that it would. But Abraham wasn't perfect. Because he lacked the knowledge of *how* God would bring about His promise, Abraham did exactly the stupidest thing a person could do. He tried to use his own knowledge to cause God's promise to come to fruition. He took Sarah's advice and slept with Sarah's servant girl Hagar, and she had a son named Ishmael.

This is, as I said, the stupidest thing a person can do, and it is precisely the thing that all of us have at some point done. When a person tries to bring about God's promises by his own efforts, based on his own knowledge without any divine directive, he isn't at all practicing faith. Not real faith anyway. He isn't trusting God, but rather he is taking what he calls faith, and subjecting it under the greater umbrella of his own abilities. Thus, he makes faith nothing more than his own knowledge, and God's promises become merely some good thing he himself will bring about. In so doing, he denies that God is a God of love who brings about all good things by His means, which are far better than ours. He puts himself in God's place, as the executor of God's promises. His "faith" then, is not a trust in God, but a trust in himself.

When we do this, we are trying to live by our own performance, all the while calling it faith. We are pretending to live by faith when we instead are slaving away like the Prodigal Brother. Only pain can come of it, just like only pain ever came by Abraham trying to substitute his own effort with Hagar for God's promise through Sarah. Wayne Jacobsen illustrates the problem with this sort of thinking:

> A friend of mine recently lost his job and is actively seeking another. One morning he told me that a plum job just escaped his grasp and that someone far less qualified got it.
>
> Knowing my friend's desire to live in God's life, I asked him if he thought anything could have prevented him from getting that job if God wanted it for him. "If I messed up, somehow," he responded.

"So you are saying that God isn't bigger than your mistakes?"

It's a misconception far too many of us indulge. If our freedom to trust God hinges on our ability to get everything right then we're really back to trusting ourselves, aren't we? If God isn't bigger than my halting attempts to learn how to walk with Him, I might as well give up now.[3]

As we said, Abraham wasn't perfect. He did indeed have faith in God. That was the over-arching principle and the under-girding foundation of Abraham's life. But Abraham was still learning what it meant to live out his trust in God. He had all sorts of messed up ways of thinking and acting, which had come to him from heredity, culture, teaching and his experiences before he had been called out. His head knowledge would always go back to things. He trusted God, but he also had to learn to live out that trust. All of us have to.

Learning to Trust in the Preposterous

Sometime after Ishmael was born, God again came to Abraham and told him, "As for your wife Sarai, do not call her Sarai, for Sarah will be her name. I will bless her; indeed, I will give you a son by her. I will bless her, and she will produce nations; kings of peoples will come from her" (Gen. 17:15-16).

When Abraham heard this, he "fell to the ground, laughed, and thought in his heart, 'Can a child be born to a hundred-year-old man? Can Sarah, a ninety-year-old woman, give birth?'" (Gen 17:17). God's promise was, according to human knowledge, utterly preposterous. It was absurd on its face. Abraham was at the century mark, and Sarah was only a decade behind him. People that old simply do not have children.

Shortly thereafter, God again came to Abraham, and told him, "I will certainly come back to you in about a year's time, and your wife Sarah will have a son!" (Gen. 18:10).

Sarah was listening in on the conversation. "She laughed to herself: 'After I have become shriveled up and my lord is old, will I have delight?'"

Both Abraham and Sarah laughed at the magnitude of God's promise. And this is the reality of faith. Faith is unreasonable. It is unreasonable because it believes what is preposterous. It believes what is preposterous because it believes in Him who is, by human reasoning, utterly absurd. Head knowledge laughs at the preposterous claims of faith. But Abraham and Sarah still believed. They believed in spite of the preposterous nature of what was promised. God's promises to us are absurd to our human minds. Thus, Paul writes of this story (Rom. 4:18-21):

> Against hope, with hope he believed, so that he became the father of many nations, according to what had been spoken: "So will your descendants be." He considered his own body to be already dead (since he was about a hundred years old), and the deadness of Sarah's womb, without weakening in the faith. He did not waver in unbelief at God's promise, but was strengthened in his faith and gave glory to God, because he was fully convinced that what He had promised He was also able to perform.

Faith is that unreasonable thing that believes, in hope, for the very thing that is humanly hopeless. Faith does not base itself on human logic or reasoning. When I was living as the Prodigal Brother, I often thought faith meant convincing myself of the strength of the evidence, trying by logic and study to narrow the gap of probability between the claims of God and the empirical evidence. The way I saw it, faith was simply knowledge. It was simply another religious hurdle I had to clear in order to earn God's acceptance.

But Abraham had learned that faith surpasses knowledge. He learned his lesson with Hagar and Ishmael. He didn't seek to determine a human way that God's promise could come true. Instead, when Abraham heard God's declaration, he could only fall down laughing. Instead of seeking, by his own knowledge, to bring about God's promises, or figure out how God intended to do so, Abraham recognized the complete absurdity of God's declaration: It was beyond human comprehension. It was a great divine foolishness.

A year later, God's promise to Abraham and Sarah was fulfilled. Sarah named the son Isaac, meaning "laughter." She explained, "God has made me laugh, and everyone who hears will laugh with me. Who would have told Abraham that Sarah would nurse children? Yet I have borne him a son in his old age" (Gen. 21:6, 7). God indeed had made her laugh. Sarah had laughed at the ridiculous nature of God's promise, and He in turn had made the ridiculous into reality. In fact, God did not give Abraham and Sarah a child until the promise could only bring laughter to them. No one finds anything odd about a woman bearing a child at 25 years of age. But that Sarah bore a child at 91 years could only indicate God's eternal favor, His loving grace towards Abraham and Sarah.

At this they had to laugh. Grace is like that: You cannot understand it, but you can live in its beauty nonetheless. Grace doesn't allow us to pretend that we are responsible for our own good fortune, but reminds us of our own smallness. Grace proves that trusting oneself to bring about true goodness, is more impossible than trusting in grace. When the love of God does the impossible, we can only laugh in joy at the results.

135

A Proof of Faith, or Faith as Proof?

Paul likens Abraham's faith in the promise of Isaac to the Christian's faith in the death and justifying resurrection of Jesus Christ (Rom. 4:22-25):

> Therefore, "it was credited to him for righteousness." Now "it was credited to him" was not written for Abraham alone, but also for us. It will be credited to us who believe in Him who raised Jesus our Lord from the dead. He was delivered up for our trespasses and raised for our justification.

We see in the resurrection how faith trusts in God's preposterous declaration. In the resurrection, the very preposterousness of the claim is evidence of its veracity: Any idiot can trust that, once a corpse is good and dead and buried, it won't hop out of the grave and start walking around and doing miracles and so forth. The Apostles actually claimed to have seen the risen Lord do just that, and what's more to have actually touched Him. Thus they went all over the world proclaiming His resurrection, and suffering harassment, insults, beatings, torture, and even death itself in defense of that claim. They had everything in this world to lose by trusting in this preposterous declaration, but they trusted nonetheless.

This, I believe, is why Hebrews tells us, "Now faith is the reality of what is hoped for, the proof of what is not seen" (Heb. 11:1). The text doesn't say, "Faith is the hope for another reality," but that faith itself *is* "the reality of what is hoped for." It is as if God in grace planted a piece of His preposterous reality into us, and that piece of His reality doesn't truly belong in human reality. Instead, like the yellow rings in *The Magician's Nephew*, it wants very much to go back to that other reality that it came from. That other reality, that city "whose architect and builder is God," is itself preposterous to humanity because it stands utterly contrary to the Babylon that the Prodigal Brother has slaved so hard to make for himself. Thus, faith is itself that reality from whence it came, and itself hopes for the reality that it is from.

Hebrews also doesn't say faith "believes in the proof it has seen," but that faith is in itself "the proof of what is not seen." When others observe a human being operating according to an utterly different reality, they either must chock it up to lunacy or stare in awe. But what is truly difficult is when faith both lives in that different and preposterous reality, and yet seems saner than those who do not. Thus faith in practice demonstrates what Kierkegaard said: "Act just once in such a manner that your action expresses that you fear God alone and man not at all—you will immediately in some measure cause a scandal."[4]

Tertullian famously said, "The blood of the martyrs is the seed of the Church." Faith does not rest on proofs. Rather, true faith is itself evidence that its object is true. Because it does the unreasonable, seems utterly sane in so doing, and conquers, faith has the power to show that the preposterous is real, and the "normal" is false. As we said, the Apostles didn't just claim Jesus rose from the grave. They endured hardship and even death for that very claim. The daily threat of death, or even the daily threat of severe physical duress experienced by the Apostles, might have caused them to renounce the resurrection if their claim were false. But this is not at all what they did. Similarly, Abraham left Haran when he had everything—in this world—to lose by so doing, and yet he indeed became the father of many nations. Real faith, faith that does the preposterous because it believes the preposterous, stands against religious ways of human thinking. Faith transcends human knowledge.

Ridiculous

The movie *Defiance* tells the story of the Bielski brothers, who saved over 1,200 of their fellow Jews from the Holocaust by creating a hiding place for them deep in the forests of modern-day Belarus. In the movie, a Rabbi named Shimon struggled deeply with his faith in God's promises to the Jewish people.

Near the end of the film, Tuvia, the oldest Bielski brother, led his pack of Jewish fugitives across a swamp to evade Nazi troops. At the end of that journey, when they all were safe on the banks of the swamp, Rabbi Shimon lay dying of tuberculosis. He said softly to Tuvia, "I almost lost my faith. But you were sent by God to save us."

Tuvia had never been religious. Whenever Rabbi Shimon quoted the Torah or the Talmud to Tuvia as a requirement for him to follow, Tuvia always responded, "I have no idea what you're talking about." But to Shimon's statement of faith, Tuvia could only respond, "Ridiculous."

Shimon replied, with his last words of life, "I know. But just in case, I thank Him, and I thank you."

Faith believes the ridiculous, and thus subjects the believer to ridicule. Faith recognizes the improbability of what it believes, and it glories in that improbability. It does not seek to convince itself of the natural probability of it, but rather it rejoices in the miraculous impossibility of God's grace. And it laughs at the world when God's grace comes to fruition. When faith does something like trusting in God to provide—to save 1,200 Jews from the Holocaust—it in the end proves itself to be true, because it brings about what is humanly impossible. Shimon knew what Tuvia had done was humanly impossible, but it had been done anyway. Thus, faith becomes "the proof of what is not seen" because it brings about the purposes of God. And God's greatest purpose for each of us is that we should be His child, resting in His arms, trusting in His love.

It Will Be Provided

To bring about His purposes in Abraham, merely giving him Isaac was not enough. God sought to show the fullness of what His promise to Abraham really meant. In so doing, He would test Abraham, so that Abraham could come to see what grace was truly about, what it meant in Abraham's life, and what it would mean for all mankind.

When God came to test Abraham, he replied: "Here I am." In fact, three times Abraham said, "Here I am," and it is this that is the key to understanding God's test of Abraham. When God first called to Abraham, he responded, "Here I am." To this, God said the unthinkable: "Take your son, your only son Isaac, whom you love, go to the land of Moriah, and offer him there as a burnt offering on one of the mountains I will tell you about" (Gen. 22:2).

God had previously called Abraham to leave his home, to give up everything he held dear, in order to go to "the land I will show you." This time, God was again calling Abraham to give up his dearest gift, Isaac, "on one of the mountains I will tell you about." God was taking Abraham full circle, bringing to perfect fruition the seed of faith He had planted in Abraham so many years ago in Haran. It was here that Abraham would finally see the ultimate point of it all.

Abraham obeyed. In so doing, he did something just as bizarre as he had when he left Haran. But he gave a bizarre obedience because of his faith in the bizarre ways of God. He trusted that whatever God was leading him to, it would not nullify God's earlier promises to him. After a life of successes and failures, of faith and then doubt and then faith again, Abraham had finally learned that God was indeed trustworthy. He had come to know that the picture of God painted by the Serpent was false: God is not selfish, malicious, and cruel, but selfless, loving, and graceful.

So Abraham packed up the necessary supplies, and together with Isaac and two servants, set out for the mountains of Moriah. When Moses arrived, he told his servants, "Stay here with the donkey. The boy and I will go over there to worship; then we'll come back to you" (Gen. 22:5). He did not say, "*I* will come back to you," but, "*We* will come back to you." This is an odd thing to say. In fact, we might even say it is a preposterous thing to say. After all, Abraham intended to go up the mountain and kill Isaac in a sacrifice. So why would he say, "*We* will come back to you"?

In the next vignette we find the second "Here I am" statement (Gen. 22:7-8):

> Then Isaac spoke to his father Abraham and said, "My father."
> And he replied, "Here I am, my son."
> Isaac said, "The fire and the wood are here, but where is the lamb for the burnt offering?"
> Abraham answered, "God Himself will provide the lamb for the burnt offering, my son." Then the two of them walked on together.

Another preposterous statement! Abraham didn't say, "God Himself will provide the *boy* for the sacrifice, namely you," but rather, "God Himself will provide *the lamb*." What was going through Abraham's mind? First he said both he and Isaac would return, and then he said God would provide the lamb. Was he lying to Isaac? If he was, Abraham was not the righteous father of the faithful, but a religious sham. The book of Hebrews gives us a picture (Heb. 11:17-19):

> By faith Abraham, when he was tested, offered up Isaac; he who had received the promises was offering

up his unique son, about whom it had been said, "In Isaac your seed will be called." He considered God to be able even to raise someone from the dead, from which he also got him back as an illustration.

Abraham could say he and Isaac were coming back down the mountain precisely because he trusted that it was a solid fact. God had told him Isaac would be the father of many offspring, and since Isaac had not yet fathered a child, Abraham knew that, whatever happened on top of that mountain, he and Isaac would be walking back down together. He believed that he would sacrifice Isaac, and that God would bring Isaac back from the dead, and then that God would provide a lamb for Abraham to make a new sacrifice in thanksgiving.

This example is central to understanding faith: Abraham could not have gone through with this entire ordeal if he did not trust God. Because deep within himself he confidently knew that God would make good on His promise, Abraham had the fortitude to go through with God's command (Gen. 22:9, 10):

When they arrived at the place that God had told him about, Abraham built the altar there and arranged the wood. He bound his son Isaac and placed him on the altar, on top of the wood. Then Abraham reached out and took the knife to slaughter his son.

In the dramatic climax of the story, we read the third and final, "Here I am." The Angel of the LORD called out, "Abraham, Abraham!" (v. 11).

Abraham again replied, "Here I am."

And to this the Angel of the LORD proclaimed, "Do not lay a hand on the boy or do anything to him. For now I know

141

that you fear God, since you have not withheld your only son from Me" (v. 12).

At this, Abraham looked and saw a ram stuck in a thicket. He captured the ram and sacrificed it to God. And then, "Abraham named that place The Lord Will Provide, so today it is said: 'It will be provided on the Lord's mountain'" (v. 14).

Here I am. Send Me.

In these three "Here I am" statements, we find the point of the story. In each, someone calls on Abraham, then Abraham replies, "Here I am," and the caller then explains or asks something about the sacrifice. In turn, Abraham's next statement expresses his trust in God's promise and grace.

First, God called to Abraham, and Abraham replied, "Here I am." Then God told Abraham to take his son to Moriah and offer him as a sacrifice on a mountain there. The next time Abraham speaks, it is to his servants: "Stay here with the donkey. The boy and I will go over there to worship; then we'll come back to you." He obeyed God's command at the same time that he knew that Isaac would survive the test and go on to fulfill the promise of God.

The second time, Isaac called to Abraham, and he replied, "Here I am." Yet he didn't say only, "Here I am," but, "Here I am, *my son*." Isaac then asked where the lamb was for the burnt offering. Abraham's additional statement of "my son," indicated that Isaac was to be the offering, because that is why Isaac "my son" was there with him. But still, in faith, Abraham replied, "God Himself will provide the lamb for the burnt offering, my son." And then the Bible tells us, "Then the two of them walked on together." In so doing, the Bible points us back to Abraham's statement that he and Isaac would walk up the mountain to worship, and both would come back down together.

The third time, the Angel of the LORD call out to Abraham, and he again replies, "Here I am."

The Angel of the LORD told him, "Do not lay a hand on the boy or do anything to him. For now I know that you fear God, since you have not withheld your only son from Me" (v. 12).

Abraham had demonstrated his complete trust in God. When he found the ram and sacrificed it, the power of his faith had been demonstrated. He said, "God Himself will provide the lamb," and that was precisely what had happened. So he named the mountain, "The Lord Will Provide," and at the time that Genesis was written, people still said, "It will be provided on the Lord's mountain."

But note here the verb tenses. Though God indeed gave a ram to be sacrificed, Abraham didn't say, "The Lord *did* provide," but rather, "The Lord *will* provide." Likewise, the people did not say, "It *was provided* on the Lord's mountain," but rather, "It *will be provided* on the Lord's mountain." God's gracious provision was not a past event, but something yet future, even to those who received the book of Genesis some 400 years after Abraham.

And what was this future provision? The text reads, "Abraham went and took the ram and offered it as a burnt offering in place of his son" (v. 13). The lamb that would be provided, was a lamb that was to be an offering "in place of *his* son." The act of Abraham foreshadowed the offering of God's Son to die in place of sinful man. Man had rejected the Tree of Life and instead chose to live by the Tree of Knowledge of Good and Evil. But this brought death to him, so that he needed someone to die in his place, to take that death for him, and in turn to give him life. Abraham believed that Isaac would be resurrected, and it is this resurrection life that the ram metaphorically provided to Isaac. Because he trusted in God to fulfill His promises, Abraham was able to obey God's command, and thus come to see in shadow form what God would do in Jesus Christ on the mountain outside of Jerusalem. Abraham saw the meaning of God's calling many years before in Haran. So Jesus would later say, "Abraham was overjoyed that he would see My day; he saw it and rejoiced" (John 8:56).

James, spoke of it this way (James 2:20-23):

Are you willing to learn that faith without works is useless? Wasn't Abraham our father justified by works when he offered Isaac his son on the altar? You see that faith was active together with his works, and by works, faith was perfected. So the Scripture was fulfilled that says, "Abraham believed God, and it was credited to him for righteousness," and he was called God's friend.

This, of course, is one of the Prodigal Brother's favorite passages, because he can misquote it to claim that a man is only granted eternal life if he does the right ethical and religious performances. But that is not at all what James says. James was not saying that we had to add works to our faith in order to be saved. Rather, context shows that James was accusing his audience of not having faith at all, and James demonstrated it by the faithless way they lived. James said that Abraham was able to offer Isaac because he first had faith, and that he was first justified by faith *before* his works brought justification, or vindication, of his faith. Faith demonstrates itself in action because one who trusts in the preposterous promises of God, will in the end do what is otherwise impossible.

The work Abraham did was not keeping a list of rules or religious rituals. His work came only because he fully trusted in God to make good what He promised, and to bring Isaac back to life. By this, his faith was transferred from the genealogical promise of offspring, to the realization that

Isaac would have a Seed who would die in humanity's place and thus bring us life from the grave. Abraham "considered God to be able even to raise someone from the dead, from which he also got [Isaac] back as an illustration." His faith was perfected, or directed toward the coming Messiah Jesus Christ, because his faith first led him to trust God's promise that Isaac would live to have many offspring.

Abraham didn't add works to his faith. That is, he didn't say, "My faith isn't good enough, so I had better add certain religious deeds and behaviors." Abraham's faith resulted in an obedience that went beyond mere rule-keeping. In him we see that trust in God transcends mere religious mandates in order to bring about the greater purpose of redemption and intimacy. Thus, faith causes the faithful ones to live out a beautiful and powerful holiness, next to which the Prodigal Brother's feigned holiness of religious ceremonies and rule-keeping are nothing but wood and rust. Sin began because Eve didn't believe what God said. Abraham was justified because he did. Faith is the opposite of living life by the knowledge of good and evil, and so the fruit of faith works in the opposite direction of the fruit of the Serpent's tree.

Justifying Faith

In Abraham's life we see why faith is inherently justifying. The Prodigal Brother may talk a lot about justification by faith, but he talks about it in the same way a cabbie might opine on how to beat the stock market: He has no idea what it means. The Prodigal Brother talks about being justified by faith as if it was merely God's slight-of-hand to get us back on track toward achieving our own righteousness by our own works. But faith is inherently justifying because it is the decision to eat of the Tree of Life, to eat and drink the body and blood of the Lord Jesus Christ. It is the power, given to us by God, to accept and live in and trust in Him.

In a single miracle, it strikes at the core of Adam's foolish choice, and abolishes it. Faith does not lead to mere rule-keeping. Rather, it restores the life lived in the true holiness of love by restoring intimacy with God. Faith in God is not a mere magic trick God uses to get us to become righteous by religious observance. It is a miracle of God that restores the relationship of trust that was lost in Eden.

Thus, the faith that justifies also demonstrates itself to be inherently justifying. Justifying faith justifies itself. It does not need to be added to, because it changes the very spiritual nature of a man. It fulfills the statement that "[Abraham] believed the Lord, and He credited it to him as righteousness" (Gen. 15:6). It shows itself to have resulted in a true righteousness that makes religious categories of righteousness pale in comparison.

Abraham's faith demonstrates the power of the "the city that has foundations, whose architect and builder is God" (Heb. 11:10). It proves that such a city exists, and that such a city is itself the warm home of safety that we all have rejected as Prodigal Sons and Daughters. Abraham, in a sense, believed in home. As Nouwen said, "Faith is the radical trust that home has always been and always will be there."[5] Abraham believed that there was an estate, beautiful and peaceful and joyous, filled with love and warmth and forgiveness. An estate with a Father whom we all ran away from so long ago, but who has been waiting for us to come home to Him. By trusting in such a place, and in such a Father, Abraham's life demonstrated the power of that trust. By faith, Abraham accepted the Father's call to come home. In so doing, Abraham's faith proved not only that he was the father of the faithful, but that the faithful themselves are of the Father.

Chapter 6

The Ministry of Condemnation

—⟨∞⟩—

> I do not obtain eternal life because I do not kill, commit
> adultery, steal, etc. Such mere outward decency does
> not constitute Christianity. The heathen observe the
> same restraints to avoid punishment or to secure the
> advantages of a good reputation. In the last analysis
> such restraint is simple hypocrisy.
>
> Martin Luther|*Commentary on Galatians*

So far, we have seen that mankind chose to live in religious ways of thinking, under the burden of religious
obligation. Man sought to become like God(s) by doing
good things and avoiding evil things. As such, he rejected
the life and holiness that comes by relational intimacy with
God. Humanity sought to secure all good things, and even
holiness, by our own efforts. We sought life by our abilities
and performances.

We have seen, in the case of Noah and Babylon, that trust
in our own efforts caused humanity to plunge himself into
horrible suffering. We sought good as a tool for something
else, and as such we rejected true goodness for a counterfeit.
We saw in God's guidance only ulterior motives, rejecting
God's gracious infinite provision and replacing it with our

own finite power. Humanity set about to conquer reality, rather than to live by trust in the One who created reality. Death was the result.

We have seen, as well, that Abraham had a righteousness before God that didn't come by his performance to a set of religious obligations or rules. He had a righteousness that was credited to him because he trusted God, and that same trust in God in turn led to a life that reflected the holiness of God. Rather than seeking to do good things in hope of securing some greater blessing, Abraham was first made right with God by His grace, and then good things came out of him.

Why the Law, Then?

If you have been brought up, as I was, in the Prodigal Brother's way of thinking, you will likely ask me the same question Paul anticipated from his audience, "Why the law then?" (Gal. 3:19). After Abraham and Isaac and Jacob, Israel endured many years of slavery in Egypt, and when God delivered them from slavery, He led them to Sinai. There He gave them the Law, 613 commands and regulations that described the essence of Old Covenant Judaism.

If you have followed the thinking to this point, you might notice that it seems the description of the Tree of Knowledge of Good and Evil also sounds a bit like the Law. The Law, after all, was a list of religious obligations given to Israel. They would receive life if they kept them (Deut. 30:19, 20), and death if they did not (Deut. 28:58-61). They were told to seek holiness by keeping the Law (Leviticus 11:44, 45; 19:2; 20:26; Deut. 28:9). They were told that they would achieve righteousness if they obeyed every command in the Law (Deut. 6:25). In other words, the Law looks very much like the idea of achieving some form of greatness by doing the right set of things and avoiding the wrong set of things.

It seems to reflect the idea that knowing good and evil can elevate one to some greater reality.

So, indeed, "Why the Law then?" I very much understand the objections you may have at this point, just as Paul's readers had objections. So I have to answer the same way Paul did: "Why the Law then? It was added because of transgressions." This statement by Paul says quite a bit. It goes a long way to demolish our religious misunderstandings.

It Was Added...

Paul first states that the Law was added. Notice the structure of this book. Man fell from grace. Then came Noah and Abraham and other patriarchs. Now we find ourselves discussing the Law. The reason this book has such a structure is that it is built on the chronology given in the Bible: Man fell, then the righteous patriarchs, then the Law. This is indeed what Paul means when he says the Law "was added." The Biblical chronology shows that the Law was given after Abraham, and not before. That is why Paul said the Law came "430 years" (Gal. 3:17) after Abraham.

One Prodigal Brother, called Covenant Theologian, disagrees with Paul. He teaches that the Law, or at least the Ten Commandments within it, were given at creation, before sin. The problem with this is that it throws the whole chronology of the Bible horribly out of alignment. Because if, as Paul said, the Law was given 430 years later, then either Adam and Eve came 430 years after Abraham, or Covenant Theologian is simply wrong.

The reason Covenant Theologian, and others like him, say the Ten Commandments were given in Eden, is that in the 13th century, a Roman Catholic scholar named Thomas Aquinas decided to re-build Christian theology on the foundation of pagan Aristotelian philosophy. As such, he tried to slice and dice the Law of Moses into what we now call moral, civil, and ceremonial parts. To define them as such, he used pagan philosophical methods rather than the Biblical text. Consequently, those who followed his thinking decided, rather arbitrarily, that the Ten Commandments were the "eternal moral law."

There are many problems with this. For one, the classification scheme implies that there is nothing immoral about disobeying God so long as the command we are disobeying is merely "ceremonial" in nature. But to disobey God is itself immorality, because it denies the goodness of God's purposes and thus seeks a goodness of purpose apart from Him that does not truly exist. All Christians agree that at least some of the commands in the Law are no longer binding on Christians. It is not because some commands are merely "ceremonial" and thus unimportant, but because the purpose for those commands in redemptive history has been reached. They've finished their work and now something new is in place. For instance, Paul described the Kosher laws, Feast days, New Moons, and weekly Sabbaths as a "shadow of the things that were to come" (Col. 2:17), but Jesus was the reality to which they pointed. Faith in Him was the point, not the commands themselves.

Further, to separate the Law into moral, civil, and ceremonial commands leaves everything up to our interpretation. Don't want to wear tassels on the corners of your garment? Just say it was "ceremonial." Don't want to be circumcised? Just call that "ceremonial" as well (even though disobedience to the circumcision command was punishable by death). The New Testament writers, in contrast, said the Law lived or died as an entire unit, the 613 rules in the Torah (Gal. 5:3, James 2:10).

But more to the point, the Bible never comes even close to referring to the Decalogue as the "eternal moral law." In fact, the Decalogue could not be eternal. Both the Old Testament narrative and Paul's epistles declare that it didn't exist until over 400 years after Abraham. Moses himself says of the Ten Commandments, "[God] did not make this covenant with our fathers, but with all of us who are alive here today" (Deut. 5:3).

The trouble is, parts of it would make no sense before the world was created, so it couldn't be eternal: "Do not commit adultery" would not have made sense to the angels, whom Jesus said do not marry (Matt. 22:30). The tenth commandment told the Israelite, "Do not covet your neighbor's ... male or female slave" (Ex. 20:17), and it then describes the slave as something that "belongs to your neighbor." But to say human slavery is part of God's eternal order is a stretch to say the least.

The fourth commandment, to cease from toil on the seventh-day of the week, would have made no sense before the earth began to rotate around its axis. Furthermore, the fourth commandment assumes the sort of toil that came only as a result of man's sin, and it points back to the time when man did not have to toil at all. And beyond that, two different reasons are given for the fourth command, and one of the reasons is that the Israelites had been delivered from slavery in Egypt, something that would have made no sense to Adam and Eve, let alone the angels before them.

The first command, to have no other gods before Yahweh, presumes that there are people going around claiming there are other gods besides Yahweh, or that Yahweh isn't the one true God. This would make no sense until the rise of pagan religions that came about after sin. The second command—"Do not make an idol for yourself, whether in the shape of anything in the heavens above or on the earth below or in the waters under the earth" (Ex. 20:4)—would not have made sense before the creations of the sky, the earth, or the seas, and it certainly would not have made sense for angels who could look on God directly. It also implies that idol worship was already a common practice in the world.

The command to honor one's father and mother only makes sense for beings who come about as a result of sexual reproduction, something neither the angels (who don't marry), or God (who is un-created) would have to deal with. The command to not murder assumes a world in which death is not only possible, but common and understood. This would not have made sense before death entered the physical world when Adam sinned. The command not to give false testimony assumes a world of courts and trials, which only occur because something bad has happened.

In fact, this sounds very much like the idea that the commandments "were added because of transgression." The Ten Commandments point back to sin that had already entered the world, not to a reality before sin was even known. This is not to say that it is or was ever okay to commit adultery or lie or steal or murder. It is to say, however, that the Ten Commandments, as a unit, could not be the "eternal moral law," but are merely a reflection of a greater moral reality.

That is why, when someone asked Jesus which was the greatest commandment in the Law, He replied (Matthew 22:37-40):

> "Love the Lord your God with all your heart, with all your soul, and with all your mind." This is the greatest and most important commandment. The second is like it: "Love your neighbor as yourself." All the Law and the Prophets depend on these two commandments.

When Jesus names the two greatest commandments, He does not point to the Ten Commandments, but rather to two commandments that were buried around other passages in the Law. The former command was given right after Moses recounted the Ten Commandments, as an underlying requirement for the Law Covenant itself (recall how Chapter 4 dealt with Paul's discussion of the "requirements of the Law"). The latter command, to love one's neighbor, appears in the Law (Lev. 19:18) surrounded by several other commandments. Some of those deal with what we might today call moral issues, like caring for the poor (v. 10) and being honest (v. 11), and others deal with sacrifices (v.5-8), cross-breeding livestock, sowing more than two kinds of seed, and wearing clothing made of two kinds of fabric (v. 19). But Jesus indicated that these two commandments, not the Decalogue, were foundational to any understanding of goodness, so that everything in the entire Old Testament (including the Law), was dependent on them.

These two commands are truly all-encompassing. They can apply to any human being anywhere, and indeed they can even apply to angels. Because of the love that exists among the persons of the Trinity, God can keep both of these commands within Himself. Or, more accurately, these commands serve as a description of the Triune God's internal relational nature. So the Law, in a sense, points back to that greater understanding of goodness, but it is not itself the very thing. Jesus' identification of the two greatest commandments means the rest of the Law must have been added on to that understanding, or derived from it. Or, just as Paul said, "[The Law] was added..."

...Because of Transgressions

As we said, many of the commandments in the Law reflect the idea that sin was already in the world. The Law assumes that a person will do something, or at least that he desires to do it, so that he must be commanded not to. This is not unlike what we saw with the difference between God's declaration to Adam and Eve before the fall and His contrasting statement to Noah after the fall. The Law assumes that the inclination to act in unloving ways towards others is intrinsic to human nature. Naturally, this wouldn't have been the case but for the fact that Adam and Eve chose sin as part of their identity.

That really seems to be the problem: All transgressions find their source in the one transgression of Adam and Eve. But for that transgression, we wouldn't today be talking about the Law or Sinai. Adam and Eve would not have needed the Ten Commandments, because they simply wouldn't have a cancer in them that needed to be constrained by the Law. Their core spiritual nature would have been perfect, as would that of their descendants. Because they would have had a perfect love for God and love for others, they simply wouldn't have acted in any other way but out of love. We would all still be in Eden together, very much enjoying God's and each other's company without a single worry about famine or murder or lying or war anything like that. In fact, we wouldn't have really even known what those things meant.

That last one I mentioned, war, is also assumed in the Law as a central part of the human experience in sinful world. In fact, an entire chapter in the Torah, Deuteronomy 20, deals with regulations regarding warfare. This conclusively demonstrates that the Law assumes a world dominated by evil, not good. Thus, it could only have been added after the fall. So it is, in fact, neither eternal nor foundational to human existence.

Imprisoned and Guarded

To explain what he means by "because of transgressions," Paul writes (Gal. 3:21-26, NRSV):

Is the law then opposed to the promises of God? Certainly not! For if a law had been given that could make alive, then righteousness would indeed come through the law. But the scripture has imprisoned all

things under the power of sin, so that what was promised [to Abraham—see vs. 6-8, 14-18] through faith
in Jesus Christ might be given to those who believe.

Now before faith came, we were imprisoned and
guarded under the law until faith would be revealed.
Therefore the law was our disciplinarian until Christ
came, so that we might be justified by faith. But now
that faith has come, we are no longer subject to a
disciplinarian, for in Christ Jesus you are all children
of God through faith.

Paul here indicates that the Law was some form of
prison, saying first that the Scripture (in Paul's day, the Old
Testament, since the New had not yet been formed) "has
imprisoned all things under the power of sin." More directly,
he says, "we were imprisoned and guarded under the law."

Paul then speaks of the Law as a "disciplinarian,"[1] or
paidagogos as it is in Greek. Today we might use the similar
pedagogue as a synonym for teacher, but in the Greek world
of the time it meant something more:

The term represents a combination of two Greek
words: *pais* meaning "boy" and *agogos*, "leader."
Thus it literally means boy-leader. It designated the
man, usually a household slave, to whom the father
of Graeco-Roman society entrusted the upbringing
of his son. He attended the boy wherever he went,
providing the needs [*sic*], guidance, and protection.
He exercised constant oversight of him from childhood to maturity and had authority to administer
discipline as required. He took the boy to the school-
master (*didaskalos*) but was not the teacher himself.
A.W.F. Blunt indicated that he was generally represented on vases and the like with a stick in his hand.
In the school situation this made certain that the boy

had a mind for learning. His task was to see to it that the boy negotiated the years from childhood to manhood in such a way as to be ready to take his place in society as a mature and responsible person.[2]

The consistent theme of Galatians is that the Law represented some form of bondage or slavery that Jesus has rescued us from. In Galatians 2:4, Paul speaks of those who wanted to bring Christians under the Old Covenant Law via the entrance rite of circumcision. He said they "came in secretly to spy on our freedom that we have in Christ Jesus, in order to enslave us." In Galatians 3, he refers to the Law as imprisonment, and as a disciplinarian who would beat a child to ensure he does the right things. In Galatians 4:25, he states that the current earthly Jerusalem, governed by the Law given at Sinai, "is in slavery with her children." In Galatians 5:1, he refers to the Law as a "yoke of slavery." In fact, were we to use the terminology familiar to this book, we might say that the Law symbolized the Prodigal Brother's self-concept as his father's slave. This odd way of referring to the Law demands that we probe to find his meaning.

The Stoicheion

One of Paul's more forceful depictions of the Law as bondage comes in Galatians 4:1-6. In fact, in that passage he is clarifying what he meant in the previously quoted passage in Galatians 3. After referring to the Law as a *paidagogos*, he explains his meaning in the next chapter (Gal. 4:1-6):

Now I say that as long as the heir is a child, he differs in no way from a slave, though he is the owner of everything. Instead, he is under guardians and stewards until the time set by his father. In the same way we also, when we were children, were in slavery under the elemental forces of the world. But when the completion of the time came, God sent His Son, born of a woman, born under the law, to redeem those under the law, so that we might receive adoption as sons.

Paul refers to "those under the law," as those "in slavery under the elemental forces of the world." The word rendered "elemental forces" is the Greek *stoicheion*. The meaning of *stoicheion* is a major point of contention among scholars. Because the word is so controversial, it is translated many different ways in different translations. Each of these translations in some way reflects the pre-existing theological bent of the translators. One of the reasons, I believe, that scholars debate this word so hotly is that, if it really means what context says it means, then the common religious idea of righteousness by performance simply falls apart.

Paul uses *stoicheion* in three other places: Once more in Galatians 5, and twice in Colossians 2. The passage in Colossians 2 is very instructive, but also rather long, so we had better get to it before we run out of space (Col. 2:8-23):

Be careful that no one takes you captive through philosophy and empty deceit based on human tradition, based on the *stoicheion* of the world, and not based on Christ. For in Him the entire fullness of God's nature dwells bodily, and you have been filled by Him, who is the head over every ruler and authority. In Him you were also circumcised with a circumcision not done with hands, by putting off the body of flesh, in the circumcision of the Messiah. Having been buried with Him in baptism, you were also raised with Him through faith in the working of God, who raised Him from the dead. And when you were dead in trespasses and in the uncircumcision of your flesh, He made you alive with Him and forgave us all our trespasses. He erased the certificate of debt, with its obligations, that was against us and opposed to us, and has taken it out of the way by nailing it to the cross. He disarmed the rulers and authorities and disgraced them publicly; He triumphed over them by Him.

Therefore don't let anyone judge you in regard to food and drink or in the matter of a festival or a New Moon or a Sabbath day. These are a shadow of what was to come; the substance is the Messiah. Let no one disqualify you, insisting on ascetic practices and the worship of angels, claiming access to a visionary realm and inflated without cause by his fleshly mind. He doesn't hold on to the head, from whom the whole body, nourished and held together by its ligaments and tendons, develops with growth from God.

If you died with Christ to the *stoicheion* of this world, why do you live as if you still belonged to the world? Why do you submit to regulations: "Don't handle, don't taste, don't touch"? All these regulations refer to what is destroyed by being used up; they are human commands and doctrines. Although these have a reputation of wisdom by promoting ascetic practices, humility, and severe treatment of the body, they are not of any value against fleshly indulgence.

There are several interesting points here. Paul identifies the *stoicheion* with circumcision, contrasting it with the spiritual circumcision "not done with hands," by which he points to our participation in Jesus' death and resurrection, so that we are born again. He identifies the *stoicheion* with the "rulers and authorities," but even more with the "certificate of debt, with its obligations," that Jesus crucified in Himself on the cross. Circumcision was the means by which a man entered into the Covenant community of Judaism, becoming indebted to keep the entire Law. That is why Paul wrote in Galatians, "Every man who gets circumcised ... is obligated to keep the entire law" (Galatians 5:3). So the "certificate of debt, with its obligations," indicates the Law that the Israelites were obligated to keep when they became circumcised. This is why, in similar language in Ephesians 2:15, Paul refers to what was nailed to the cross as the "law of the commands in ordinances" (YLT). By erasing this "certificate of debt, with its obligations," Paul says that Jesus "disarmed the rulers and authorities and disgraced them publicly."

Paul further identifies the *stoicheion* with the annual Jewish festivals, monthly New Moon observances, and weekly Sabbaths. This is quite similar to his second use of the term in Galatians 4, where he also adds the Sabbatical years: "How can you turn back again to the weak and bankrupt *stoicheion*? Do you want to be enslaved to them all over again? You observe special days, months, seasons, and years" (vs. 9, 10).

He also identifies the *stoicheion* with food and drink commandments, the kosher laws. He once again refers to the *stoicheion*, characterizing them according to the Law's regulations regarding handling, tasting, and touching. He refers to these "ascetic practices" as "human commands and doctrines" that are "not of any value against fleshly indulgence."

When we bring it all together, we find something curious: Paul is writing Galatians and Colossians to Gentiles (Gal. 1:15, 2:2-5, 7, 5:2; Col. 1:27).[3] Paul is telling them that all peoples were, in their respective religions, under the power of the *stoicheion*. In parallel to being "under the *stoicheion*," Jesus was "born under the Law" (Gal. 4:3, 4). By taking its curse in Himself, He crucified the Law and freed the believer from the *stoicheion*. Paul tells them that returning to the Jewish festivals would be returning to the *stoicheion* they were under. He tells them the circumcision by the flesh is part of the power of the *stoicheion*.

We find some remarkable conclusions: 1) Living to the Law is the same as living under sin. Paul says the Law has "imprisoned all things under the power of sin."[4] 2) Living to the Law has the same underlying principle as all human realities, so that for a Christian to seek righteousness by observing the Torah would be the same as seeking holiness through a false religion. 3) Jesus put the Law to death in Himself on the cross, and 4) in so doing He triumphed over the powers of darkness and freed us from their bondage.

These are simply very strong words. Marcion, a second century Christian teacher, tried to make sense of this seeming contradiction by arguing that the Law was not actually given by the true God, but by a sort of demonic imposter. The problem with this, of course, is that Paul attests to the fact that the same God who gave the Law, also put it to death in Himself in Jesus Christ. But what is more difficult to understand is that, by killing the very Law He gave, God "disarmed the rulers and authorities and disgraced them publicly; He triumphed over them by Him" (Col. 2:15)

This has led to a great deal of scholarly speculation on exactly what Paul meant by "the elemental forces of this world," or the *stoicheion* as it is in the original Greek. For some, these *stoicheion* are angelic or demonic beings, but that brings us back to the very silliness taught by Marcion. If God did indeed give the Law, which Paul describes as the *stoicheion*, then to say the *stoicheion* are spiritual beings opposed to God is an obvious contradiction. But, as DeLashmutt points out, the use of *stoicheion* to refer to spiritual beings did not begin until the third of fourth century AD, long after Paul.[5] Still, many scholars hold this view today while at the same time denying they are Marcionites.

Some scholars have argued that the *stoicheion* represented the idea that certain angelic beings were responsible for steering planets in their orbits, and that somehow this, in Paul's mind, symbolized man's bondage. They get this from Paul's discussion of the *stoicheion* in relation to the calendar Sabbaths and feasts of the Jewish people, which were determined by astronomical observations. Such arguments smack of the kind of secular chauvinism with which the modern mind approaches ancient writings: "We are so much smarter now." Paul's writings show him to be an extremely intelligent individual. Even in his day, only a fool would think that man's central problem was that angelic beings were pushing planets around. And Paul certainly wasn't so foolish as to think that the point of the cross was to stop the angels from doing so.

Rather, the key in all this is that *stoicheion* is derived from the Greek word *stoicheo*, which has to deal with marching or walking. Paul uses *stoicheo* elsewhere to detail how a Christian walks out his new life in Jesus (Rom. 4:12; Gal. 5:25, 6:16; Phil. 3:16). Hebrews 5:12 also uses the term *stoicheion* to denote the basic spiritual principles of the Gospel of Jesus. *Stoicheion*, then, literally denotes the underlying principles of something, the basic way of looking at life. So the *stoicheion* of the world are the "basic principles of the world," as the NIV properly translates the term.

Quite Simple, Really

If you are at all bothered by the idea that the Law operated by the same basic underlying principles—*stoicheion*—of this sinful world, then perhaps you assume I am saying more than I mean to. I do not mean that the commands in the Law are somehow evil. Nor do I mean that the God who reveals Himself in the Old Testament is not one and the same God who revealed Himself in Jesus Christ in the New. That is not at all the point. God did not change between the Old and New Testaments, but the audience of the writings did.

Consider an illustration: Only a great fool would treat a wild wolf the same way he would a domesticated retriever. You do not let a wolf lie down at the foot of your bed. You do not let him play with your children. You do not feed him Kibble. You feed him raw meat. And heaven help you if you try to put a leash on him and take him for a walk! Instead, you keep him locked up in a cage or enclosure, and you do not let him near anyone who isn't properly trained and protected. You certainly don't put any kind of leash on him. Rather you tranquilize him when you want to transport him.

The wolf has one foundational instinct: Survival. You do not try to motivate him by his love of you. He doesn't love you. He thinks you are his captor, and if he had a chance, he might very well make a meal of you. Instead, you use his instinct to control him. You give food to him conditional on his willingness to play his part, and in so doing you constrain him. You may punish him for misbehaving, so that he fears you and will not attack you. But, again, you don't govern him on the basis of his love for you. He is hostile towards you.

But if, somehow, you could turn him into a tame domesticated dog, then you would relate to him entirely differently. His motivation would not primarily be survival, but love for his master. You would not feed him raw meat, but dry food. He would enjoy going for walks with you, and a leash would not bother him. He would be completely safe around your children because he knows how valuable they are to you, and he loves you. You would not cage him up at night, nor would you use his survival instinct to control him. His love for you would constrain him, and he would learn to do your bidding out of love in the context of relationship.

Stiff-Necked and Rebellious

The thing we must understand about the Law is to whom it was given. It was given only to the Israelites (Deut. 5:3). But more to the point, it was given to a people whom the Torah calls "stiff-necked" a total of eight times (Ex. 32:9, 33:4, 5, 34:9; Deut. 9:6, 13, 10:16, 31:27). In fact, rather than referring to the Israelites as good and special and uniquely obedient, Moses called them "rebellious" (Deut. 31:27). Echoing this, we read in the New Testament, "We know that the law is not meant for a righteous person, but for the lawless and **rebellious**, for the ungodly and sinful, for the unholy and irreverent" (1 Tim. 1:9)

The highest of high holy days in the Jewish calendar, the Day of Atonement, was given to purify the tabernacle because of Israel's "rebellious acts" (Lev. 16:16, 21): When God gave the Law, He assumed that Israel would simply go on being rebellious for generation after generation, so that they would have a special ceremony to remind them of their rebelliousness. The charge of rebelliousness was echoed 15 times by God Himself to the prophet Ezekiel (2:5, 6, 7, 8, 3:9, 26, 27, etc.). The Law was not given to a people who were born again, indwelt by God and thus constrained by their love for their heavenly Father. It was given to a rebellious people for whom the phrase "born again" had no meaning. It was given to wolves, not domesticated retrievers.

Once we come to understand this, we can see what Paul meant when he referred to the Law as slavery. He said the Law "imprisoned everything under sin's power" (Gal. 3:22). The Law simply allowed for the reality that humanity had in itself, not truly abrogating it, but using human reality for a greater purpose. It made use of politics, war, religion, fear, and punishment, in order to prepare a path for Jesus to come and subvert all those things with grace. It turned all of those basic principles of man back against man himself, so that a new reality, a new Kingdom of God, could come and replace the old principles of the world.

That, in a sense, is the difference between Law and Grace. We have spoken a bit about John 1:16 and 17. When you read John's introduction, he is stating that, in the incarnation of Jesus Christ, God began to relate to humanity in a completely different way than before. Up to that point, God had been working within the confines of the world man had made for himself, in a sense respecting Adam and Eve's choice. We might say God was working within the basic principles of this world, rather than outright contradicting them with another world altogether. He was dealing with wild wolves according to their wolfish nature.

But in Jesus Christ, God invaded this world with an altogether different one, the Kingdom of Heaven. God meant to overturn Adam's world with a new one. He meant to turn men from wild wolves into humble, gentle retrievers, so that He might relate to them as He truly desired. Or as John put it (John 1:12-13):

> To all who did receive Him,
> He gave them the right to be children of God,
> To those who believe in His name,
> Who were born,
> Not of blood,
> Or of the will of the flesh,
> Or of the will of man,
> But of God.

As Paul said in Galatians, the Law ideally was to keep the Israelite people under guard, as free as *humanly* possible from pagan influences, so that Jesus could come to them and fulfill the promise made to Abraham. In this it worked acceptably. The Law promised life to its recipients, but never *eternal* life, only a better mortal life and a degree of safety

from unnatural and violent death. The righteousness promised by the Law was not an *eternal*, saving righteousness, but
only a temporal one. Paul explains the difference between
the righteousness in the Law and the eternal righteousness
of God (Rom. 9:30-32, 10:3-4, NRSV):

> What then are we to say? Gentiles, who did not strive
> for righteousness, have attained it, that is, righteous-
> ness through faith; but Israel, who did strive for the
> righteousness that is based on the law, did not succeed
> in fulfilling that law. Why not? Because they did not
> strive for it on the basis of faith, but as if it were based
> on works... For, being ignorant of the righteousness
> that comes from God, and seeking to establish their
> own, they have not submitted to God's righteousness.
> For Christ is the end of the law so that there may be
> righteousness for everyone who believes.

The Law did not offer the eternal righteousness of God,
the eternal salvation that comes only by faith. The Law was
instead a temporary contract between Israel and God. So the
Law only offered a form of right relation—righteousness—to
the contract. Keeping that contract only meant the Israelites
were in right relation to the Law itself, not eternally saved
by God. The Law was not concerned with saving humanity,
but with making use of human reality to keep Israel under
guard until the time came for the Messiah to appear with a
heavenly reality.

To offer an extreme illustration, a German citizen during
World War II who served as a private in the Wehrmacht
might have been righteous in regards to his legal duty to
his government, but he would certainly not be considered
righteous in an eternal, salvific sense for doing so. In fact,
possibly the opposite. When the Allies over-ran Germany
and the war ended, they certainly would not have punished a

mere private for serving in the German infantry, but neither would his service in the army would in any way ingratiate him to the conquering Allies. Similarly, the Law only offered a temporal righteousness that is based on the realities of this world, not an eternal and saving righteousness that could only come from an invasion of this world by One who is beyond it.

Because the Law was meant to keep Israel under guard, it was based on the *stoicheion*, the basic principles upon which this human world operates. It used those principles—reward, punishment, control, fear, violence, and so on—in order to achieve the goal of guarding Israel. The unregenerate people it guarded could only walk according to those human principles. They did not have the born-again nature that would allow them to live by a truly other-worldly way of walking. So the Law was, as Luther put it, "material, mundane, earthly."

Unlike God's promise of salvation to Abraham, the Law was not unilateral, but bi-lateral, and as such had to reflect the unredeemed nature of the human parties to the agreement. For instance, Jesus said the Law's treatment of divorce did not capture the fullness of God's ideal for us: "Moses permitted you to divorce your wives because of the hardness of your hearts. But it was not like that from the beginning" (Matt. 19:8). The Law, as we said, also allowed for warfare and slavery, both clearly derived from the fallen reality of the *stoicheion*, and not God's ideal. Martin Luther sums up the meaning of the *stoicheion* quite well:

> By the elements of the world [*stoicheion*] the Apostle does not understand the physical elements, as some have thought. In calling the Law "the elements of the world," Paul means to say that the Law is something material, mundane, earthly. It may restrain evil, but it does not deliver from sin. The Law does not

justify; it does not bring a person to heaven. I do not obtain eternal life because I do not kill, commit adultery, steal, etc. Such mere outward decency does not constitute Christianity. The heathen observe the same restraints to avoid punishment or to secure the advantages of a good reputation. In the last analysis such restraint is simple hypocrisy. When the Law exercises its higher function it accuses and condemns the conscience. All these effects of the Law cannot be called divine or heavenly. These effects are elements of the world.[6]

The Condemnation

The Israelites, like Abraham, could only receive the *eternal* righteousness of God by having it credited to them because of their faith. Having a whole relationship with God might have enabled them to keep the underlying requirements of the Torah, but not because they sought a right *eternal* relationship with God via Torah observance. Rather, keeping the underlying requirements of the Law—loving their neighbors—would have happened only if the Israelites first sought God according to the faith of righteous Abraham, and not according to the commands of the Law. David, for instance, was one such man whom Paul said sought the righteousness that comes by faith instead of the righteousness that comes by the Law (Rom. 4:6-8). Thus, he was a man after God's own heart.

But the slavish Prodigal Brother within us who rules the fallen nature always seeks to achieve something by means of his own performances and merits and works. When the Law came, the natural inclination of the unregenerate Israelites was to attempt to use it to gain God's eternal favor, completely ignoring the right relationship that could only come by the faith of Abraham. Indeed, the full reality of that

167

faith was not revealed until Jesus Christ. So they sought the *eternal* righteousness credited to Abraham, not by trusting in the *eternal* God, but by means of keeping the *temporal* Law. Fallen humanity will not, left to itself, accept a free gift of reconciliation with God that comes by faith. Instead, fallen humanity will always try to achieve some form of merit before God by its own performance. Unless God intervenes, there is no other possible outcome, because slavery to the "knowledge of good and evil" is intrinsic to the Prodigal Brother's very nature.

Because of who he is, the Prodigal Brother will place the Law in his conscience as the thing he must use to get what he wants. He will try and try and try to keep the Law, thinking that somehow this will secure greater blessings from God or greater wealth or power. When God gave the Law, He also knew humanity would seek righteousness by it, and in a sense He intended humanity to try this and fail. He intended them to fail, not because He wanted them to fail to be righteous, but because He wanted them to conclusively realize righteousness can never come by performance. As Luther said in the quote above, "When the Law exercises its higher function it accuses and condemns the conscience."

Eugene Peterson paraphrases the first beatitude in Matthew by saying, "You're blessed when you're at the end of your rope" (Matt. 5:3, The Message). If a fool wants to hang himself by the means of his own folly, the best way to illustrate his error is to hand him a rope. In Chapter 1, we saw Jesus use the Law this way with the rich young ruler. Trying to obtain righteousness by works is very much the basic principle of human religion. But the Law was given with such a very high standard of moral uprightness, that the Law itself would prove the impossibility of achieving righteousness through performance. It became the rope by which the fools of this world might hang themselves (Rom. 3:19-24):

Now we know that whatever the law says speaks to those who are subject to the law, so that every mouth may be shut and the whole world may become subject to God's judgment. For no flesh will be justified in His sight by the works of the law, for through the law comes the knowledge of sin. But now, apart from the law, God's righteousness has been revealed—attested by the Law and the Prophets—that is, God's righteousness through faith in Jesus Christ, to all who believe, since there is no distinction. For all have sinned and fall short of the glory of God. They are justified freely by His grace through the redemption that is in Christ Jesus.

In this sense, the Law demonstrated to the "whole world," through the example of the Jews (those "subject to the law") that it was impossible for man to achieve true righteousness by religious performance. Man sought to be like God(s) in Eden, yet the Law leaves no choice but for us to admit that we "fall short of the glory of God." Instead, trying and failing to achieve righteousness by the Law only demonstrates to the sinner the utter impossibility of being like God by his own efforts. The only hope left for such a person is to repent of the whole "Knowledge of Good and Evil" foolishness, and instead embrace the Tree of Life by faith in Jesus Christ.

We can begin to understand why Paul referred to the Ten Commandments as the "ministry of death, chiseled in letters on stones" and the "ministry of condemnation" (2 Cor. 3:7). We can see why Paul said "all who rely on the works of the law are under a curse" (Gal. 3:10). The Law was given to an unregenerate, "stiff-necked" and "rebellious" people, specifically to show the world the curse sinful man created for himself in Eden. The Law is not, solely in itself, the complete definition of sins. Nor is it, in itself, the original source of man's condemnation. After all, Paul said that,

"In fact, sin was in the world before the law, but sin is not charged to one's account when there is no law. Nevertheless, death reigned from Adam to Moses..." (Rom 5:13-14). Sin existed before the Law came to define a list of sins and non-sins. More, the curse of death that man chose for himself in Eden came to us even before the Law was given at Sinai. The Law came in order that God might charge sin to one's account, bringing that person under His judgment, so that the person would see his need for the mercy in Jesus Christ. As such, the Law wasn't an eternal means of defining sin. Rather, the Law was a means to give us "the knowledge of sin," implying that sin was already in us ("sin was in the world before the law") but we didn't really know it. The rules are not the point. They are merely a tool to point to a greater truth. We are broken.

As Wayne Jacobsen puts it, the world uniformly holds to what he calls the "do, to be." The world says we must do this, that, and the other, and that by properly performing such things, we win God's approval and become right with Him. In contrast, Jacobsen says, the Gospel reflects the idea of "be, to do." We are first adopted as His children utterly by grace, and then by living in that relationship God brings about His goodness in us. The Law, and every human religion, clearly reflects the former understanding, while only the Gospel reflects the latter. But God chose to give the Law in such a way that the Law itself would make clear both that God is righteous, and man is not.

But Paul Said...

If you have been taught the Prodigal Brother's version of Christianity, then you might immediately reply by quoting his favorite proof-text from Paul's epistle to the Romans, "The law is holy, and the commandment is holy and just and good" (Rom. 7:12). Paul indeed said this, but the conclusion he drew from it is the opposite of the Prodigal Brother's thinking.

First, Paul's statement doesn't rule out the possibility that there could be a new law, or new principles, or new ideas, or in fact a new Messiah, that would be more holy, more just, and better than the Old Covenant Law. As we saw, Paul argued that it was better to fulfill the underlying requirements of the Law by loving one's neighbor, than to seek after the commandments themselves. Loving others is more holy, more just, and better than keeping a list of rules. Moreover, there is an entire book of the Bible, Hebrews, which shows how the new revelation that came in Jesus Christ is superior to what came in the Law. We also recall those famous words of John: "Although the law was given through Moses, grace and truth came through Jesus Christ" (John 1:17). Just because the Law Covenant was holy, does not mean there could not come a new reality that was more holy than the Old Covenant Law.

But more centrally, Paul writes (Romans 7:7-12):

What should we say then? Is the law sin? Absolutely not! On the contrary, I would not have known sin if it were not for the law. For example, I would not have known what it is to covet if the law had not said, "You shall not covet." And sin, seizing an opportunity through the commandment, produced in me coveting of every kind. For apart from the law sin is dead. Once I was alive apart from the law, but when the commandment came, sin sprang to life and I died. The commandment that was meant for life resulted in death for me. For sin, seizing an opportunity through the commandment, deceived me, and through it killed me. So then, the law is holy, and the commandment is holy and just and good.

Paul states, if I may paraphrase, that the cancer of sin within him wrapped itself around the Law and used it to bring about greater and greater sin in him. This, it seems, is what Paul meant when he said the Law had "imprisoned everything under sin's power" (Gal. 3:22). Paul goes further, declaring that by using the Law, sin in him "deceived me, and through it killed me." Elsewhere, Paul writes similarly, "Through the law I have died to the law, that I might live to God. I have been crucified with Christ; and I no longer live, but Christ lives in me" (Gal 2:19-20).

We can see how the Law put the old Saul to death: In the rest of Romans 7, Paul tells how the very goodness described in the tenth commandment—"You shall not covet"—caused him to try to achieve the holiness in the command by his own efforts. Sin in him believed, pridefully, that he had the means in himself to be good just like God is good. But in trying to live this out, he found he had no goodness in himself at all by which he could do the good described by that command-ment. Goodness was intrinsic only to God, not to Paul.

Within him instead was something vile and evil. He learned that you cannot do good to become righteous, because you must be righteous first before you can do good. The Law led Paul to look for someone to rescue him from this "body of death," (v. 24) and he found that someone in Jesus Christ (v. 25). According to Romans 7, the Law was holy *because* it drove Paul to die to his own religious efforts and trust instead in Jesus Christ to save him. The Law ceases to be holy to us if we divorce it from its intended function of convicting lost sinners of the impossibility of achieving righteousness by human effort.

In keeping with this function, we find that the better the essential goodness in the commandment, the more likely it would be to cause the very crisis that Paul went through. For instance, no Jew ever had a real problem with circumcision, since he was circumcised the eighth day and would never remember it. Simply put, it wasn't his decision. Instead, Paul got to the very core of a command that dealt with what went on within him, in his very mind—desiring something that didn't belong to him. He spoke of a command that showed the essential un-lovingness that was Saul of Tarsus.

The burden of the Law is the fact that a person who loves God and others perfectly will be able to keep these hard commands like not coveting. But a person who doesn't love, cannot. Love, not mere technical violations of the Ten Commandments or the other 603 rules, is really the key moral deficiency in humanity. The Law simply points that out. Love is why you cannot do good in order to become good. You must first have love within you, in order to act it out in life. You must first love in order to act lovingly.

But in order to love, you must be loved by God first, before you even love Him in return. Because it is His love in us—His indwelling—that He gives us by grace because He first loves us. So His love in us is what must come out of us, resulting in true goodness of action. That is why Paul told the born-again Roman Christians not to focus on keeping the commandments in the Law, but on loving others.

Bringing It All Together

So we can see why Paul describes the Law as a reflection of the *stoicheion* of this world. The Law demonstrated to mankind, through the Israelites, that we cannot do good in order to be good. The Serpent, as we said, conveniently left out that part about how simply knowing what is good and what is evil doesn't actually make you like God. The missing step was that God doesn't merely know good and evil, but He is good and not evil, and it is because of this that He does good and not evil.

Israel's neighbors didn't tend to bother with an understanding of holiness as strict as that of the Law. For example, instead of condemning sexual immorality, Israel's pagan neighbors made it a part of their religious systems. They instituted temple prostitutes with whom one could perform all sorts of debauchery under the guise of service to the gods. In order to deal with the fact that they had no goodness within themselves, the pagans merely re-defined their "knowledge of good and evil" in a way that accommodated their sinfulness. As Paul said in Romans 1, God simply gave the Gentiles over to that sort of evil. In so doing evil they would realize their brokenness by experiencing the results that sin brings: Sexual disease, murder, war, poverty, depression, and so forth.

But God did something different with Israel. By giving Israel a sort of impressionist portrait of what God is like in His essential righteousness, the Law gave them something inflexible and truly good to shoot for: A shadowy (Col. 2:17) representation of God that was given by God Himself. It gave them, in that sense, a truly divine "knowledge of good and evil" instead of a merely human one. But, as Paul explains in the beginning of Romans 2, the Jews had no means of condemning the Gentiles for their perversions, because Jewish history is riddled with the exact same sorts of immoral behavior as the pagans practiced. The Law did not make them live righteously. Mere commands and penalties and rewards and fear—the basic principles of this world— cannot make one good. Rules may show us our hatred, but they cannot cause us to love.

And that was the problem. God's holiness cannot be achieved by means of human effort. The Law proved to man that this entire business of trying to be like God through the "knowledge of good and evil," had not resulted in a man like God at all, but rather more like His opposite. You must first have God's goodness in you by grace, in order to reflect His love in your life.

It is not that God was being dishonest. If you were truly good, truly unmarred by sin and had goodness intrinsic to you, you could keep any set of commandments God might give. You could do this because supreme love of God would be the core of who you were. As such, the Law would not so much grant such a person righteousness or holiness or life, as it would merely attest to the fact that he was good in the first place. So, in that sense, the rewards attached to Law-keeping were indeed true. A person who perfectly kept the Law would indeed have life and righteousness and holiness, but only because all those things were there in the first place and enabled him to keep the Law. Only One Person has ever lived that way.

The Law came to guard Israel until the time of the Messiah, and to show to us the inability of achieving righteousness by human efforts. Both of these functions are temporary, not eternal. They are results relegated to this world, not to the next. When a person comes to faith in Jesus Christ, the Law of Sinai is through with him. He has died to it, and instead risen to live by the Reality outside this world, God the Son. The Law served to demonstrate our emptiness, so that Jesus could come to fill us with Himself. The Law served to demonstrate our unrighteousness, so that we might freely receive the righteousness of God in Jesus Christ. The Law served to bring us to death, so that Jesus could rise from the grave and make us alive. The Law came to demonstrate our slavery to the principles of the world, so that Jesus could liberate us from the "knowledge of good and evil." And to that liberty, we shall turn now.

Chapter 7

Anno Domini

—⟨⟩—

Grace is the only force in the universe powerful
enough to break the chains that enslave generations.
Philip Yancey/*What's So Amazing About Grace?*

W e separate the modern from the ancient era by dividing
time into two segments, BC ("Before Christ"), and
AD ("Anno Domini"). Many Christians have commented on
how this shows the Christ-event as the central dividing line
of human experience. This, I agree, is true, but I suspect the
religious world misses the point hidden in those two time
notations.

We don't denote time after Jesus' advent as AC, for "After
Christ," though that would be the most obvious response to
the phrase "Before Christ." We mark our modern era with
the term "Anno Domini," Latin for "the Year of the Lord."
That can't help but make me think of another "year of the
Lord" spoken of by Isaiah in a prophecy about the Messiah
(Isa. 61:1, 2, NKJV):

The Spirit of the Lord God is upon Me,
Because the Lord has anointed Me
To preach good tidings to the poor;

He has sent Me to heal the brokenhearted,
To proclaim liberty to the captives,
And the opening of the prison to those who are
    bound;
To proclaim the acceptable *year of the Lord.*

If we were to write Isaiah's prophecy in Latin, we might say the Messiah would "proclaim the acceptable *Anno Domini*," and two of the four Gospels distinctly couch Jesus' ministry on earth in such terms: Matthew and Luke explain who Jesus is by showing His ministry as the fulfillment of Isaiah 61:1-3.

The Year of the Lord

The "year of the Lord" was the Jewish Jubilee year. In addition to their weekly Sabbath, the Jews had an annual Sabbath every seventh year. On that year, the land would lie fallow, no one would work in the fields, and instead God would ensure that the land brought forth enough food for them to live on. But every 49 years, after the seventh Sabbatical year, there would be an additional rest year, the Jubilee.

On that year, no one would work. It was a year to "proclaim freedom in the land for all its inhabitants" (Lev. 25:10), or as Isaiah had it, "To proclaim liberty to the captives." When the Israelites came into Canaan, each family was given a specific plot of land that would be theirs for every genera-tion onward. They were free to buy or sell these plots from each other. Those who had become very poor would often sell their land, and if that didn't give them enough to live on, they would sell themselves into indentured servitude to another Israelite family. But in the Jubilee year, the original reality was restored: The impoverished indentured servants were not only set free, but given back their original land.

Everyone was back before God on an equal footing, the same as when they had entered Canaan: They all lived because God had, in His grace, given each of them a land to live on.

The Israelites were not to sow or harvest during the Jubilee. Instead, they were to eat directly out of the field. God would provide a triple harvest in the sixth year: Enough food to eat in the seventh Sabbatical year, the following Jubilee year, and the year after that (Lev. 25:21, 22). In the United States, workers usually receive two weeks paid vacation. In Europe, it can be as much as six weeks. But in Israel, every seventh year was to be a year of paid vacation, and the 49th and 50th years of the cycle were to be two straight years of vacation. It was the annual equivalent of over eight weeks of vacation.

Just like the Jews' seventh-day Sabbath, the Jubilee year was filled with Edenic symbolism. The children of Israel were not to toil in the fields, sowing and harvesting. Instead, they were to eat the food directly in the field, just as Adam and Eve were able to eat directly from the trees of the Garden without having to go through the arduous cycle of planting and reaping. Because of his choice to live outside of God's gracious provision, Adam cursed himself to toil every year in the fields, in a back-breaking slavery to his basic needs. But in the Jubilee year, all the slaves who toiled in the field would be set free! By rejecting God's grace, Adam had lost his special land, Eden, the basis of his material provision. In the Jubilee year, every impoverished Israelite would have his land restored to him!

All of Israelite life was meant to look forward to the great year of release, the year of the Lord when all Israel could rest and everything would be restored. It was the climax of the Jewish religious calendar. Certainly every family sold into indentured servitude would groan for the time when they would finally be liberated from bondage. No doubt the poor landless families yearned for the proclamation of Jubilee, when their ancestral lands would be returned to them and they would have a means of provision and freedom from want. Jubilee was the year when all servitude would cease and each Israelite would be, economically speaking, truly free.

My Slaves

As we saw in Chapter 2, unlike the pagan gods of Israel's neighbors, the true God did not create man to live in the slavery of religious obligation to Him. He created man to live freely in His grace. His grace would give man food and life. His grace would even make man holy by His indwelling. But man chose, not what God desired to give him at creation, but what the pagans instead believed about creation. Adam chose a life of slavery to the performance of the intrinsically impossible, seeking to achieve the holiness of God in his life by his actions.

And that is why the Jubilee commands in the Law are of particular interest. God first tells the Israelites that they are to sell and buy each other only as indentured servants, workers who would be freed from servitude on the Jubilee year. He tells them the Israelite servants are not to be seen as permanent slaves. It is the reasoning He gives that is so fascinating: "They are not to be sold as slaves, because they are My slaves I brought out of the land of Egypt" (Lev. 25:42). God declares this once again at the end of the chapter regarding the Jubilee: "For the Israelites are My slaves. They are My slaves I brought out of the land of Egypt" (Lev. 25:55).

In fact, in the next chapter, God tells the Israelites, "I am the Lord your God, who brought you out of the land of Egypt, so that you would no longer be their slaves. I broke the bars of your yoke and enabled you to live in freedom." But He tells them that, unless they perfectly keep all 613 commands in the Law, He will give them curses and punishments and diseases and plagues. He in fact describes far worse punishments for disobedience than the Israelites ever experienced from the Egyptians. He says, for example (Lev. 26:16, 17):

I will bring terror on you—wasting disease and fever that will cause your eyes to fail and your life to ebb away. You will sow your seed in vain because your enemies will eat it. I will turn against you, so that you will be defeated by your enemies. Those who hate you will rule over you, and you will flee even though no one is pursuing you.

But more than that, He describes attacks by wild animals, famine, starvation, and the sword of vengeance. All this He couches in terms of a master's punishment of his slaves, saying, "I also will strike you seven times for your sins," (Lev. 26:24), and, "I will also discipline you seven times for your sins" (Lev. 26:28).

So it is no surprise, if you think about it, that God ends His discussion of Jubilee by telling the Israelites, "You are My slaves." Man chose, as his nature, to be a slave. God's description of Israel as "My slaves" did not so much reflect some divine desire to enslave humanity, as it did the fact that fallen man thinks of himself as a slave. As shown in Leviticus 26, God's ultimate desire is for man to be free, but unless man is born again, he can only live to God as a slave. The Prodigal Brother was truly a son in his father's estate, but he could only think of himself as a slave. The only way he knew to live to his father was by slaving to earn his father's affection and avoid his father's wrath. The Law did not so much make Israel slaves, as it treated them like the slaves they by nature were. The entire Israelite system seemed to remind them of their intrinsic slavery, to make them yearn for the time when God would free them from legalistic bondage to the Covenant at Sinai.

The Two Yokes

In the aforementioned movie *Defiance*, two men, Ben Zion and Krensky, died on a mission to secure medicine for the fever-ridden Jewish band. At their funeral, Rabbi Shimon gives a prayer that powerfully demonstrates the anguish of the community:

> Merciful God, we commit our friends
> Ben Zion and Krensky to your care.
> We have no more prayers, no more tears.
> We have run out of blood.
> Choose another people.
> We have paid for each of your Commandments.
> We have covered every field and stone with ashes.
> Sanctify another land.
> Choose another people.
> Teach them the Deeds and the Prophecies.
> Grant us but one more blessing –
> Take back the gift of our holiness.

In a great irony, Rabbi Shimon's prayer echoes the words of another Shimon, 1900 years before. Shimon Peter said that the Law was "a yoke that neither our forefathers nor we have been able to bear" (Acts 15:10). And another Rabbi, Saul of Tarsus, described the Law as slavery in Galatians 3 and 4:

> Now I say that as long as the heir is a child, he differs in no way from a slave, though he is the owner of everything. Instead, he is under guardians and stewards until the time set by his father. In the same way we also, when we were children, were in slavery under the *stoicheion* of the world. But when the completion of the time came, God sent His Son, born of a

181

woman, born under the law, to redeem those under the law, so that we might receive adoption as sons. And because you are sons, God has sent the Spirit of His Son into our hearts, crying, "Abba, Father!" So you are no longer a slave, but a son; and if a son, then an heir through God.

Paul again refers to the Law as the *stoicheion*, or the "basic principles of this world," (NIV) that Jesus was born under. He declares that we were in slavery to the *stoicheion*. According to him, because of our spiritual immaturity, we were by nature slaves, so the Law treated us as such. By being born under the Law, Jesus chose to be born into this slavery to the *stoicheion*. As someone who was not by nature a sinful slave, but *the* Son, Jesus could thus "redeem those under the law."

Rabbi Shimon's prayer, Shimon Peter's declaration in Jerusalem, and Saul's statement to the Galatian Christians each represent the sort of response God intended by the Law. The Law was meant to demonstrate to us the slavery we have taken upon ourselves, an unbearable yoke of trusting in human performance. The last portion of Leviticus 25, as well as the proceeding Leviticus 26, paint exactly such a picture. If we fail to see the Law as a sort of metaphorical slavery, then perhaps we have missed the very essence of what God, in both the Old and New Testaments, says about the Covenant of the Law given at Sinai.

After telling the New Covenant Christians not to seek to be bound by the Old Covenant Law, Paul says, "Christ has liberated us into freedom. Therefore stand firm and don't submit again to a yoke of slavery" (Gal. 5:1). Context clearly points to the "yoke of slavery" as one and the same yoke spoken of by Peter, the Law given at Sinai. The Old Moses had liberated the Israelites into a greater slavery than the one they had left, the spiritual slavery of religious obligations they had no hope of ever living up to. These obligations operated on unregenerate slaves, and therefore had to be given in accordance with the world's basic principles. These are the only principles the slave-minded Prodigal Brother can understand, so long as he has not been born again. So it was with unregenerate Israel.

But the New Moses—Jesus Christ—came to liberate humanity into a freedom from religious enslavement. He came so that we might be born again, not born according to the world's basic principles, but born by the Spirit of God as Abba's children. That is why Jesus mentions another yoke. In Matthew 11, after Jesus describes His Jubilee ministry by quoting Isaiah 61:1—"The poor are told the good news"— He implores us (Matt. 11:28-30):

Come to Me, all of you who are weary and burdened, and I will give you rest. All of you, take up My yoke and learn from Me, because I am gentle and humble in heart, and you will find rest for yourselves. For My yoke is easy and My burden is light.

The Law was a "yoke of slavery," (Gal. 5:1) and Jesus responded with a yoke of rest. The Law was "a yoke that neither our forefathers nor we have been able to bear," and Jesus came to replace it with a yoke that is easy and a burden that is light. The Jubilee was a declaration of rest to the indentured slaves. No one planted or harvested in the Jubilee year. So when Jesus came with the hope of a spiritual Jubilee, He came with a message of rest. He came to replace the slavery of Sinai with the adoption as children. He came to take the Prodigal Brother out of the fields and return him to the celebration in his father's house.

Unforgiven and Unloved

First-century Israel was dominated by scribes and Pharisees who functioned like the morals police of today's theocratic Islamic states. Every violation, even (to the modern mind) a seemingly minor one like carrying a bed roll on the Sabbath, was cause for severe chastisement. The result could be excommunication from the synagogue, the center of Jewish social and religious life. Or punishment could be as severe as stoning for crimes like adultery. The problem with the Pharisees wasn't that they were disloyal to the Law's demand for punishment, but that they were fiercely loyal to it. Consequently, everyone lived in fear of them.

Those who had done some form of moral evil— "tax-collectors and sinners"—were shunned by their communities, unforgiven and unloved. For all the down-trodden and guilt-racked, who needed the grace of God and could not receive it through the Law, the Covenant of Sinai had indeed become "a yoke of slavery" that "neither our forefathers nor we have been able to bear."

Mercy, and Not Sacrifice

It was to these the broken and sick and guilt-ridden "My slaves" who were in bondage under the Law, that Jesus proclaimed His Jubilee. When Matthew describes Jesus' Jubilee ministry, he book-ends the symbolism with Jesus' quotation of Hosea 6:6, "I desire mercy and not sacrifice" (Matt. 9:13, 12:7).

Just before Jesus said it the first time, a group of men had brought a paralytic to Him. Rather than healing him out-right, Jesus first said to him, "Have courage, son, your sins are forgiven!" (Matt.9:2) This seems, on its face, an odd thing to say to a man who wanted freedom from paralysis. But in the religious mindset of the day, the man's paralysis was a result of God's displeasure for his sinfulness. The religious establishment might have categorized him as unclean, and thus he would be cut off from his community.

There is a difference between seeing sickness as the tragic result of Adam's foolish choice, and seeing it as God's angry judgment against a particular individual. When Paul pleaded with the Lord to remove his own physical ailment, Jesus said, "My grace is sufficient for you, for My power is perfected in weakness" (2 Cor. 12:9). Physical ailments are something the Law cannot cure, because true freedom from suffering can only be given by God's grace. Jesus did not see illness as God's anger at the afflicted, but rather as an opportunity for God to demonstrate the power of His grace.

Sickness may remind us that something in our world is not as it should be, but the symptoms themselves do not constitute a cure. They in some sense pose a question that only grace can answer. Similarly, the Law reminded man of his own fallenness, so that he would see his need for the mercy of God. As the author of Hebrews puts it (Heb. 10:1-4):

> Since the law has only a shadow of the good things to come, and not the actual form of those realities, it can never perfect the worshipers by the same sacrifices they continually offer year after year. Otherwise, wouldn't they have stopped being offered, since the worshipers, once purified, would no longer have any consciousness of sins? But in the sacrifices there is a reminder of sins every year.

The Law didn't truly forgive sins. It didn't allow for sins to be completely wiped away. All it allowed for was that sins would be sort of temporarily passed over. In fact, all the sacrifices and ceremonies only covered "unintentional" sin,[1] accidents of clumsiness and not failures of conscience. For intentional sin, *real* sinfulness, the Law only promised a forestalled judgment, not a complete atonement. And that is why offerings had to be made "year after year."

Now, if you have ever lived with this kind guilt-inducing religious obligation, you can understand how horrible it is. I myself grew up in a brand of Law-based Christianity that taught that sins were never forgiven. They were only conditionally pardoned. Jesus would wait to see if, in our lives, we had done a good enough job keeping the Ten Commandments. Then, if we had, He would permanently blot out our sins.

One of the many problems with all of this is that you never really knew if you were good enough to merit having your sins blotted out. You would constantly be reminded of your own sinfulness as you worked to keep every one of the Ten Commandments, as well as several other rules that came from here or there in the Law, or from held-over Victorian cultural prejudices. Forgiveness, in that Old Covenant-focused system, was always conditional on how hard you worked, on what religious acts you did, and so forth. I remember, from a very young age, being told by more than one adult that God would only forgive my sins if I did X or Y or Z.

This assertion wreaked havoc in my young mind. I constantly felt the terrors of guilt and lived in fear that God would completely reject me. In fact, this thinking, coupled with other factors, led to a deep clinical depression between my fifth and sixth grade years. I was suicidal. The psychiatrist said I was perhaps the worst case he had ever seen in an adolescent. I was constantly worried about all of my sins, always seeking to apologize just right and ask forgiveness, hoping that somehow God would forgive me. I worried that if I died, I would not have done the right things that would convince God to forgive my sins.

In fact, this way of thinking stayed with me even into adulthood, when thankfully Jesus rescued me from that prison. When I was in death under the Law, forgiveness was not a free gift of God, but something I had to earn. I knew that the fear of God's wrath for unforgiven sins was something far worse than any physical ailment. It haunted my fears, kept me awake at night, caused me to be bitter, angry, and always afraid.

Similarly, because of the religious culture of his time, the paralytic's ailment reminded him that the Law left him unforgiven, outside of the religious system of Judaism and thus separate from God. His daily social life in the Jewish community would have been a constant reminder of his shame and spiritual inadequacy. So you can understand exactly what it feels like when Jesus says to you, as He said to me and to the paralytic, "Have courage, son, your sins are forgiven!" It is positively liberating.

That is why Jesus' healing of the paralyzed man comes in close proximity to His later statement that "I desire mercy and not sacrifice." The sacrifices could never bring mercy. They could only remind of sin. That is the very nature of religious obligation. It only awakens the shame in us at the same time that it tries to cover that shame with religious works. But it can never really cover shame. Like Adam and Eve's itchy and uncomfortable fig leaves, it continually reminds us that something about us isn't as it should be. I think that is why the author of Hebrews 10 goes on to say (vs. 8-10):

After He says above, "You did not desire or delight in sacrifices and offerings, whole burnt offerings and sin offerings," (which are offered according to the law), He then says, "See, I have come to do Your will." He takes away the first [covenant] to establish the second. By this will, we have been sanctified through the offering of the body of Jesus Christ once and for all.

God never truly desired to bind us with religious obligation that only reminds us of shame. Sinai was not His ultimate desire, but merely a means of bringing us to see that only His grace, and not our abilities, could bring about true life. God has always desired to give us grace and not religion, and that was the will of God that God the Son came to bring about.

That is why, when Jesus told the paralytic, "Your sins are forgiven," He incurred the rage of the scribes and Pharisees. They thought it was blasphemy that He would claim the authority to forgive sins. The Prodigal Brother in us cannot accept grace. Grace is contrary to his very nature. He can only trust in his own religious slaving. Like most Prodigal Brothers, the Pharisees saw ailments as God's judgment for sins in people's lives. So for Jesus to tell the paralytic that his sins were forgiven was mind-boggling to them indeed. It was as if Jesus was seeking to overthrow the established order. In fact, He was.

And this act of healing demonstrates the overwhelming grace of Jesus' Jubilee. He indeed healed the man of his paralysis, but He did so in order to demonstrate that He had the authority to do the greater deed, forgiving the man's sins. That is why Isaiah wrote of the Messianic Jubilee, "He has sent Me to heal the brokenhearted" (Isa. 61:1).

The Scandal of Grace

From there Jesus went to call Matthew, a tax collector, as His disciple. Tax collectors were absolutely despised. On Israel's religious ladder, they must have been the lowest of the low, just a notch above uncircumcised Gentiles, and two notches below navel lint. They were collaborators, collecting taxes for the hated Roman government. These taxes had to be paid in addition to the tithes and Temple taxes paid to Israel's religious establishment. And that is why Matthew's name is so important. The Bible doesn't just call him "Matthew." It also calls him "Levi." He was a Levite, a member of the priestly tribe. For him to collect taxes for the Romans, rather than live in service to the religious system, was a horrible affront to the religious order. It was no small thing for Jesus to call a tax collector to be His disciple. It was even more scandalous that He called a *Levite* tax collector.

The scandal continued as Jesus went to eat at Matthew's house. "Many tax collectors and sinners came as guests to eat with Jesus and His disciples" (Matt. 9:10). In the first century Jewish religious culture, eating together was a sign of friendship and close emotional intimacy. For an up-and-coming Jewish rabbi to eat with tax collectors and sinners would have been utterly scandalous. Even today, it would not go over well with the Prodigal Brother if he saw a Christian befriending and loving a homosexual despite his sin. But that was exactly the sort of scandalous thing Jesus was doing.

And that is precisely what grace is. It is scandalous to the religious thinking of the world. Our word *scandal* comes from the Greek word *skandalon*, literally meaning a stumbling block. This word was used to denote something offensive. The scandal of the word *skandalon* is that Paul used it to describe the Gospel: "We preach Christ crucified, a *skandalon* to the Jews and foolishness to the Gentiles" (1 Cor.1:23).

It was in sight of the divine scandal of grace that the Pharisees asked, "Why does your Teacher eat with tax collectors and sinners?" And it was to this question that Jesus retorted, "Those who are well don't need a doctor, but the sick do. Go and learn what this means: 'I desire mercy and not sacrifice'" (Matt. 9:12-13).

These are the words Matthew's Gospel uses to characterize Jesus' Jubilee ministry. "I desire mercy and not sacrifice." Sacrifice was the basis of the Jewish religious system. Everything was grounded on the Temple. It touched every facet of life. Several times a year a Jewish family might go to the Temple to offer the sacrifices required by the Law. Mercy was something to be purchased by sacrifice, not something offered freely. So when Jesus said, "I desire mercy and not sacrifice," He was striking at the very foundations of first century religious thinking.

The Prodigal Brother would have you think that God cannot be around sinners, but the Bible tells us that it is sinners who can't stand to be around God. If God cannot stand to be around sinners, then why did He come to earth eating with "tax collectors and sinners"? We desired sacrifice, and spurned His grace. So it is we who made ourselves unclean and left ourselves unable to bear His presence. But God desired an offering that religion could not give. An offering only He could give. A free mercy. Grace. Reconciliation.

The Fermented Wine of Grace

In the next vignette, Jesus' disciples ask Him about fasting, and He turns it into a lesson about "mercy and not sacrifice." He tells them, "No one puts new wine into old wineskins. Otherwise, the skins burst, the wine spills out, and the skins are ruined. But they put new wine into fresh wineskins, and both are preserved."

There is something in this metaphor that hits us right between the eyes: Jesus says the new wine would burst old wineskins. I can guarantee you that if you put grape juice into a first century wineskin, and keep it fresh in your refrigerator, it will never burst. But add a bit of yeast and leave it on the countertop, and soon you will have, not juice, but wine bubbling out of the skin and bursting it. To burst a wineskin, you need fermentation, because fermentation produces excess carbon dioxide. In first century Judea, fermentation was done in wineskins. And unless the leather wineskin was fresh and flexible and supple, the carbon dioxide would burst the brittle wineskin, and both the wine and the skin would be lost. The point: Jesus' grace is intoxicating.

You cannot pour grace into a religious way of thinking. Before I understood grace, I tried to marry it to my religious way of thinking, and it always had to take a backseat to the Law. The Law that God intended to drive me to Christ, became the very thing that kept me from Him. Both the sweet wine of grace and the bitter judgment of the Law were destroyed to me.

It was only when wine was poured into a new wineskin, into a new way of thinking, that I could fathom grace. It was only then that I knew grace's rich taste, oaky aroma, and intoxicating effects. It was only then that I could fully grasp what Jesus meant when He said, "I desire mercy and not sacrifice." And that really is the point: You just cannot combine the old sacrifices of religious obligation with the new mercy of grace. They are incompatible. Jesus offered the latter to free us from the former. The spiritual Jubilee did not come so that we could continue living as indentured servants.

Cleansing Grace

But the mercy of grace doesn't merely forgive. It cleanses from defilement where the old system of religious obligation could not. Sin brought shame, and religion feasts on the shame of its slaves. But grace rids us of shame and in its place brings a holiness that the Law could not. As Paul put it, in Jesus Christ "the grace of God has appeared, bringing salvation to all, training us to renounce impiety and worldly passions, and in the present age to live lives that are self-controlled, upright, and godly" (Titus 2:11-12, NRSV). Grace first saves us, ridding us of shame, and then grace, not the Law or religious obligation, cleanses us from the power of evil. That is precisely what Matthew's Gospel shows in the next two miracles of Jesus Christ.

As Jesus was talking to His disciples about wine and wineskins, a synagogue leader came imploring Him to heal his dying daughter. Jesus recognized the man's faith and began following him to his home. But as He went, a woman grabbed a tassel on His robe. Jesus was of course a Jew. He was born under the Law, as Paul said, and those who were under the Law were to wear tassels on the edges of their garments.

The woman had a flow of blood that had lasted for twelve years, making her unclean according to the Law. No one could touch her, or they too would be unclean (Lev. 15:25). For 12 agonizing years, this woman had known little or nothing of the loving acceptance symbolized by human touch. To a Jew of the time, her uncleanness was a mark of God's disfavor, a sign of defiling sin. It was a great scarlet letter of shame.

But God had said through the Prophet Hosea: "I desire mercy and not sacrifice." God's ultimate desire wasn't for her to give Him an offering. His ultimate desire was to give her mercy in her brokenness, healing in her sickness, love in her loneliness. It was this God of grace whom she recognized in Jesus Christ, and that is why she said of Him, "If I can just touch His robe, I'll be made well!" (Matt. 9:21).

The woman had risked a great deal in touching Jesus' robe. Had He been like all the other rabbis, He might have responded in anger. The woman, after all, would have made Him "unclean until evening" (Lev. 15:19). It was by faith that she had touched His garment. By faith she trusted him to be a Messiah of grace, a Christ who ultimately desired "mercy and not sacrifice." But what if she was wrong?

When the woman was discovered, she was so afraid that she had incurred Jesus' anger that she fell before Him trembling (Luke 8:47). But rather than be angry with her, Jesus looked on her with all the love of His gentle heart. He wasn't angry she had touched Him. He was delighted by her faith. He didn't merely call her "woman," a term of respect, but "daughter," a term of tender affection. Jesus was traveling to cure the daughter of the synagogue leader, knowing all the while that He would cure this daughter as well. Jesus indeed had cured her, and in so doing He showed her the meaning of His Gospel: "Your faith has made you well. Go in peace."

Rather than her defilement infecting Him, His grace cleansed the source of her uncleanness, overcoming the defilement that caused her shame. For 12 sad years she lived daily with the Law's accusing finger, shouting to her, "You are unclean! You are unclean!" For 12 terrible years she could not know the touch of a human hand! For 12 horrid years this woman was locked in a dungeon of religious shame! But Jesus broke down the bars that held her in and destroyed the chains that bound her. His *Anno Domini* had set her free from her captivity under the Law. Indeed, His grace had triumphed over religion. Mercy had triumphed over sacrifice.

After this, Jesus arrived at the synagogue leader's home. The man's daughter was dead. She must have died while Jesus was healing the broken woman. Jesus didn't bring the girl to life the same way He did later with Lazarus. He didn't just speak life to her. He took her by the hand. When Jesus touched the body of the dead girl, He was risking defilement according to the Law (Num. 19:11-13):

> The person who touches any human corpse will be unclean for seven days.... Anyone who touches a body of a person who has died, and does not purify himself, defiles the tabernacle of the Lord. That person will be cut off from Israel.

There is a reason Jesus told the mourners around the girl to leave the house. There is a reason that, after He healed the girl, Jesus told those present, "Be sure that no one finds out!" (Matt. 9:30) His enemies could have used the act as a weapon against Him, claiming He was a false Messiah because He did not purify Himself and thus was "cut off from Israel."

But He could not be unclean. God, you see, can never be made unclean. Were He to undergo the rituals of cleansing, He would be denying both His divine nature and His mission. His grace is not defiled by our sin, but His grace cleanses us of our sin. Death came into the world because of sin. But Jesus came with grace, and rather than being defiled by the death of that little girl, His grace overcame her death. His grace overcame the Law's charge of "unclean." By bringing an authentic holiness that religion cannot, God's grace over-throws the Prodigal Brother's entire world, and himself with it. That is the *Anno Domini* of Jesus Christ.

From Death to Life

Jesus didn't see death as merely a physical phenomenon. He would call people dead whose bodies were still living (Luke 9:60), and He said that even those who died physi-cally would still live (John 11:25, 26). As Ravi Zacharias often says, "Jesus did not come to make bad people good. He came to make dead people alive." Jesus came to make us "alive with the Messiah even though we were dead in tres-passes" (Eph. 2:5). In Jesus, God "has rescued us from the domain of darkness and transferred us into the kingdom of the Son He loves" (Col. 1:13). By raising the girl from death, Jesus showed that we can no more make ourselves accept-able to God than a dead man can bring himself to life. But what we cannot do, the Jubilee of grace does for us. This is indeed a mystery, and this mystery is the meaning of Jesus' Jubilee ministry (Isa. 61:2-3):

To proclaim the year of the Lord's favor,
And the day of our God's vengeance;
To comfort all who mourn,
To provide for those who mourn in Zion;
To give them a crown of beauty instead of ashes,
Festive oil instead of mourning,
And splendid clothes instead of despair.

Jesus did not come to heap fire and brimstone on us, but to "comfort all who mourn." He did not seek to condemn us to death by religious obligation, but to give us "festive oil instead of mourning and splendid clothes instead of despair." Jesus did not come to bring a religion of ethical merit. He came to turn water into wine.

The One Who Is to Come

While this was happening, John the Baptist was rotting away in Judean prison. Hoping to know for sure that all his work had not been in vain, John sent disciples to ask Jesus, "Are You the One who is to come, or should we expect someone else?" (Matt. 11:3).

Jesus, in response, described His ministry according to the prophecies of Isaiah. First, He mentioned Isaiah 35: "The blind see" (Isa. 35:5), "the lame walk" (Isa. 35:6), "those with skin disease are healed" (possible reference to Isa. 35:8). Jesus then said that "the dead are raised," a reference to a phrase in Isaiah 61 that is not found in modern manuscripts, but was found in the ancient Dead Sea Scrolls.[2] Then, Jesus quoted from Isaiah 61:1, regarding the Messianic Jubilee: "The poor are told the good news."

This last statement becomes the basis for the sermon that follows. The Jubilee was to be announced with a trumpet after the Day of Atonement (Lev. 25:9). Following the trumpet sound, the Israelites were to "proclaim freedom in the land for all its inhabitants" (Lev. 25:10). For those who had lived for years in indentured servitude, or lived in poverty without a land of their own, it would be good news indeed. All debts were forgiven.

Imagine if, during the recent mortgage crisis, someone had miraculously appeared and paid off every mortgage in America. Every single homeowner in America would own his or her land outright. One of the biggest drains on disposable income would disappear overnight. Americans would no longer have to worry about how to provide for themselves. The menacing financial Grim Reaper would have been turned away and all would be free from the fear of foreclosure and poverty. Undoubtedly Americans would have been celebrating in the streets. It would have been a modern-day Jubilee.

But if mortgage debt was done away with, Americans could buy and sell houses without much, if any, additional financing. If Americans no longer required what was once their biggest financing need, banks would lose their business model. To be sure, there are sometimes financial benefits to borrowing even when you technically don't need to (a principle you can learn in any college investments course, but I won't bore you by explaining it here), but certainly there would be a dramatically lower demand for mortgage financing in such a scenario. The powers-that-be might have survived the short-term credit debacle, only to find their long-term business prospects destroyed. Simply put, if your livelihood depends on the continued indebtedness of others, then the Jubilee is not good news to you.

In a sense, that is illustrative. Jesus said, "Those who are well don't need a doctor, but the sick do" (Matt. 9:12). There are two groups of people in this world. Those who only think they are well, and those who know they are truly sick. So when Jesus came to "preach good tidings to the poor," as Isaiah put it, He was preaching something that would divide humanity. It would only be "good tidings" to the "poor in spirit" (Matt. 5:3) who knew they needed His grace. But the grace of God is not good news to those who have built a comfortable life out of their own self-righteousness. Jesus chose to hang around with "tax collectors and sinners" because they were the only ones who would receive Him. They, after all, were the only ones who knew they needed grace and not religion, mercy and not sacrifice. To the Pharisees, on the other hand, the religious system offered prestige and power. They had learned to play its game by fooling everyone, especially themselves, that they had the ability to fulfill the debt of religious obligation. This is always and ever the way it is in human religion. Those who know they need help are pushed aside in favor of those who think they do not. Those who seek human righteousness by the sacrifice of religious performance cannot receive the divine righteousness that is given freely by God's mercy. So Jesus says (Matthew 11:25-26):

I praise You, Father, Lord of heaven and earth, because You have hidden these things from the wise and learned and revealed them to infants. Yes, Father, because this was Your good pleasure.

Those who think they know, do not see the grace of God as "good tidings." Only the lost—those who do not presume to know how to save themselves—will see grace as "good tidings." Jesus' Jubilee Gospel—the "good tidings"—offers free reconciliation between God and man. Consequently, it grows the rift between Ishmael and Isaac, between the Prodigal Son and the Prodigal Brother.

God's grace calls out to the Prodigal Son and not his self-righteous brother. Thus, Jesus offered His new yoke—not to the religious and self-righteous—but to "all of you who are weary and burdened" (Matt. 11:28). By freeing the indentured servants and returning the land from the rich to the poor, the Jubilee robbed the wealthy and powerful of the means of their prosperity and prestige. Likewise, Jesus' Jubilee calls out to those who are in slavery to religious obligation, held down and exploited by the Pharisees of our world. His Jubilee heals those who know they are sick, and thus brings shame on those who think they are well.

Restoring "My Rest"

Jesus gives the sick and weary a kind of rest that religious obligation cannot. Jesus said, "Come to Me, all of you who are weary and burdened, and I will give you rest" (Matt. 11:28). And Matthew continues, telling us (Matt. 12:1-2):

> At that time Jesus passed through the grainfields on the Sabbath. His disciples were hungry and began to pick and eat some heads of grain. But when the Pharisees saw it, they said to Him, "Look, Your disciples are doing what is not lawful to do on the Sabbath!"

The Jewish Sabbath symbolized the rest in grace that had been lost in Eden, and it foreshadowed the return of grace in Jesus Christ. It pointed forward to a time when "again He sets a certain day—today" (Heb. 4:7, NRSV). There would be a day when God's "My Rest" would be restored to humanity: "For we who have believed [in the Gospel] enter that rest" (Heb. 4:3, NRSV).

When Jesus offered rest to those who were weary and burdened, He was offering the rest of grace, the easy yoke of His love. While the chapter markings, added long after the Bible was written, would cordon off Matthew 12:1-8 from Matthew 11:28-30, the author plainly saw a connection between the spiritual rest Jesus offered and the Pharisee's jealousy for the rules of the Jewish Sabbath. It is part of the greater theme of chapters 9 through 12, the theme of the triumph of mercy over sacrifice, or grace over the Law.

Jesus had just finished describing His ministry as the fulfillment of the Jubilee prophecy of Isaiah 61. In the Jubilee commands, we find, "The fiftieth year will be your Jubilee; you are not to sow, reap what grows by itself, or harvest its untended vines... you may only eat its produce directly from the field" (Lev. 25:11-12). The fact that the disciples were eating grain directly from the field, on the Sabbath, showed that the new yoke of spiritual Jubilee triumphed over the old yoke of the Law. The Jubilee of Jesus Christ brought a freedom that the Law could not provide.

The Pharisees could not accept the new wine of grace because they were jealous for the old wine of religious slavery. They could not accept the greater, every-day rest of grace because they desired to pursue righteousness by the religious forms and shadows of the Old Covenant Law. So Jesus used the Old Testament to show that there was always a greater righteousness beyond the Law (Matt. 12:3-8, NRSV):

Have you not read what David did when he and his companions were hungry? He entered the house of God and ate the bread of the Presence, which it was not lawful for him or his companions to eat, but only for the priests. Or have you not read in the law that on the Sabbath the priests in the Temple break the Sabbath and yet are guiltless? I tell you, something greater than the Temple is here. But if you had known what this means, 'I desire mercy and not sacrifice,' you would not have condemned the guiltless. For the Son of Man is Lord of the Sabbath.

It is important to read the Lord's words closely. He referred to the time when David took the showbread in the Tabernacle and fed it to his men, and He pointed out the special Sabbath sacrifices of the Levitical priests. Jesus was clear that these two acts were indeed violations of the Old Covenant Law. In His own words, David's actions were "not lawful," and the priests "break the Sabbath."

The showbread represented His body, which would be broken for us. David, in keeping his line alive, kept alive the line through which the Messiah would come. He was serving "something greater than the Temple." When the priests performed their sacrifices, they were symbolizing the coming of the Messiah who would die as a sacrifice for all. Thus, they were pointing toward "something greater than the Temple."

Jesus did not try to argue that His disciples could be justified by the Law, but rather He said "something greater than the Temple is here." The Temple was to house the Ark, the various sacrificial instruments, and the Ten Commandments. In the middle of the Ten Commandments was the very Sabbath command Jesus' disciples were accused of violating. But because they were living in the new reality of Jesus' eternal Jubilee, they could not be condemned by the old power of the "ministry of condemnation" (2 Cor. 3:11). They lived in the freedom of His grace, and in His Jubilee they were free to "eat its produce directly from the field" (Lev. 25:12) without fearing the "ministry of death, chiseled in letters on stones" (2 Cor. 3:7). When the Sabbath commandment was given at Sinai, an Israelite violated it by picking up sticks on the Sabbath. He was immediately stoned to death (Num. 15:32-36). But it could not be so for the disciples of Jesus. They lived by trusting in His grace. And He saved them because He was "Lord of the Sabbath," greater than the Sabbath Law of Sinai, and thus greater than the Law it came from. Rather than claim that the Law allowed what His disciples were doing, Jesus claimed a source of authority greater than the Law.

Eating from the Field

Had the Pharisees understood what God meant when He said, "I desire mercy and not sacrifice," they would have known that God had a greater purpose than could ever come by mere rules as embodied in the Law. The Jubilee of Jesus Christ came to free us spiritually to "eat... produce directly from the field," to live in the grace of God's provision, free of the debts imposed by religious obligation. Jesus came to give us a rest in His grace, to free us from the slavery we had brought to ourselves, to return us spiritually to the time when we could eat from the trees and fields without the arduous task of planting and harvesting that came when Adam fell.

And that is what is meant by *Anno Domini*, the year of the Lord. That is why the prophet Isaiah described Jesus' ministry as the ministry of the great antitypical Jubilee year. That is why Matthew and Luke couched it in such terms. In the Law, God was foreshadowing a time when His grace, rejected by Adam, would return in Jesus Christ. He demonstrated, through Israel, that man had sold himself into indentured servitude to religious duties. Israel was meant to groan and cry out in their slavery, yearning for the time, the eternal jubilee, when they would be set free from the religious bondage of Sinai.

Jesus came running after those who had wandered off His Father's estate—those who, like the Prodigal, had chosen slavery over sonship. He embraced them and freed them from their chains. In Jesus Christ, the same God who once called the Israelites "My Slaves" (Lev. 25:42, 55) had now said to them, "I do not call you slaves anymore." (John 15:15).

Chapter 8

Broken and Beloved

—⟨◦◦◦⟩—

I'm all out of faith. This is how I feel:
I'm cold and I am shamed, lying naked on the floor.
Natalie Imbruglia/"Torn"

One of the most surprising things about Jesus of Nazareth
is the prepositional phrase "of Nazareth." Nazareth
was nothing. Archaeologist James Strange writes, "Nazareth
is not mentioned in ancient Jewish sources earlier than the
third century AD. This likely reflects its lack of promi-
nence both in Galilee and in Judaea."[1] Decades later, Paul's
enemies would pejoratively refer to him as "ringleader of
the sect of the Nazarenes" (Acts 24:5). Simply associating
someone with Nazareth was enough to disqualify him in the
eyes of first century Jews. It is no wonder that Nathanael
asked, "Can anything good come out of Nazareth?" (John
1:46).

Jesus was born as one of the "unmentionables," the
"untouchables." The world often glosses over the true
scandal of Jesus' birth story and societal status. The world
doesn't want to admit that Jesus was born any other way but
as you see Him in medieval paintings and icons: His mother
bedecked in the finest gold-fringed clothes, a golden halo

around his head, all the world looking on in awe. This is a Jesus who is part of the Prodigal Brother's world, a Jesus who ascents to his value system, a Jesus who does not stand as an indictment of everything he stands for.

But that is not the picture the Gospels paint. Jesus was not born into the upper crust of human society. The King of Kings was not born to a noble family. He was born to a family that descended from royalty, to be sure. But the throne had long since departed from their ancestors, and in their place was a cruel man installed by the hated Roman conquerors.

Instead of living in the marble halls of royalty, Jesus' family lived in poverty in the most irrelevant little village in the most contemptible province of the despised country in all the Roman world. They didn't even have the dignity of working their own land as farmers. Jesus' father was a mere carpenter. But if that wasn't enough, Jesus was born into a culture of what we might today call "hillbillies" or "rednecks." All other Jews of the time looked on Galileans with contempt: They didn't speak Hebrew. They weren't, by Jewish standards of the time, very religious. They were uneducated. They were poor. They couldn't even speak Aramaic without an embarrassing accent.

Mercy Triumphs over Judgment

Not only was Jesus born into a Galilean and Nazarene family, but His birth story was wrought with what Yancey called "nine months of awkward explanations, the lingering scent of scandal."[2] He was conceived outside of wedlock, a harsh stigma to attach to a young Christian boy in our day, let alone a Jewish one in first century Israel. Certainly Mary was not able to hide her pregnancy from everyone. Yancey asks, "How many times did Joseph second-guess his own encounter with an angel—*just a dream?*—as he endured the hot shame of living among villagers who could plainly see the changing shape of his fiancée?"[3]

This says a lot about Joseph. The Law of Moses prescribed death for a female fiancée who slept with a man to whom she wasn't betrothed (Deut. 22:23-24). Though Mary did not actually qualify as an adulterer, Joseph did not know it at the time. Still, rather than defend his rights by raising a charge against Mary, "Joseph, being a righteous man, and not wanting to disgrace her publicly, decided to divorce her secretly" (Matt. 1:19).

In the beginning of his Gospel, written to first century Jews, Matthew proposes a new definition of righteousness. Rather than being righteous because he sought to bring down on Mary the penal requirements of the Law, Joseph was called righteous because he desired to treat an alleged sinner with mercy and compassion. The Apostle James would later characterize this new kind of righteousness by saying, "Judgment is without mercy to the one who hasn't shown mercy. Mercy triumphs over judgment" (James 2:13).

If I had only four words to describe Jesus' life on earth, I would have to choose those words of James: "Mercy triumphs over judgment." Perhaps Jesus chose to be born into Joseph's family because, in his own way, Joseph desired "mercy and not sacrifice." Just as Joseph, before he knew the whole story, decided to let Mary live when the Law would have condemned her to death, so Jesus freely offered mercy to those who knew only the condemnation of others.

A Tax Collector's Gospel

If you are trying to reach first century Jews, choosing a hated tax-collector (Matthew) to write that Gospel might serve to alienate large portions of your intended audience. So why did God choose Matthew? Neil Cole mused:

If I were to choose a man to write my Good News for the Jews, I would choose a man of utmost integrity who would have ready credibility among the Jewish leaders. I would probably go to the Temple and find the wisest and most respected young Pharisee I could and choose him to be my Gospel writer. Jesus went to the tax office and chose the most hated and disrespected man He could find. When He wanted to bring the good news to the Gentiles, then He went to the temple and chose a Pharisee.[4]

But this all depends on the sort of Jew you are seeking out. By beginning his story with Jesus' virgin birth, Matthew immediately disqualifies a certain kind of Jew. A well-heeled and respected self-righteous Pharisee, reading the account of Jesus' conception, would see only a slipshod farce intended to cover ignoble and illegitimate origins. Indeed, one second-century Jewish critic named Celsus delivered exactly such a charge. Even in His own day, Jesus' birth story had disqualified Him in the eyes of the religious establishment. The Pharisees once said to Him, "*We* weren't born of sexual immorality. *We* have one Father—God" (John 8:41).

No, Matthew's Gospel was written to a different kind of Jew. God chose Matthew because Matthew was the kind of Jew for whom that Gospel was intended: A Jew whom the Jewish religious world condemned. Jesus came for those who, like Matthew, were "tax-collectors and sinners." Matthew shows Jesus to be their merciful champion, "the sinless friend of sinners."[5]

Neither Do I Condemn You...

When I think of Jesus' mother, ever after suffering from charges of immorality by non-Christians, I can't help but remember another woman accused of adultery. The scribes and Pharisees brought this woman before Jesus in order to trap Him (John 8:6). They said, "Teacher, this woman was caught in the act of committing adultery. In the law Moses commanded us to stone such women. So what do You say?" (vs. 4-5). The Romans only gave the Jews authority to exercise the death penalty in cases of a sin against the Temple. All other cases had to be brought to the Roman authorities. But Moses required that such a woman be stoned. If Jesus said she must be stoned, He would be rebelling against the Romans. If He said she wasn't to be stoned, the Pharisees would charge Him with disobedience to Moses.

It seems significant that this woman was charged with the same sin that the Pharisees would accuse Mary of. One has to wonder if, in this cowering woman, Jesus saw a bit of His mother, 30 odd years before, cowering in fear before an angel who announced that she, an unmarried and betrothed virgin, was bearing the promised Messiah. By bringing this woman into the Temple, the Pharisees were exposing her sin to the entire nation, as it were. There would have been hundreds or thousands of onlookers. I wonder if Jesus saw, in their lurid stares of shame, the townspeople of Nazareth staring judgmentally at His own pregnant mother when she was bearing Him.

So rather than play the religious game of shame and blame, Jesus did something entirely unexpected: Nothing. He just stooped down and began writing on the ground. Several commentators have argued He was writing the sins of the scribes and Pharisees, but the fact is the Bible does not say what He was writing. The content of His writing doesn't matter. It simply isn't the point.

The point is that He refused to sit in judgment over the woman. "For God did not send His Son into the world that He might condemn the world, but that the world might be saved through Him" (John 3:17). Instead of engaging the Pharisees in a religious chess game with the life of a woman as their pawn, He simply had nothing to do with them. One has to wonder how long Jesus sat there writing. I can imagine Him writing for several minutes, perhaps writing a Psalm or a Messianic prophecy from Isaiah. Perhaps He wrote the statement from Hosea: "I desire mercy and not sacrifice."

Whatever He wrote, it would have become an embarrassment for His opponents. They had hoped to confront Him, in front of the entire nation of Israel, with an unwinnable game. Hundreds or thousands of onlookers were now staring, not simply at the woman, but at the rabbis surrounding her. One can imagine the sheepish looks that must have grown across their faces as Jesus just sat there writing, seemingly oblivious to their presence.

I suppose, as they became increasingly embarrassed by His silence, that they began to badger Him more intently. The Gospel records, "When they persisted in questioning Him, He stood up and said to them, 'The one without sin among you should be the first to throw a stone at her'" (John 8:7). With one statement, Jesus entirely turned the table on the scribes and Pharisees. He moved the central issue from her sins to theirs. He required them, not Him, to decided whether or not to defy the Romans and begin stoning her.

And it puts them in a terrible theological conundrum. If they took up rocks against her, they would be claiming that they were without sin. But they knew well that no one could truly claim to be without sin. As Pharisees, they surely thought their sins were only minor, trivial matters, but they were sins nonetheless. On the other hand, if they didn't stone her, they would be admitting their sinfulness in the very center of the Jewish religious establishment. And by bringing the woman to Jesus for Him to stone her, yet not stoning her themselves, they would be tacitly admitting that He was sinless and thus the only human who could render a truly righteous judgment.

Faced themselves with an impossible theological catch 22, Jesus' opponents merely walked out. To do so was to admit their own sinfulness before the entire nation. On top of that, their little trap had come back to bite them. They had been outsmarted and shamed in front of everyone. This national embarrassment must have constituted the defining low point in their rabbinical careers. We can't help but remember what James said: "Judgment is without mercy to the one who hasn't shown mercy."

Eventually, only Jesus and the woman remained, alone in the center of the courtyard. He asked her, "Woman, where are they? Has no one condemned you?" (v. 8).

She replied, "No one, Lord" (v. 11).

At that Jesus said, "Neither do I condemn you. Go, and from now on do not sin anymore" (v. 12). By choosing not to condemn someone for whom the Law demanded punishment, Jesus showed Himself to be greater than the Law. As the divine Son of God, the decision to condemn or pardon was ultimately His. Like his earthly father Joseph, Jesus showed that there is a greater righteousness than the judgment and condemnation of religious ideology. By extending mercy to this sinful woman, He had umasked the greater unrighteousness of judgmental religious thinking. Religion, at its core, cannot show mercy, and yet mercy is what all of us, as sinners, need most desperately. None of us, if we really think about it, is qualified to cast the first stone, yet all of us seem to want to. That, in itself, is an indictment of who we are, but Jesus triumphed over all of it by extending a mercy to us that we could never earn.

But more startling for the religious mind is Jesus' last statement. "Go, and from now on do not sin anymore." The Prodigal Brother, when he tells this story, will often focus in on this statement, apply it to everyone else (except himself), and state that God is angry with us for our sins and we had better stop, or else. But that isn't at all what Jesus says. He tells her He does not condemn her, at the same time that He recognizes that she had done something for which she deserved condemnation. Jesus does not give us the Prodigal Brother's pagan god Zeus, who seeks to rain lightning bolts down on us for not doing the right things. In the Bible, Satan, not God, is called "the accuser." Rather, God in Jesus Christ comes as one seeking to protect us from condemnation by exercising His mercy when we have least deserved it, and thus most need it.

Jesus did not try to frighten the woman into holy living by threatening her with condemnation. Instead, the mercy He had shown her would be the foundation of her new life. Grace, and not religious fear, was the basis for His admonition to avoid sin. The fear of judgment and death in the Law was evidently not enough to keep this woman from committing adultery. Fear has never been a successful long-term solution to sin.

That is why Jesus came. He came for broken people like the woman caught in adultery. Jesus makes the reception of God's grace the basis for us to have true life. The woman, marked for death by religion, was given a new life by Jesus Christ. And more, He made His free gift of life the means of breaking the power of sin over her. Grace, and not religion, would make the woman holy. Goodness would come out of her, not in order for her to gain life, but because life had already been granted to her by God's grace. Grace both forgave her and made her holy. Mercy indeed triumphed over judgment.

The Pleasing Perfume of a Broken Heart

When we read this story, we are reminded of yet another woman who had been accused of immorality, Mary Magdalene. Some commentators have said Mary and the woman at the Temple were one and the same. We really don't know for sure. Still we cannot help but see in Mary Magdalene a similar triumph of Jesus' mercy.

The story begins in the house of a Pharisee, Simon, who had invited Jesus to a dinner party. Mary Magdalene (John 12:3) came into His presence, poured fragrant perfume all over His feet, and washed them with oil. Wearing sandals and walking on dusty roads, Jesus' feet would have been covered in dirt and filth. To wash someone's feet was an act of humiliation and submission so dishonorable that not even slaves would do it. Not only did Mary wash Jesus' feet, but she did so with a fragrant perfume that cost a year's wages, and she wiped His feet with her hair (Luke 7:37-38):

> And a woman in the town who was a sinner found out that Jesus was reclining at the table in the Pharisee's house. She brought an alabaster flask of fragrant oil and stood behind Him at His feet, weeping, and began to wash His feet with her tears. She wiped His feet with the hair of her head, kissing them and anointing them with the fragrant oil.

Mary's love and appreciation for Jesus truly puts so much of modern religious ceremonialism to shame. Today we stand up in a building on Sunday and sing a hymn chosen by someone else, repeating the words like mind-numbed robots. We call this "worship." But Mary went much further. She came into the house of a Pharisee who would only look on her with disgust. She knelt weeping before Jesus in the middle of a meal. She utterly debased herself by washing— even kissing!—His filthy feet, and anointed them with a fragrant perfume that cost her more than any of the offerings given by anyone in our buildings today. All this, not because some law or some ceremony or some pastor or priest or elder demanded it, but simply because her love for Jesus had so overwhelmed her.

I think about the symbolism of the fragrant perfuming, rising up from the floor to Jesus' nostrils. It reminds me of how the burnt offerings were so often described as "a pleasing aroma to the Lord" (Ex. 29:25; Lev. 1:9, 13, 17). And it makes me think of how another immoral sinner, King David, talked about those burnt offerings (Ps. 51:16-17):

You do not want a sacrifice, or I would give it;
You are not pleased with a burnt offering.
The sacrifice pleasing to God is a broken spirit.
God, You will not despise a broken and humbled heart.

The perfume of Mary Magdalene was the pleasing aroma of a "broken and humbled heart." She came to Him in her naked brokenness. To God the Son, this was a greater gift than any that had been given to Him by the priests on the altars of the Temple. His most desperate desire is to wrap His arms around us as He glues together the pieces of our broken hearts with the blood of His cross.

To the Pharisee Simon, though, this was not a pleasing aroma of love and mercy, but a foul stench of unholy defilement. Simon said to himself, "This man, if He were a prophet, would know who and what kind of woman this is who is touching Him—she's a sinner!" (v. 39) His tone sounds very much like the Prodigal Brother, furious at the father's love because he deserved it so much more than his immoral and profligate younger brother.

That is the thing about grace. The father knew full well what the Prodigal Son had done. He didn't need the older brother to remind him. The fact is, the father just didn't care. The point was that the Prodigal Son had returned. Similarly, Jesus knew full well that Mary was a sinner. In fact, it was principally because she was a sinner that He was so moved by her actions. She had answered the call to return to His Father's estate.

Jesus turned to Simon and explained the ways of the Kingdom of Heaven (Luke 7:41-43):

> "A creditor had two debtors. One owed 500 denarii, and the other 50. Since they could not pay it back, he graciously forgave them both. So, which of them will love him more?"
>
> Simon answered, "I suppose the one he forgave more."
>
> "You have judged correctly," He told him.

Jesus' parable must have knocked Simon for a loop. After all, Jesus said the creditor forgave his debtors *because* they could not pay it back. The creditor didn't forgive the debtors because they earnestly made a good-faith effort to pay their debts, yet came up a little short. He didn't forgive them because they offered some other service in its place. He forgave them because of the utter impossibility of repayment.

But Jesus went even further. He demonstrated how Mary's act was an indictment of Simon himself (v. 44-48):

> Turning to the woman, He said to Simon, "Do you see this woman? I entered your house; you gave Me no water for My feet, but she, with her tears, has washed My feet and wiped them with her hair. You gave Me no kiss, but she hasn't stopped kissing My feet since I came in. You didn't anoint My head with oil, but she has anointed My feet with fragrant oil. Therefore I tell you, her many sins have been forgiven; that's why she loved much. But the one who is forgiven little, loves little." Then He said to her, "Your sins are forgiven."

In a culture that prized hospitality, Jesus publically shamed Simon for having shown Him no real hospitality. The respected Pharisee had not even offered Jesus a basin in which to wash His own feet, but this "sinner" Mary had not only given Him water for His feet, but gave Him her very tears and washed His feet herself! Simon had not offered any affectionate greeting to Jesus, not even kissing Him on his cheek as was often done. Mary kissed, not His clean face, but His grimy, dirt-covered feet! Simon had not anointed Jesus head with olive oil as a highly honored guest, but Mary poured very expensive perfume all over His feet. Simon, the pious Pharisee, had been shown-up in his own home by a whore. Truly Jesus words to the religious establishment had been demonstrated in the home of Simon: "Prostitutes are entering the kingdom of God before you!" (Matt. 21:31)

Jesus did not stop there. The greater righteousness demonstrated by Mary came as an authentic expression of a forgiven heart. Mary did not do what she did because religion required it. She did what she did because Jesus of Nazareth was everything to her. She had come to Him in her weakness, and He had forgiven her. Just like the woman in the Temple, the grace of God in Jesus Christ formed the basis of her holiness. His righteousness was hers because she had admitted her own unrighteousness. He said to her, "Your sins are forgiven," and "Your faith has saved you" (v. 50). She was told to "go in peace" (v. 50) because she had rejected the false peace of religious obligation and accepted instead the greater peace of the grace of God. Mercy had triumphed over judgment.

Paul in the Temple

The Pharisees' judgment against Jesus was that He hung around with tax collectors like Zaccheus and Matthew, and sinners like Mary Magdalene. To these Pharisees, "who trusted in themselves that they were righteous and looked down on everyone else," (Luke 18:9) Jesus delivered one of His most poignant parables (Luke 18:10-14):

> Two men went up to the temple complex to pray, one a Pharisee and the other a tax collector. The Pharisee took his stand and was praying like this: "God, I thank You that I'm not like other people — greedy, unrighteous, adulterers, or even like this tax collector. I fast twice a week; I give a tenth of everything I get."
>
> But the tax collector, standing far off, would not even raise his eyes to heaven but kept striking his chest and saying, "God, turn Your wrath from me — a sinner!" I tell you, this one went down to his house justified rather than the other; because everyone who exalts himself will be humbled, but the one who humbles himself will be exalted.

The parable is entirely subversive. The Jewish religious establishment greatly honored the Pharisees. They seemed so very holy, so pious and devoted to the Law. This man gave a tenth of everything he had to the Temple, showing his loyalty to God and to the people of Israel. He would never think of appearing greedy. He was clean cut, wearing fine robes and large phylacteries (boxes worn on the head containing texts from the Torah). Not only did he abstain from the sexual immorality that so characterized the pagan Romans, but he fasted twice a week, demonstrating a powerful religious discipline. He seemed, in short, to be the perfect Jew.

The tax collector, on the other hand, was hated as a vile traitor. He was greedy and cruel. No doubt the immorality of his Roman masters had rubbed off on him. He had betrayed God's covenant people by collaborating with the Roman regime, and thus had shown his disloyalty to the Torah and

God. Certainly he did not tithe. Tithe was paid principally from livestock and agriculture, and if he had tried to give currency to the Temple, I doubt the Priests would have accepted his defiled blood money. If the Pharisee seemed the perfect Jew, this tax collector was his perfect opposite, friendless and unrighteous

Some might argue that the Pharisee's prayer was a normal prayer that Jesus' audience would not have gasped at. But the very scandal of the parable is what comes out of the Pharisee's mouth: The Jews knew they were to give thanks to God for His beneficence, not to talk up their showiness and pride. All the best prayers of the Old Testament reflected such a spirit. The normal human response to this prayer is to see in it a prideful, arrogant contempt of God's gifts. This Pharisee was not truly thanking God for His goodness, but thanking himself for his own. He was blaspheming.

In contrast, the prayer of the vile tax collector would have seemed like poetry right out of the Psalms or the prophets, a lamentation that cries out for God's mercy and depends utterly on His goodness. In fact, it seems very much like the prayer in Daniel 9, when Daniel pled with God to free his people from captivity, not because they had earned that gift, but because they were terrible sinners desperately in need of God's mercy. Certainly the tax collector's prayer could not have impacted Jesus' audience any differently than it does us. It is a beautiful, humble, and heart-breaking cry for help from a God he trusts to be merciful and gracious.

In the minds of the religious system, God must have admired the Pharisee for his devotion to the Torah, and He must have despised the tax collector for his collaboration with the Romans. But the story going on within each of them was different indeed. The prayer of the Pharisee showed him to be a blasphemer, self-righteous and full of pride. No one likes a braggart. In contrast, the tax collector admitted his utter moral hopelessness and rested on the grace of a compassionate God. Everyone likes an underdog.

The Pharisee was one who built his life on the judgment of others. He even went out of his way to thank God that he wasn't like that disgusting tax collector over there. But the Jews of the day knew the words of Psalm 51. They knew they should always approach Yahweh in humility. Clearly the Pharisee, in his self-righteous judgmentalism, was not doing so. He even took a stand to raise himself up to God. But the tax collector, in his plea for mercy, was broken and humble. He stood far off, daring not to approach God in his uncleanness.

God showed grace to the tax collector. He showed mercy to the one who begged for mercy. The man was justified—literally, declared innocent—by God. The one who stood far away because of his uncleanness, was brought close to God by divine mercy. Mercy again had triumphed over judgment.

Oddly, the Greek term Jesus used when He called the tax collector "justified"—*dikaioo*—is the same word Paul used when he said we were "justified freely by His grace through the redemption that is in Christ Jesus" (Romans 3:24). I have to wonder if this parable had at all influenced Paul's theology. After all, it appears only in the Gospel written by Luke, Paul's trusted friend and assistant. It is riddled with ideas later attributed to Paul. It speaks of those who lived by the Law as those who "trusted in themselves that they were righteous." This reminds us of Paul's words in Romans 9 that his countrymen had rejected the Gospel because they sought righteousness by their religious efforts. The tax collector was a horrible sinner whom the Law could only condemn. But he trusted in God's mercy, asking that God "turn your wrath from me." Literally in Greek he asks God to "be propitiated," surprisingly similar to Paul's statement that God "presented [Jesus] as a propitiation through faith in His blood" (Romans 3:25).

We also find a Pharisee who sought righteousness by works, and boasted before God about his Law keeping. This sounds like many of Paul's statements that, in truth, all were sinners and no one had a right to boast. In contrast, the tax collector had no works of the Law upon which to boast. He had utterly violated the Torah. Yet, having done nothing by the Law to win justification before God, he was freely justified by grace. In fact, were I to sum up the theological point of this parable, I would use Paul's words in Romans 3:27-28:

> Where then is boasting? It is excluded. By what kind of law? By one of works? No, on the contrary, by a law of faith. For we conclude that a man is justified by faith apart from works of law.

A Home for the Broken

Imagine a house filled with men and women, some sitting on the floor, others on sofas, a few standing. Together they are eating an evening meal, drinking wine from a cup that they pass amongst themselves, and eating bread. In the back right corner you will find a man who used to work as a male prostitute, selling himself to women *and* especially to men. Next to him is a banker who used to give loans to poor widows, only so he could evict them from their homes and steal their property. At his feet sits a woman who used to sell her body in sexual rituals at the local pagan temple. As you scan the room, you see near the door a man who used to make a living by swindling people with ponzi schemes. Continuing, you find a woman who lived as a lesbian, and next to her a man who has slept with so many other men that he long ago lost count. Close to another corner you see a man who was a rampant alcoholic, and beyond him a drug addict who wasted away his family fortune on his habits.

This is not a reunion of former members of the United States Congress. It is a gathering of the believers in the church at Corinth, "those who are sanctified in Christ Jesus and called as saints" (1 Cor. 1:2). The wine they are passing around represents the blood of Jesus Christ, and the bread they eat is His body. Paul knew well the lessons of Jesus' mercy that we read today in the Gospels. He probably did know about the parable of the Pharisee and Tax Collector. That is why, when Paul sought out people for his churches, he didn't seek the morally upright, the respectable, the wealthy, or the educated. Instead, he chose the weak, the addicted, the despised, the poor, and the sexually broken.

Today, in judgmental self-righteousness, some Pharisees will condemn homosexuals and other deviants with Paul's words in 1 Corinthians 6:9-10: "Do not be deceived: No sexually immoral people, idolaters, adulterers, male prostitutes, homosexuals, thieves, greedy people, drunkards, revilers, or swindlers will inherit God's kingdom." Certainly the Prodigal Brother would never be caught dead in a meeting of such unclean people. But what today's Pharisees don't know is what is written in the very next verse: "Some of you were like this; but you were washed, you were sanctified, you were justified in the name of the Lord Jesus Christ and by the Spirit of our God." Paul isn't describing the world of sinners in contrast to those who have earned God's favor by moral performance. He is describing the power of the blood of Jesus Christ to reconcile what was at enmity, heal what was broken, and raise what was dead.

It seems very much that God wants it that way. He doesn't want to waste His grace on people who think they are too good to need it. He wants those who know they are too awful to deserve it. Adam and Eve rejected God's grace because they didn't realize how centrally important it is to their joy and happiness and existence. Only those who have felt the harsh cruelty of life by the "knowledge of good and evil," will know the utter failure of human efforts. Only these can realize, in their brokenness, that they are not "like God, knowing good and evil." Only these can understand that His grace is the only means to receive the joy of true holiness. And only these can realize that the holiness of God is not a holiness of empty ceremony and external behaviors, but the holiness of a Father cuddling a little child on His lap as the child drifts off to sleep in sublime peace.

I had a pastor who once described the church as "a hospital for sinners, not a hotel for 'saints.'" It seems this was always central to Jesus' message of mercy triumphing over judgment. In Neil Cole's book *Organic Church*, he tells a story of a brother in one of his house churches whom the body had made an elder. The man soon got into an illicit affair with one of the church members, and the affair was uncovered. Rather than respond with condemnation and judgment, Cole followed the Biblical remedy: In tears, the man confessed his sin openly in a gathering of the whole church. In a touching scene, the believers immediately expressed their forgiveness, rose from their seats, and to a person embraced him in tears: The entire body of Christ, weeping and embracing in a tender celebration of the triumph of the mercy of Jesus of Nazareth.

The Prodigals

This is the very thing that Jesus came to bring. When the early Church proclaimed "Jesus is Lord," they weren't simply stating some abstract theological supposition. They were proclaiming God's indictment of this graceless world. Throughout the Roman Empire the cry was, "Caesar is Lord."[6] Jesus was born at a time when the first Roman Emperor, Caesar Augustus, was calling himself a god and proclaiming his reign as "the Good News," the Gospel.[7] Jesus came as the Son of God heralding His own "Good News," a new Kingdom, not of this world, but of heaven. When the Romans crucified the only innocent man to ever live, He rose from the grave and turned the greatest symbol of human oppression—the cross—into the greatest symbol of divine mercy. "He disarmed the rulers and authorities and disgraced them publicly" (Col. 2:15). The Roman Empire was a world where the broken were trampled, the weak were oppressed by the strong, and the guilty were flogged and tortured and crucified. Jesus led an invasion of this world by another one, another Kingdom where the broken are embraced in tears, the weak cherished in love, and the guilty forgiven in mercy.

When Jesus tells the story of how His Kingdom works, He uses the parable of the son who took his inheritance early and left his father's house to make his own way in the world. He wallowed in licentious immorality, only to find himself penniless, broken, and starving. So he set out for his father's house, hoping beyond hope that his father would take him back, not as a son—that was too much to ask—but as a hired servant, slaving in the fields.

At this Jesus' Jewish audience must have seen something of their own religious world. They knew that they were to be a light to the Gentiles. Many Jewish proselytizers would tour the Roman world, seeking to make converts of the Gentiles. The Jews must indeed have seen the Prodigal Son as the many Gentiles who had rebelled against Yahweh, given themselves over to immoral excesses, and come to realize their own sinful brokenness. In the synagogues of the dispersion, a side room was created to house the many uncircumcised Gentiles—God-fearers as they were called—who were unfulfilled in paganism and wanted instead to hear the message of the One God Yahweh. These God-fearers, who could not bring themselves to go through the humiliation of circumcision, still believed in Yahweh and sought to live by the "Noahide Laws" that the Rabbis of the time had crafted for Gentiles.

In contrast, the Jews must have seen in themselves the older son, the one who had remained faithful to his father, faithful to Yahweh: The one who hadn't given himself over to immorality and instead worked dutifully in the moral kingdom of the Torah. I imagine they fully expected the father to take back the prodigal, not as a full-fledged son, not as a full-fledged child of the chosen, but instead as a hired servant: A sort of second-tier Yahweh worshipper, not quite good enough to be a real Jew, but not like the immoral pagans in the world outside the father's estate. This was their definition of mercy.

But Jesus described a meeting unlike anything they would have expected. He told the story with characteristic words of love, compassion, and tenderness (Luke 15:17-20):

> When he came to his senses, he said, "How many of my father's hired hands have more than enough food, and here I am dying of hunger! I'll get up, go to my father, and say to him, Father, I have sinned against heaven and in your sight. I'm no longer worthy to be called your son. Make me like one of your hired hands." So he got up and went to his father. But while the son was still a long way off, his father saw him and was filled with compassion. He ran, threw his arms around his neck, and kissed him.

This scene would have been simply beyond the pale. For a wealthy and respected Jewish man, running was a shameful act: He would have to hike up his robe, exposing his legs and possibly his private parts. Moreover, the father didn't scold his child as the Jewish audience might have expected of Yahweh. Rather, he was "filled with compassion," and he "threw his arms around his neck, and kissed him." The Greek literally says the father "fell on his neck," evoking imagery of the two men falling to the ground, rolling in the dirt in a joyous embrace, one of them clean and stately, and the other filthy and wretched beyond description. Jamieson, Fausset, and Brown describe the scene in a wondrous incredulity:

> What!? In all his filth? Yes! In all his rags? Yes! In all his haggard, shattered wretchedness? Yes! "Our Father who art in heaven," is this Thy portraiture? It is even so! And because it is so, I wonder not that such incomparable teaching hath made the world new.[8]

Jesus' audience must have thought this depiction of Yahweh bordered on the blasphemous. But what is worse for their world-view is what came next. The son tried to choke out his practiced speech, "Father, I have sinned against heaven and in your sight. I'm no longer worthy to be called your son" (v. 21). But the father wouldn't even allow him to get to the part about making him a hired servant. Instead, the father interrupted the son. He immediately directed his servants to put the finest robe on his son. His son was in tattered rags, dirty, perhaps hairless from malnourishment, utterly shamed. His father removed his shame by cloaking him in a robe of luxury. The son was nothing in the wider world, but his father gave him the family ring with the seal that symbolized authority. And even more, the father told his servants to kill the choice calf and prepare a party. The son who had been starving would feast on the finest steak.

The older son, the Jewish son, was taken aback at his father's mercy. In a seemingly prophetic statement about the Israelites' rejection of Christ, the son "didn't want to go in" (v.28) to the party. Just as the father had previously come out to meet the younger son, so he came out to retrieve the older.

But the older son would not have his father's love. Instead, he told his father, "Look, I have been slaving many years for you, and I have never disobeyed your orders, yet you never gave me a young goat so I could celebrate with my friends. But when this son of yours came, who has devoured your assets with prostitutes, you slaughtered the fattened calf for him" (v. 29).

But the father replied, "Son, you are always with me, and everything I have is yours. But we had to celebrate and rejoice, because this brother of yours was dead and is alive again; he was lost and is found" (vs. 31, 32). Everything the father had was always there for the older son. All he had to do was ask, and his father's grace would have poured out parties and blessings freely. But instead, the older son had relied on his efforts as a hired hand, seeking only the wages he could earn, and not the gifts of love that came unearned and free. So he never knew the grace his father wanted to give him.

The younger son had left his father's house, and now that he had returned, the older son would not. Both sons were prodigal in this regard. Both had rejected their father's love and sought to live outside his provision. But only the younger son knew that the father's grace could not be earned, because only the younger son had done everything possible to *not* deserve it. Only the younger son truly knew what it was like to live in his father's love, because only he knew the impossibility of living outside it. Only the younger son knew what it meant for mercy to triumph over judgment.

Cold and Shamed

That is the amazing thing about the grace that came to us in Jesus Christ. He didn't come looking for people who were well-fed, well-clothed, and full of their own virtue. He came for those who were starving, naked, and sick. He told them, "Blessed are the poor in spirit, because the kingdom of heaven is theirs" (Matthew 5:3). He came to give His kingdom to those who were spiritually broken, hungry, guilt-ridden, and despairing. He came for the cold, coughing and malnourished souls whose clothes were in tatters and whose hair was falling out. He looked down at the sorry wrecks we had become that sad day in Eden, and He was "filled with compassion" (Luke 15:20). He came running for humanity, for us who had been so long away from Eden that we did not even remember our Father's name.

In His mercy for the women of this world who are caught in adultery, Jesus triumphs over their accusers. In His mercy for the Mary Magdalene's of this world, Jesus triumphs over the judgmental Simons. In His mercy for the tax collectors of this world, Jesus triumphs over the self-righteous Pharisees. And, above all else, in His mercy for the prodigal sons of this world, Jesus triumphs over their religious Prodigal Brothers.

If there is one picture of the Father we should keep always on our minds, it is that one. Jesus does not paint a picture of a Father who always wanted religious obligation and empty external behaviors. Instead, Jesus shows us a Father who always wanted to give us His love freely, not asking us to earn it, but merely desiring us to receive His warm embrace. Jesus paints a picture of a Father whose greatest hope is to pick up His sobbing little children, and hold them close to His chest. Jesus paints a picture of a Father who finds us at our most beautiful, when we think we are at our most broken and dirty and ashamed.

Chapter 9

The Prodigal Son's Punishment

—◦◦◦—

Is punishment really an appropriate response to a rejection of intimate *friendship*? One would not have thought so, especially if the parties involved were attempting to restore the relationship.

Bayne and Restall *"A Participatory Model..."*[1]

A man had two sons. The younger of them said to his father, "Father, give me the share of the estate I have coming to me." So he distributed the assets to them. Not many days later, the younger son gathered together all he had and traveled to a distant country, where he squandered his estate in foolish living.

After he had spent everything, a severe famine struck that country, and he had nothing. Then he went to work for one of the citizens of that country, who sent him into his fields to feed pigs. He longed to eat his fill from the carob pods the pigs were eating, but no one would give him any. When he came to his senses, he said, "How many of my father's hired hands have more than enough food, and here I am dying of hunger! I'll get up, go to my father, and say to him, 'Father, I have sinned against heaven and in your sight. I'm no longer *worthy to be called your son. Make me like one of your hired hands.'"*

So he got up and went to his father. But while the son was still a long way off, his father saw him and was filled with wrath. He ran, pointed his finger at his son, and began to berate him. So the son said to him, "Father, I have sinned against heaven and in your sight. I'm no longer worthy to be called your son."

But the father, clutching the handle of his sheathed sword, replied, "You are right that you aren't worthy, you filthy urchin! You have wasted half my fortune with prostitutes and booze, and I have half a mind to remove your head from your shoulders so that I may be satisfied."

The son stammered, "No father! Make me like one your hired servants instead. Let me work my debt off."

"You fool!" the father shot back. "Don't you realize the extent of your debt? You could never work long enough as a hired hand to pay me back what you owe! At a hired hand's wages, you would have to work for ten lifetimes to pay me back! No, my wrath must be appeased!"

At that, the father unsheathed his sword, lifting it high above his head as he towered over his kneeling and groveling son. Suddenly, the older son appeared, stepping in between the father and the younger son.

"Father, do not do this to my brother. I have worked perfectly for you all this time. Certainly, in my work for you, I have earned more than enough to compensate for my brother's profligacy. Please, be reconciled to my brother. Don't you see he has come back? Don't you see that we thought he was dead, but he is alive!"

The father, seething with rage, hissed at the older son, "Love him?! I am so angry with him that I must be allowed to punish him! If I am not allowed my justice, my rage will go on within me, eating me up, for the rest of my life."

The older son, looking on his brother with pity, calmly replied, "Very well father. Then kill me. Beat me into a pulp and rend my head from my shoulders. Then your rage can be quieted and you will be able to love my brother."

With that, the father grabbed a whip and began to thrash the older son, producing gaping wounds and bruises and welts all over the older son's body. He continued to beat him for hours, before, finally, in a fit of rage that has not been seen since the world began, he lifted his sword above his head and brought it down on the older brother's neck.

"There, I feel so much better," the father sighed, smiling at the younger brother. "How about you and I go have a cup of coffee and get to know each other again? I do love you very much, now."

You have just read the story of the Prodigal's Punishment, and no doubt you noticed that it differed severely from the parable of the Prodigal Son. The father in the original story of the Prodigal Son is very much the kind of father you would want to celebrate with. He loved the son even when the son rejected him and went off wasting the inheritance. He came running, filled with compassion, when he saw the son far off. He embraced his son in his brokenness and wouldn't even hear of his son's desire to work as a hired hand. Instead, he wrapped his son in royal clothing and held a grand celebration for him.

But the father in the parable of the Prodigal's Punishment is entirely different. He was seething mad with his son the whole time the son was away. He ran to meet his son, but only because he was filled with wrath. When he came near his son, the first thing he wanted to do was kill him, such was the father's rage. The father's primary concern was not for the son he loved, but for the treasure he lost. He desperately needed something to make him feel compensated for his son's profligacy, and the only thing he could come up with was being allowed to beat someone to death. But in the true story, the father doesn't even care about his fortune and won't even hear of the son's attempts to ingratiate himself through economic means.

In the true parable, killing the fattened calf was the means whereby the father reconciled this son to himself and welcomed him into the estate. But in the Prodigal's Punishment, it was only because the older son offered to be the father's whipping boy, that the father was able to get out his pathologically irrational anger. In order to feel better about the Prodigal Son, he had to purge his rage by beating someone, anyone. He could not love the Prodigal Son until he had exercised his wrath. This father, having satiated his desire for brutal suffering, then invited the younger son out for a cup of coffee, proclaiming his new-found love for the son. But the question is, if you were the Prodigal, is this the sort of insanely angry psychopath with whom you would like to cement a new relationship?

The Cross: What It Isn't

If you have been raised in a Christian background, the Prodigal's Punishment is a story you have probably heard countless times, but not in the same way I told it. It is precisely the explanation of the cross that is often taught in Christian circles. Wayne Jacobsen explains the obvious problem with this theory of the cross:

> Don't get me wrong. I want as much mercy as I can get. If someone else wants to take a punishment I deserve and I get off scot free, I'm fine with that. But what does this narrative force us to conclude about the nature of God?[2]

That really is the question. What does this say about who God is? Would you decide to go have a cup of coffee with a father like that? Would you let him live in your heart? I, for one, would not even leave such a father alone with my cat. Who knows what he would do to it if it stepped out of line! This view of the cross makes it look as if the primary nature of God's character is wrath, not love. This view of atonement means that many Christians mistakenly think they have been reconciled to a God they are afraid of, not a Father they love.

Further, this story claims that sin is somehow God's problem, His set of arbitrary behavioral standards that, if violated, bring Him to such an irrational boiling point that He simply must beat the snot out of someone in order to feel better. As such, this view claims that the cross is simply God solving His own rage, correcting the problem within *Himself* so that He can feel okay about human sinfulness: But if God does not change, does the cross effect some change in God's heart, or in mine?

It is no wonder that the New Testament never uses such imagery to explain the atonement of Calvary. (In fact, the Old Testament doesn't use such imagery either, as we shall find in our discussion of Leviticus 16 and Isaiah 53 in the next chapter.) Paul makes clear that, even before Jesus came to die, God loved us: "But God proves His own love for us in that while we were still sinners Christ died for us" (Rom. 5:8). If there is one foundational text for the entire Christian faith, it is John 3:16: "For God so loved the world that He gave His only begotten Son, that whoever believes in Him should not perish but have everlasting life" (NKJV). Jesus didn't say God gave His Son *so that* He could love the world. Jesus says that, because God already loved the world, He gave His Son. The cross demonstrated a love that God already had for us before Jesus gave Himself. In fact, it was God's love for us that made Him come running for us in the person of Jesus Christ.

Anselm's Mafia God

The traditional view of the atonement, called "Penal Substitution" or "Penal Satisfaction," is not as traditional as some people think. Some honest folks ignorantly claim that it was always the foundational Christian view of the cross, and that anyone who thinks differently is a heretic. But it is a solid historical fact that Penal Substitution only dates back to the medieval era. There have been, and still are, many other theories of atonement in Christianity that have been afforded status as orthodox. Some of them—for instance the Christus Victor view exemplified in C.S. Lewis's *The Lion, The Witch, and the Wardrobe*—have a far longer history than Penal Substitution.

The doctrine of Penal Substitution traces its roots back to Anselm, a Roman Catholic who was born about 1033 AD, long after Peter, Paul, and John. *Cur Deus Homo*, the work in which Anselm advanced his doctrine of atonement, is not based principally on the Biblical explanation of the cross, but on the power of Anselm's philosophical argumentation. For instance, his initial assumption is that man owed God a debt of honor. This sounds like the medieval feudal concept of fealty popular in Anselm's day. It doesn't keep with Scripture, which says that God has always desired to have us *love* Him, not merely give the dry religious sorts of acts that pass for "honoring." True love goes much further than mere "honoring" ever could. Anselm's assumption doesn't keep with the Bible's view of God's eternal purpose, to have someone to whom He could express His love and whom He could dwell within. As Bayne and Restall put it:

> If the obligation to honor God is the ground of our obligations, then God's relation to us is akin to that of a petty bureaucrat, whose relations with his infe-riors are controlled by whether or not those inferiors

show him the appropriate amount of respect. This is not to deny that respect may be appropriate in a right relationship, but to analyze the rightness of the relationship in terms of respect is to conceive of God's desires for His creatures in terms of their compliance and deference. This does grave injustice to the Gospel imperatives for the believer to love God and love neighbor.[3]

Anselm's theory makes the cross God's means of solving His offended ego, as if He needed the cross in order to save face. He had to have His honor, regardless of who gave it to Him, and He recovered His honor among us by torturing His Son to death. This God doesn't seem like the loving Father of Jesus. He seems like a mafia don who has to restore his honor among his peers by making an example of one of them, so that they would know to honor him and not cross him again.

A Few Problems

Penal Substitution explains the cross as a solution to God's inability to fully accept us, as if it cured God's problem. It does not see the cross as solving *our* problem. But who had the problem? God did not eat the forbidden fruit. Penal Substitution argues God no longer has a problem with my sins because He got His anger out of His system. The argument states that, by expressing His wrath against sinners, His understanding of divine justice has been met, so He can be at peace with us. Yet we find nowhere in Scripture where divine justice is explained merely as God solving the problem of His temper by punishing an innocent man in place of a guilty one. To use an extreme example, would it have made sense if God had punished the Israelites with the plagues, instead of the Egyptians, because He was angry with

Egypt? As we shall see in a fuller discussion of Romans 1 to 3, such a view is not in keeping with Paul's understanding of God's justice.

There is a central difficulty with this view that its proponents don't like to discuss: If the cross was merely God getting His wrath out of His system, to satisfy a concept of divine justice that we find nowhere else in Scripture, why did the One who died have to be God? Why did God have to be incarnate in Jesus Christ, live, die, and rise from the grave, in order to provide for atonement? If all that was needed was for an innocent being to take God's wrath in our place to satisfy God's need for punishment, then why not pick an angel? Indeed, one can be an Arian (one who does not believe Jesus is God) and still believe in Penal Substitution. But "an account of the atonement should at the very least draw a meaningful connection between the atonement and the incarnation."[4]

As many theologians now recognize, Anselm's view is not in keeping with the understanding of the Christian Trinity: It puts the persons of Jesus and the Father as, in a sense, combatants. But the historical doctrine of the Trinity asserts that God is one essence, one Being who exists eternally as a mutual indwelling of three co-equal persons. If He is one Being, He cannot have some sort of discord within Himself. God is not a house divided against Himself. Penal Substitution gives us a "good cop, bad cop" view of the Father and Son. But when Jesus came to earth, He told his Jewish countrymen, "The Father and I are One" (John 10:30). In the upper room before His arrest, Phillip asked Him to show them the Father. He replied, "Have I been among you all this time without your knowing Me, Philip? The one who has seen Me has seen the Father" (John 14:9). There is no disconnect in character between the person of Jesus and the person of the Father. Jesus Himself described the Father as "filled with compassion."

Rather, the Bible says Jesus voluntarily submitted to the pain of the cross. Romans 8:3 presents the cross as something the Father did *in* His Son, not *to* His Son. Paul also explains that in the cross, Father and Son were working together for the reconciliation of the world (2 Cor. 5:17-20).

To get around these problems, many proponents of Penal Substitution will recast the issue into God making a demonstration of His wrath, so that man would know that you can't just break His commands and get off "scot free." That means the relationship we are reconciled to is one built on fear of God's punishment, not one built on the acceptance of His love. But John tells us (1 John 4:14-19):

> We have seen and we testify that the Father has sent the Son as Savior of the world. Whoever confesses that Jesus is the Son of God—God remains in him and he in God. And we have come to know and to believe the love that God has for us. God is love, and the one who remains in love remains in God, and God remains in him.
>
> In this, love is perfected with us so that we may have confidence in the day of judgment; for we are as He is in this world. There is no fear in love; instead, perfect love drives out fear, because fear involves punishment. So the one who fears has not reached perfection in love. We love because He first loved us.

John doesn't present a Savior whose method of salvation drove us to fear God's punishment for sin, but whose loving act drove us to love God in return and to have His love in us for others. In fact, rather than the cross reminding us of the terrors of God's wrath against us, Jesus' saving act was to remind us of God's love and thus drive fear of punishment out of our relationship with Him.

Charles Spurgeon, whom I otherwise highly respect, exemplified the un-Biblical, fear-based thinking tied up in Penal Substitution. Concerning Christ's death on the cross, Spurgeon said:

> When God saw Jesus in the sinner's place, He did not spare Him; and when He finds the unregenerate without Christ, He will not spare them. O sinner, Jesus was led away by His enemies: so shall you be dragged away by fiends to the place appointed for you. Jesus was deserted of God; and if He, who was only imputedly [sic] a sinner, was deserted, how much more shall you be?[5]

But that's not how the Bible puts it. Rather, Paul said, "He did not even spare His own Son, but offered Him up for us all; how will He not also with Him grant us everything?" (Rom. 8:32). The cross was not a basis for a fear of God's anger, but God's act of giving to us the thing we most needed. Because He did that for us, there is no reason to doubt that He will give us everything that is truly good. The cross does not bring us to repentance by making us afraid of an angry God. It brings us to repentance by demonstrating the amazing power of God's love for us, a love we have spurned since Eden.

Here we see how Penal Substitution confirms us in our Phariseeism. It says that the way to God's heart is through outward behaviors, not inward love. It merely writes off our failures to earn God's favor, so that we can try again to earn His favor by our own efforts. It does not reconcile us to an intimate relationship based on God's unmerited love for us and our trust in Him. Instead it keeps us in the same old religious world view that says that God's principle concern is merely following a list of externally-focused rules. Thus, it engenders a motivation for doing good that is rooted, not in the love God has planted within us, but in our fear of God's anger: If His wrath led Him to do that to His own innocent Son, think of what He might do to us if we don't try to do the right things!

Symbol, or Power?

Among some theologians who hold a Penal Substitution view, it is popular to characterize the cross as a symbol of God's punishment for sin. Since sin had been symbolically punished, the thinking goes, God can now be at peace with us. The idea of the cross as a symbol is exactly that: It only "symbolizes" something. Such a view supposes a cross that isn't actually real. In 1 Corinthians 1:17-18, Paul explains the cross as God's power that has an effect on our lives:

> For Christ did not send me to baptize, but to preach the gospel—not with clever words, so that the cross of Christ will not be emptied of its effect. For to those who are perishing the message of the cross is foolishness, but to us who are being saved it is God's power.

In fact, the entire epistle is full of references to God's power in the cross and the resurrection (1 Cor. 1:18, 24; 2:4, 5; 4:19, 20; 5:4; 6:14; 15:43). Rather than offering the cross as a mere symbol that demonstrates to the immoral Corinthian Christians that God is angry with sin, Paul expressed the cross as the powerful solution to the moral and doctrinal problems that had plagued that church: The cross is God's means of solving the deep spiritual problems of humanity that get expressed in sins.

And that leads us to another problem with Penal Substitution: It has no tie to the initial sin in Eden. In Eden, as many evangelical scholars will agree, mankind rejected

God's grace and love, and instead chose to live by his own ability expressed through his own "knowledge of good and evil." For God to merely beat His Son senseless in order to get out His anger or exemplify His wrath or whatever, does not answer the problem created in Eden. During Ronald Reagan's first year in the White House, he said of the wasteful budget passed by his predecessor, "Cures were found for which there were no known diseases." In essence, that is Penal Substitution, a cure in search of a disease, a solution in search of a problem. If anything, as the story of the Prodigal's Punishment shows, such a cross would only confirm Adam's suspicions: This is an irrational and temperamental God who cannot at all be trusted.

God's Passion

The Penal Substitution view of the cross largely stems from an incorrect interpretation of Romans 1 to 3. Penal Substitution says that God is horribly enraged at us for sinning, and that His wrath must somehow be satisfied by destroying an object of punishment. This is simply not the Bible's explanation of God's wrath. In fact, Paul explains God's wrath in Romans 1: "God's wrath is revealed from heaven against all godlessness and unrighteousness of people" (Rom. 1:18). God's wrath is not revealed against "all godless and unrighteous people," but against "all godlessness and unrighteousness *of* people." The ultimate object of God's wrath is the sin within us, not ourselves directly. In His mercy, He seeks to find a way to separate the sin within man, from the man himself whom God loves. He is angry with the sin itself that is within us and has us as its dutiful slaves. This indeed is reflected in the life of Jesus Christ, where He seemed to see sin as something that twists, victimizes, and enslaves the people He loved so dearly. It isn't just that God "hates the sin, but loves the sinner." God hates sin precisely *because* He loves the sinner.

The word we translate as "wrath" in Romans is the Greek word *orge*. It literally means "passion" or "desire," and it denotes something much more than mere fleshly anger or a temper tantrum or anything like that. In fact, if we were to replace *wrath* with *passion* in Romans 1:18, we might view the text entirely differently: God's passion is to rid this world of the destructive power of sin.

Paul continues his explanation of God's wrath in Romans 1 by stating what God did about it: "Therefore God delivered them over in the cravings of their hearts to sexual impurity…" (v. 24). And again, "Because they did not think it worthwhile to have God in their knowledge, God delivered them over to a worthless mind to do what is morally wrong" (v. 28). In order to demonstrate His passion, God simply gave man over to the sin within him, so that man might experience the natural result of his self-destructive behavior and come to agree with God about the problem. This illustrates one central truth about God's wrath: It isn't focused simply on behaviors. If, as religious thinking says, God's biggest issue with humanity is our external behaviors, He would never have delivered us over to do even more bad behaviors. God's problem isn't our behaviors, but the broken and hostile spirit within us that causes them.

Paul further explains, "Although they know full well God's just sentence—that those who practice such things deserve to die—they not only do them, but even applaud others who practice them" (v. 32). Now, this might at first sound like Penal Substitution. After all, God's just sentence is that "those who do such things deserve to die." But we have to follow Paul's line of reasoning. Right before this, he says of humanity, "They are filled with all unrighteousness, evil, greed, and wickedness. They are full of envy, murder, disputes, deceit, and malice. They are gossips, slanderers, God-haters, arrogant, proud, boastful, inventors of evil, disobedient to parents, undiscerning, untrustworthy, unloving, and unmerciful" (v. 29-31). Paul is saying we are "filled with" something horrible, "full of" very evil things. Thus, the fact that "those who do such things deserve to die," is evidentiary language. Paul refers to it as "God's just sentence," meaning a very reasonable declaration that this twisted thing called man should not be around. It is not at all unlike what happened in Noah's day. Such a creature who is filled with the things Paul mentioned, and thus does the things Paul describes, is not safe to have around. I wouldn't want a murderer in my house, nor could I trust a gossip with my most intimate secrets. I cannot trust a deceitful and malicious man at all. Such a person should not be allowed in polite society, but the problem is that "polite society" is entirely made up of such people: "Such people" are me and you and everyone else. To simply punish the only innocent One with God's just sentence is to make that sentence unjust, because then it would do nothing to address the evil things we are "filled with" that result in condemnation in the first place.

The Parable of the Faulty Computer

To understand what I mean by this, consider a tale I heard while working in the financial industry. A few fine mathematicians and programmers decided to create a computer program that could sense patterns and anomalies in short term stock price movements and exploit them for profit with automatic trading. So they plugged the program into the market, giving it $50 million in investment capital to play with.

It immediately sold 15,000 S&P 500 futures contracts. Let me put that in laymen's terms: Within a few seconds, the program had decided to place a $750 million bet against the

U.S. stock market! Even a 1% increase in the stock market, as often happens in the span of a mere hour or two, would cause the model to lose 15% of its $50 million capital. For most traders, a 15% loss is horrible for an entire *year*, let alone an *hour*. The programmers immediately unplugged the machine and closed out its positions. The program was junked.

That is, in a sense, why humanity deserves to be junked. We have sin within us, a core deficiency in of our very nature. The silly bets the computer program made were not the true *reason* the program had to be junked. They merely demonstrated to everyone that within the program there was a deficiency that meant the program wasn't right. The evidence proved the program's creators were justified in destroying it.

Similarly, we are a horribly malfunctioning machine. God's judgment—His righteous declaration—that those who do such things deserve to die, is not an arbitrary decision, nor the result of His arbitrary squeamishness at certain outward actions. Rather, it is His correct conclusion (if we may use such a word about God), proved to us by the evidence, that something is wrong with us. In choosing sin as part of our nature, we have chosen a divorce from a loving intimacy with God. This turns us into something quite dangerous and awful, a species that inflicts suffering on itself and thus breaks God's heart. That is why God's passion comes against the sin within us that causes us to be so.

Paul the Rabbi

In a sense, our unrighteousness—the evil that we do, and the hatred and violence that we pour out on one another—illustrates that God is correct when He says that we should be destroyed. Paul deals directly with this in Romans 3:4-6:

God must be true, but everyone is a liar, as it is written: "That You may be justified in Your words and triumph when You judge." But if our unrighteousness highlights God's righteousness, what are we to say? I use a human argument: Is God unrighteous to inflict wrath? Absolutely not! Otherwise, how will God judge the world?

Paul was a Jew before he was anything else. He was one of the most accomplished Rabbis of his day. And in the letter of Romans, we find certain Jewish characteristics that are not present in his other writings. This is probably because Romans is the only Pauline epistle whose audience had a sizeable contingent of Jewish Christians. All of his other letters were written principally to Gentiles.

So in Romans 1 to 3, we find him describing a characteristically Jewish understanding of judgment: In that view, a trial (for lack of a better word) is a two-sided affair. One of the two parties must be judged correct, and the other faulty. In the Torah, if a person falsely accuses someone else of a crime, and the adjudication demonstrates the innocence of the accused, then the false accuser was to be punished with the punishment that would have gone to the one he accused (Deut. 19:16-20):

> If a malicious witness testifies against someone accusing him of a crime, the two people in the dispute must stand in the presence of the Lord before the priests and judges in authority at the time. The judges are to make a careful investigation, and if the witness turns out to be a liar who has falsely accused his brother, you must do to him as he intended to do to his brother. You must purge the evil from you.

In essence, Paul is discussing a sort of court case in which man and God are sitting opposed to each other, each one claiming that the other is somehow in the wrong. In a way, Paul is echoing God's statement to Israel through the prophet Micah (6:2-3):

Listen to the Lord's lawsuit,
You mountains and enduring foundations of the earth,
Because the Lord has a case against His people,
And He will argue it against Israel.
My people, what have I done to you,
Or how have I wearied you?
Testify against Me!

This is basically how Paul is dealing with Romans 1 to 3. The Jewishness of this sort of court case could baffle the Western mind. In Western courts, the person who brings a lawsuit never starts out by asking the accused to testify against *him*! Because he is the accuser, *he* is not the one on trial. Thus, a trial like the one in Micah 6 would make no sense to us.

The results of sin demonstrate in this court setting that God is in the right, and thus that everyone else is a liar, or in the terms of the Torah, a "false witness." Our unrighteousness, resulting in self-destruction and suffering, demonstrates God's righteousness. Thus, God is justified in His judgment: The entire history of humanity proves that He was correct in His warning to Adam and Eve. He was not lying about the fruit, as Satan and Adam and Eve accused Him. The evidence bears God out on this.

The Parable of the Old Russian

Paul's argument about man's utter sinfulness reaches its culmination in Romans 3:19 and 20. Paul writes, "Now we know that whatever the law says speaks to those who are subject to the law, so that every mouth may be shut and the whole world may become subject to God's judgment. For no flesh will be justified in His sight by the works of the law, for through the law comes the knowledge of sin" (Romans 3:19-20). This is the point of it: As we saw in Chapter 6, the Law came to give man a knowledge of sin. It was given to prove to man that the reality he had chosen for himself was doomed to a horrible, painful, and heart-rending failure.

When the Communists began to foment a Marxist revolution in Russia, they offered an absolutely idyllic world devoid of pain, malice, hatred, anger, war, starvation, and so on. Truly, Marxism was offered as the solution to every single human evil except death from old age. Suppose that, as the people were thinking of supporting the Marxists, a very wise old Russian had come and told them something like this: "You think you want this Utopia they are offering. You think it will give you a wonderful, amazing world so full of happiness that you can hardly imagine it. But here is exactly what will happen: So awful will be the tyranny to come, that you will someday dream of being under the yoke of the tsars. Millions of you will starve to death. Tens of millions more will be murdered in political purges under mere suspicion of disloyalty to the head of the party. Children will be used as spies against their parents. You will plunge yourselves into such wretched poverty that you will yearn for the paltry food you have now. And your government will be so corrupt it will make the tsars look like the epitome of virtue." The citizens didn't at all like this man's pessimism. They accused him of lying to protect the greedy capitalist oppressors. So they kicked him out of Russia and followed after the Marxists.

In 1942, twenty-five years later, this wise old Russian returned. To be sure, another 25 years is a long time for an old man, but let's pretend he stayed alive. He says to them,

"Alright, since after 25 years you still don't believe me, I'm going to institute a system that will prove my point. I am going to tell your regime not to murder another innocent person. On top of that, I'm going to hold you to your claims about eradicating poverty. If you can ensure that from now until I return, no more than 1,000 innocent people will be murdered, and if you also ensure that you have successfully destroyed poverty, then I'll agree you were right about communism. If not, you must admit I was right, and you must submit to my solution." The problem is, 1942 would have been square in the middle of the reign of Stalin, the most murderous of all Russian tyrants. Stalin himself would have murdered millions of innocent people in the years after 1942. That, in itself, would be proof of the utter failure of Russian communism.

Suppose now that 45 years after he first returned, the wise old Russian came back, still miraculously alive. It would now be 1987, close to the end of the Soviet regime. The old Russian sat down with the people, looked at the sort of system of account that they had agreed to with him, and began to tally up the score: Not only were more than 1,000 innocents killed, but millions were. Far from being exterminated, poverty and starvation were rampant throughout the Eastern Bloc.

There would be absolutely no denying it. It was all there in the tally card, in black and white. They were horribly wrong, and he was very right. Those who had disagreed with the old Russian, who had said he was lying to them about the effects of communism, simply would not have a leg to stand on in the final meeting. The old man was right, and every communist was a liar. They could not return any accusation against the old man, because it was undeniably clear that he was correct. To paraphrase Paul, "every mouth would be shut."

In the same way, the Law causes us to be subject to God's judgment, to in a sense agree with God on why He has demanded that this malfunctioning thing should be done away with. It gives man the knowledge of the sin within himself. There was poverty and murder in communist Russia before the old Russian came back in 1942 to set up a tally system, but it wasn't until 1942 that such poverty and tyranny were used as evidence against Russian communism. Similarly, Paul says, "Therefore, just as sin entered the world through one man, and death through sin, in this way death spread to all men, because all sinned. In fact, sin was in the world before the law, but sin is not charged to one's account when there is no law. Nevertheless, death reigned from Adam to Moses..." (Romans 5:12-14). Like the old Russian's tally system, the Law created a means of charging sin to man's account, so that he could see his deficiency and admit the evil within him.

Punishment, or Solution?

As we have seen, Romans 1 to 3 represents a Jewish understanding of judgment and justice. Now, there is a central difference between the Western view of judgment, and the ancient Jewish view that was informed by the Torah. The Western view, held by Anselm and the Reformers, sees judgment as a punishment problem: Someone must be punished. Our systems of punishment are devised principally to create negative rewards (punishments) for crimes. The idea is that, if we take away the incentive, people will be less likely to do it, and thus we will keep further crimes from occurring.

But the problem is, simply punishing someone with jail time after he has, for instance, burnt my house down, doesn't solve the problem that I am out a perfectly good house. Somehow, there is a sense within me that I should have my house back. And that is where the ancient Jewish view of judgment differs from ours. Their view wasn't principally about punishment, but about equity: Restoring what was wrong, fixing the problem, putting people back on the footing they would have had if the evil had not been done. In fact, as we shall see in Chapter 10 when we discuss Isaiah 53, even the death sentences in the Torah reflected a view of punishment by death that removed evil from the community, restoring it to holiness. They were punishments that cured the evil within the community, not punishments that merely allowed God to feel better about the sins of the community.

We see the ancient Jewish understanding of judgment in Jeremiah's prophecies against wicked men who "judge not the cause, the cause of the fatherless, yet they prosper; and the right of the needy do they not judge" (5:28, KJV[6]). Further, we find God exhorting the nation of Judah to "learn to do well; seek judgment, relieve the oppressed, judge the fatherless, plead for the widow" (Isa. 1:17, KJV). Judgment was inextricably tied to relieving the oppressed. Were we to put over our Western concepts onto the texts of Jeremiah and Isaiah, we would find God perversely saying to punish the fatherless. But context indicates that this judgment is not simply punishment, but setting things right. God is directing Israel to care for the poor and broken and down-trodden in the kingdom, because their unwillingness to do so stood as contradiction to God's loving and merciful nature. In the Bible, justice does not simply mean "punishment." It means fixing what is wrong.

Further, we read of the Messiah, "With righteousness shall he judge the poor, and reprove with equity for the meek of the earth: and he shall smite the earth with the rod of his mouth, and with the breath of his lips shall he slay the wicked" (Isa. 11:4, KJV). The Messiah is said to judge the poor, but not punish them. Instead, he slays the wicked. And that is central to Biblical judgment. Slaying the wicked is a means of destroying those who oppress the poor, so that the poor can live in safety from the oppressors. Thus, the Messiah would "reprove [the wicked] with equity, for [the sake of] the meek of the earth." This is not merely, as we see it today, a show of punishment to dis-incentivize future acts of sin by others, but a means of protecting the innocent.

We see this also in the apocalyptic prophecy of Daniel 7, in which a horn persecutes the people of God. Daniel records, "I beheld, and the same horn made war with the saints, and prevailed against them; Until the Ancient of days came, and judgment was given to the saints of the most High; and the time came that the saints possessed the kingdom" (Dan. 7:21-22, KJV). Because the horn oppressed the saints, God gave them judgment, removing the kingdom from the evil horn, giving it to the saints, and destroying the horn. To merely punish the horn, without setting things right as they should be, would not fulfill God's concept of justice. It would be like executing Hitler but allowing the Nazi Regime to continue to stand.

In his renowned book *The Knowledge of the Holy*, A.W. Tozer explains the Biblical view of God's judgment:

> Holy men of tender compassion, outraged by the inequity of the world's rulers, prayed, "O Lord God, to whom vengeance belongeth; a God, to whom vengeance belongeth, shew thyself. Lift up thyself, thou Judge of the earth: render a reward to the proud. Lord, how long shall the wicked, how long shall the wicked triumph?" And this is to be understood not as a plea for personal vengeance but as a longing to see moral equity prevail in human society.

God's justice doesn't seek to simply make an example of someone. Nor is His justice somehow a mere irrational emotional response to something that, for a reason that we don't fully understand, irritates Him deeply. God's judgment is the means by which He makes things right. It is His means of making the created order reflect the pure, peaceful, and loving goodness that is intrinsic to Himself.

Unless we understand God's Biblical concept of justice, Romans 1 to 3 will have no meaning to us. We will be left only with a selfish human understanding of wrath as a mere angry tantrum. For instance, recall that Paul says, "Is God unrighteous to inflict wrath? Absolutely not! Otherwise, how will God judge the world?" (Rom. 3:6-7). When I first read this, I came at it from my modern Western thinking. So to "inflict wrath" and to "judge," in my mind, both meant to exercise some form of punishment on the wrongdoer. It appeared Paul was quite foolishly saying, "Is God unrighteous to inflict punishment? Absolutely Not! Otherwise, how will God punish the world?" If we read this with our modern glasses, we will think that it is somehow intrinsic to God that He just needs to punish for some reason we don't understand. Thus, we will have a view of the cross that is entirely about God's need to torture someone, perhaps anyone, in order for His wrath to be subsided.

That is why we must understand the Biblical definitions of God's justice and His judgment. Paul is really saying, "Is God unrighteous to destroy the wicked? Absolutely not! Otherwise, how will God set the world right?" God's wrath—His passion—is not a mere angry feeling within God that requires some divine catharsis. It is His desire to set the world right by removing that which will not submit to His righteous and holy love.

Justice, Apart From the Law

As we have seen, the Law merely proves to man his utter failure. Though he sought to be "like God, knowing good and evil," we find Paul declaring that "all have sinned and fall short of the glory of God" (Rom. 3:23). The Law gave man a knowledge of the sin within him, silencing his claims against God in judgment. In Romans 3:20, Paul leaves us in the lurch by detailing God's judgment of man from the beginning up to the time before Christ: "For no flesh will be justified in His sight by the works of the law, for through the law comes the knowledge of sin." In the court case between God and man, we cannot use the Law to show that we are in the right. We cannot show that we have achieved the glory of God. Instead, we are left simply knowing the sin within us.

And, but for the cross, that is where we would be left: We are left with the Russian man and Soviet communists, sitting at the table and staring at the tally card. Both know the irrepressible verdict: Communism was an utter failure, just as the old man had warned. However, Russia is still an absolute political, social, and economic disaster. The Russians need something more than the tally card. And to beat the Old Russian's innocent son to death would not fix the problem. They need something to solve Russia's pressing difficulties, to restore it to the right state and thus solve the situation that the tally card points to. And that is what Paul says happened in Jesus Christ (Rom. 3:21-26):

> But now, apart from the law, God's righteousness has been revealed—attested by the Law and the Prophets—that is, God's righteousness through faith in Jesus Christ, to all who believe, since there is no distinction. For all have sinned and fall short of the glory of God. They are justified freely by His grace through the redemption that is in Christ Jesus. God presented Him as a propitiation through faith in His blood, to demonstrate His righteousness, because in His restraint God passed over the sins previously committed. He presented Him to demonstrate His righteousness at the present time, so that He would

be righteous and declare righteous the one who has faith in Jesus.

Now, any scholar will tell you that the terms "righteousness" and "justice" are, in the original languages, essentially one and the same. This reflects the Biblical view of justice, which sees justice as things being the way they ought to be. In other words, the Biblical view of justice is "just-ness": The idea that the order of things is just. Similarly, "righteousness" essentially implies "right-ness," the idea that things are right, and especially that man is in right relationship to God, and that God is consistent with Himself. Consequently, we could just as easily translate the Greek as, "But now, apart from the Law, God's *justice* has been revealed..." That, really, is the central point of Paul's discussion here. God's justice, His means of setting things right, is revealed in Jesus Christ.

God's righteous solution comes "apart from the Law." That last part is quite important. Up to that point, Paul's focus had been on the law court, on the Law as condemning man in a lawsuit between man and God. In the final verdict, God had been convincingly shown to be right and man had been shown to be wrong. The solution, though, to man's condemnation did not come through the legal concepts of the law court, but "apart from the Law."

Penal Substitution interprets Romans 3:21-26 this way: "Because man could not obey the Law, he incurred a moral debt. The debt the Law incurred was a debt of punishment by God's wrath, so Jesus stepped in and took that punishment for us, paying our debt." There are several major Biblical problems with this, most centrally that it reads Penal Substitution into the text in order to get it from the text, and that it is based on the medieval European concepts of justice that Americans like myself have inherited.

As we saw from Romans 5, the Law came to "impute" sin, or to "charge sin to one's account." Those who hold to the

Penal Substitution theory argue that, since sin was charged to man's account through the Law, Jesus came to pay that incurred debt by allowing God to exercise His wrath against Christ. But the problem is that there is no mention anywhere in the Law that somehow the debt incurred by the Law can be satisfied simply by God torturing an innocent. In fact, we would not at all think of that as revealing God's justice. But more to the point, the debt was not man's chief problem. As we saw in Romans 5, sin and death reigned from Adam to Moses, even when there was no Law to create a debt. Just as communism was Russia's problem and the tally card was the means of pointing to the problem, so the debt was merely a tool to point to man's problem of sin.

Rather than presenting a righteousness that was "apart from the Law," Penal Substitution makes Sinai the point of Calvary. This creates a huge disconnect with the human race that lived before Sinai, and with the Gentiles after Sinai who were not given the Law. In an attempt to deal with the tally card, Penal Substitution fails to deal with the under-lying problem that made the tally card look so bad. Penal Substitution forgives sins, but doesn't solve the inner spiritual problem that created them. It deals with the symptoms, but doesn't offer a cure. But God's wrath is directed principally against sin within us, not merely its outward behavioral manifestations.

Penal Substitution is right that Israelites who broke the Law were to be punished. Its proponents are right that Paul spoke of man knowing God's just determination that those who do evil should die. But they ignore the fact that the solution came "apart from the Law," apart from the justice within the Law. As we saw, in order to be consistent with God's justice, a just solution must not merely punish evildoers, but set the reality back to the way it should be. God's ultimate justice is a justice that always existed, but was revealed to us "apart from the Law" in Jesus Christ. God's justice is His desire that man be restored to the loving relationship with Him that existed in Eden, a relationship that eventually bears fruit in holiness. That is the relationship God always wanted, but man rejected.

That is the chief problem of Penal Substitution. It doesn't truly bring me to reconcile with a loving God. It doesn't allow for the cross to set right the relationship that man rejected, resulting in the "godlessness and unrighteousness *of* people." Rather, Penal Substitution simply allows for God to sort of self-medicate His mind, to quiet His internal desire for things to be truly good. But it wasn't God who rejected intimacy. It was us.

Paul says God presented Jesus "as a propitiation through faith in His blood, to demonstrate His righteousness, because in His restraint God passed over the sins previously committed" (v. 25). The cross, in the Penal framework, was a propitiation because it allowed God to quiet His wrath by punishing someone. Thus, in this view, God is now able to pass over sins. So Penal Substitution reads the text this way, "In order to continue to pass over the sins committed after the cross, God presented Jesus as a propitiation, because He passed over the sins committed before the cross." If God could pass over sins before the cross, why does the cross suddenly enable Him to pass over sins thereafter? Why, indeed, does Jesus die merely to allow God to continue doing what He had already been doing for thousands of years? And if the cross was Jesus taking the Father's wrathful punishment so that the Father could be appeased, why does Paul say that *God* presented Jesus as a propitiation? Would it make more sense to say *Jesus* presented *Himself* before God the Father as a propitiation?

What, instead, does Paul mean by the propitiation? There is, to be sure, no scholarly consensus on this. The exact meaning of the word "propitiation" in this text is hotly disputed. But a simple way to look at this is to note that the Greek word rendered "propitiation" is *hilasterion*. In the common usage of the day, *hilasterion* meant a gift one party gave to another in order to settle a dispute between the two of them.[7] If this common meaning is intended (and there is little reason to suspect it isn't), then this would *not* imply that Jesus presented Himself as gift to God, offering to appease the Father's wrath by taking punishment and thus reconciling God to humanity. Instead, Paul says "*God presented Him,*" meaning that God presented Jesus as gift *to us,* in order to take away our hostility towards Him. In fact, as we shall discuss in the next chapter, Paul explicitly says in Colossians 1:21-22 that the cross came to reconcile us to God because we were "hostile in mind."

The context of Romans up to this point has focused on an adversarial dispute between God and man, and a *hilasterion* was a gift given to amend such a dispute and reconcile the adversaries. The entire context is God revealing Himself to mankind, not God revealing Himself to Himself or giving Himself something. Rather than Jesus giving Himself to God as a willing victim of divine punishment, the *hilasterion* must be a gift He offers us to reconcile us in our enmity against Him and thus remove sin's power over us. Such a gift must not merely be a symbol or a token. It must have a power to overcome sin in sinful humanity. We will discuss the nature of that gift in the next chapter.

Demonstrating His Righteousness

Paul speaks of the death and resurrection of Jesus as God demonstrating His righteousness, or justice. As we read above, some interpret that statement as meaning God had to demonstrate His anger against sin by punishing Jesus, so that He could give us mercy and yet let us know that sin still angers Him. This, of course, comes from the perspective that justice only means punishment. But how does punishing an innocent for the sins of a guilty man demonstrate God's justice? When you ask someone this, he will reply, "Well, God's justice is incomprehensible." But if God was demonstrating His justice to us, how does it help us if His demonstration of His justice is incomprehensible to us? The point is that it has to be comprehensible for it to be a demonstration to us.

The cross demonstrates something to us about God that we could not have understood in any other way, and it causes His righteousness to triumph instead of sin, so that He can both be just and justify us. He demonstrates His righteousness to us by curing our enmity towards Him through the perfection of His love, by sending Jesus to die for us so that we can live to God. He demonstrates His righteousness by redeeming His creation in Jesus Christ, rather than continuing on allowing humanity to destroy itself one generation after another. By redeeming us, He justifies Himself against the charge that He has done nothing to solve the problem, and His solution to the problem also justifies us.

We shall see in Chapter 10 how God does this. We shall see that cross is God's justice against the destructive power of sin, His reconciliation for the broken relationship that occurred in Eden, and His cure for the sin that man accepted into his nature at the fall. In later chapters of Romans, Paul details exactly how the cross reveals God's righteousness or justice "apart from the Law." Rather than divorce Romans 3 from the rest of the letter, as is often done, we will instead let Romans interpret Romans, Paul interpret Paul, and the Bible interpret the Bible. Thus, we shall see that the cross doesn't solve God's problem with sin by making Him feel better about it, and us. The cross solves humanity's problem of sin by destroying its power to enslave us.

Chapter 10

If One Died for All

—∂∕∂∕∂—

Jesus Christ didn't come to begin a new religion. He
came to begin a new creation.

Frank Viola/From Eternity to Here

On a cool desert night, a wealthy and powerful Rabbi
named Nicodemus approached a man named Jesus ben
Joseph, a lowly carpenter-cum-sage from the Galilean dump
of Nazareth. As if to demonstrate Nicodemus' theological
vacuity, Jesus spoke abruptly, "Unless someone is born
again, he cannot see the Kingdom of God." So confused was
this great rabbi Nicodemus, that he incredulously asked Jesus
how it was possibly to crawl back into his mother's womb
and come out again. Jesus explained that we must be "born
of the Spirit" (John 3:8). For Nicodemus, a non-Trinitarian
first century Jew, this only further complicated the issue.

So finally, Jesus declared, "No one has ascended into
heaven except the One who descended from heaven—the
Son of Man. Just as Moses lifted up the snake in the wilderness, so the Son of Man must be lifted up, so that everyone
who believes in Him will have eternal life" (John 3:13-15).
Jesus saw a fundamental connection between His death on
the cross—His being "lifted up"—and the new birth. But

how are they connected? That is the mystery of the cross that we must discover here.

Trying Harder, or Born Again?

In the Garden of Eden, God did not say to Adam, "If you eat from the Tree of Knowledge of Good and Evil, I will get so angry that I will kill you." Rather, He said quite matter-of-factly, "On the day you eat from it, you will certainly die" (Gen. 2:17). Death was the natural spiritual result of rejecting the source of Life. Man's great problem is that he is a spiritual zombie, the walking-dead. He rejected trust in God and instead chose trust in himself as part of his nature. He spurned God's grace and plunged into a spiritual "domain of darkness" (Col. 1:13). As Paul said in Romans, "Sin entered the world through one man, and death through sin." Only a few paragraphs later, Paul said, "And what fruit was produced then from the things you are now ashamed of? For the end of those things is death. But now, since you have been liberated from sin and become enslaved to God, you have your fruit, which results in sanctification — and the end is eternal life!" (Rom. 6:21-23)

As we saw in the previous chapter, a cross that merely gives someone else our deserved punishment does not solve the deadness inherent in our spiritual essence. It doesn't give us a new fruit, or take away the old fruit in us. Reflecting the religious thinking that spawned it, Penal Substitution leaves sin as a problem we must solve by a sheer act of will. All the cross did, in that view, was fix God's anger at our failings. The message of Penal Substitution is not that God has made us a new creation in Jesus Christ. The message is that God's anger in torturing Jesus should scare us into trying harder to achieve certain behaviors by our own power.

Cleansing Our Consciences

In the Roman Empire of the first century, Judaism had a legal right to exist, but the separate Christian faith did not. Faced with persecution, some Christians of a Jewish background were leaving Christianity to return to Judaism. The book of Hebrews was written to such people, showing them how the New Covenant of Calvary was far superior to the Old Covenant of Sinai.

Hebrews presents the cross as the true sacrifice foreshadowed by the Old Covenant rituals. In Hebrews 9, the author compares Jesus' sacrifice to the annual Day of Atonement ritual in the Levitical system. He explained the difference by showing that the cross was truly effective in solving the sin problem, while the Old Covenant rituals were not (Heb. 9:13-14):

> For if the blood of goats and bulls and the ashes of a heifer sprinkling those who are defiled, sanctify for the purification of the flesh, how much more will the blood of the Messiah, who through the eternal Spirit offered Himself without blemish to God, cleanse our consciences from dead works to serve the living God?

The power of the cross, according to Hebrews, was not that it merely covered our sins externally, but that it was effective in fixing something wrong in us. It didn't simply allow God to satisfy His temper. Instead, it had the power to "cleanse our consciences from dead works to serve the living God." The author continues by stating, "But now He has appeared one time, at the end of the ages, for the removal of sin by the sacrifice of Himself" (Heb. 9:26-27). Jesus didn't merely allow God to love us despite our sins. Rather, His sacrifice offered a "removal of sin." Not *sins* in plural, but *sin*. The cross is God's means to remove the brokenness in human nature that makes us trust in ourselves instead of in Him. Hebrews does not present the cross as solving God's problem. It presents the cross as the solution to *our* inability to trust God. The cross serves as the only effective means of bridging a broken relationship.

The Day of Atonement was the highest day in the Jewish religious calendar. As Hebrews 9 states, it directly foreshadowed the atonement Christ brought on Calvary. The Day of Atonement was not presented in the Old Testament as a ritual meant to appease the anger of a vengeful God. Rather, it is presented as a means of cleansing the Israelites of the defilement of sin: "Atonement will be made for you on this day to cleanse you, and you will be clean from all your sins before the Lord" (Lev. 16:30). The Day of Atonement symbolized the way the Messiah's death would cleanse us of sin. Thus, the author of Hebrews interprets the cross in exactly the same way, as a gift God gave to cleanse our consciences and remove sin's power over us. The cross cures us. It doesn't merely punish someone in our place.

The New Creation

But how does the cross do this? If you were to read everything Paul says about the cross (and I strongly suggest you do so), you will find a uniform understanding: The cross sets right the relationship that was broken in Eden by removing from us a spirit that is hostile to God. Read what Paul says of the cross in 2 Corinthians 5:14-21:

> For Christ's love compels us, since we have reached this conclusion: If One died for all, then all died. And He died for all so that those who live should no longer live for themselves, but for the One who died for them and was raised.

From now on, then, we do not know anyone in a purely human way. Even if we have known Christ in a purely human way, yet now we no longer know Him like that. Therefore if anyone is in Christ, there is a new creation; old things have passed away, and look, new things have come. Now everything is from God, who reconciled us to Himself through Christ and gave us the ministry of reconciliation: That is, in Christ, God was reconciling the world to Himself, not counting their trespasses against them, and He has committed the message of reconciliation to us. Therefore, we are ambassadors for Christ; certain that God is appealing through us, we plead on Christ's behalf, "Be reconciled to God." He made the One who did not know sin to be sin for us, so that we might become the righteousness of God in Him.

As we shall see, this passage is representative of the Pauline view of the cross, and it is also explicitly affirmed by Peter. I hope you will join me in breaking this statement into its constituent parts, studying these parts individually, and then bringing it all together at the end. To do this, we should first note the following parallel texts:

- Romans 6:6-11: "For we know that our old self was crucified with Him in order that sin's dominion over the body may be abolished, so that we may no longer be enslaved to sin, since a person who has died is freed from sin's claims. Now if we died with Christ, we believe that we will also live with Him, because we know that Christ, having been raised from the dead, no longer dies. Death no longer rules over Him. For in that He died, He died to sin once for all; but in that He lives, He lives to God. So, you too consider yourselves dead to sin, but alive to God in Christ Jesus."

- Romans 7:4-6: "Therefore, my brothers, you also were put to death in relation to the law through the crucified body of the Messiah, so that you may belong to another—to Him who was raised from the dead— that we may bear fruit for God. For when we were in the flesh, the sinful passions operated through the law in every part of us and bore fruit for death. But now we have been released from the law, since we have died to what held us, so that we may serve in the new way of the Spirit and not in the old letter of the law."

- Galatians 2:19-20: "For through the law I have died to the law, that I might live to God. I have been cruci- fied with Christ; and I no longer live, but Christ lives in me."

- Galatians 5:24-25: "Now those who belong to Christ Jesus have crucified the flesh with its passions and desires. If we live by the Spirit, we must also follow the Spirit."

- Galatians 6:14-15: "But as for me, I will never boast about anything except the cross of our Lord Jesus Christ, through whom the world has been crucified to me, and I to the world. For both circumcision and uncircumcision mean nothing; what matters instead is a new creation."

- Colossians 1:21-22: "And you were once alienated and hostile in mind because of your evil actions. But now He has reconciled you by His physical body through His death, to present you holy, faultless, and blameless before Him."

- Colossians 2:20-3:3: "If you died with Christ to the elemental forces of this world, why do you live as if you still belonged to the world? Why do you submit to regulations: 'Don't handle, don't taste, don't touch'? ... So if you have been raised with the Messiah, seek what is above, where the Messiah is, seated at the right hand of God. Set your minds on what is above, not on what is on the earth. For you have died, and your life is hidden with the Messiah in God."

- In 2 Timothy 2:11: "This saying is trustworthy: 'For if we have died with Him, we will also live with Him.'"
- In 1 Peter 2:24-25: "He Himself bore our sins in His body on the tree, so that, having died to sins, we might live for righteousness; by His wounding you have been healed. For you were like sheep going astray, but you have now returned to the shepherd and guardian of your souls."
- In 1 Peter 3:18: "For Christ also suffered for sins once for all, the righteous for the unrighteous, that He might bring you to God, after being put to death in the fleshly realm but made alive in the spiritual realm."

If one died for all, then all died.

This is an odd statement, to say the least. Some might argue this is purely metaphorical because Paul elsewhere tells the Romans, "Consider yourselves dead to sin, but alive to God in Christ Jesus" (Rom. 6:11). Perhaps Paul is merely saying we should act or think *as if* we died in Jesus' death, even though we didn't. But if you read Romans 6:11 in context, Paul is telling them to consider themselves dead to sin precisely *because* that is the actual fact of the matter. He starts off in Romans 6:6 by saying, "For we *know* that our old self was crucified with Him..." He expects the audience to have already known this as a fact. So in verse 11, Paul is telling them to live in the reality to which they have been delivered. We see parallels to this in many of the passages above, where there is a call to holiness based on the new identity of the Christian.

In the context of 2 Corinthians 5:14, Paul is defending and explaining his work as an apostle. Rather than speak of the believer's death in Christ as merely metaphorical, he says that this one truth—"If One died for all, then all died"—is the foundation of his apostolic ministry (see the preceding vs. 11-12, where the context is clearly Paul's ministry as an apostle). We witness the foundational nature of this credo throughout the Pauline corpus: While the idea of Penal Substitution is based only on (a mis-interpretation of) Romans 3:21-26, Paul repeats the idea of sharing in Jesus' death eight different times in four separate epistles. Paul does not state it as a mere symbol or metaphor, but as a basic fact of the Gospel that he, in most instances, expects the believer to know. Further, in Romans 6 and 7, Paul makes this doctrine of the cross the basis of his most systematic discussion of salvation. Not only that, but Peter also states it twice in his first epistle.

Moreover, Paul tells Timothy that this statement of us dying in Jesus' death is trustworthy. If that isn't enough, we also find Peter explaining what it means for Jesus to bear our sins by stating that *we* have died to sin. Neither Peter nor Paul seems to think of this as some symbol. We should accept it as a fact, however mysterious and mechanically incomprehensible it may be.

Therefore if anyone is in Christ, there is a new creation; old things have passed away, and look, new things have come.

This flows from the previous statement that "if One died for all, then all died." Paul makes the death on the cross, and the participation in Jesus' resurrection, the basis for the new birth. In order for the believer to be a new man, somehow the old man must be destroyed. This is accomplished on the cross, where the cancer of sin in us is exposed to God's wrath, and through Jesus' resurrection life, we are born again a new man, a new creation.

We see why Paul cannot be speaking metaphorically about all believers participating in Jesus' death. After all, if our participation in Jesus' death were a metaphor, then so would be our new birth. The new birth, then, would not truly mean being born of the Spirit, as the Bible teaches, but rather it would be just a metaphor for a good feeling in us. But the Gospel is not pop psychology. It is "God's power for salvation to everyone who believes" (Rom. 1:16).

Paul discusses his own conversion experience on the Damascus road by stating, "I no longer live, but Christ lives in me." Similarly, later in Galatians, Paul tells us that we have been crucified with Christ, and thus, "If we live by the Spirit, we must also follow the Spirit." Through the Holy Spirit, Jesus pours into us His resurrection life, regenerating our spirits. Thus, Paul's and Peter's appeals for Christian holiness are not based on the idea that we should fear God's anger against us as allegedly displayed on the cross. Rather, we are, in Christ, a new creation, so that we should live out the reality that has been made real in us through Jesus' death and resurrection. Thus, Paul says, "He died for all so that those who live should no longer live for themselves, but for the One who died for them and was raised." Peter affirms this view when he says, "Having died to sins, we might live for righteousness."

The implications for this are far-reaching. Recall that Paul describes his conversion by saying, "For through the law I have died to the law, that I might live to God" (Gal. 2:19). Hebrews similarly tells us that the "blood of the Messiah" will "cleanse our consciences from dead works to serve the living God" (9:14). In context, the dead works were the Old Covenant Law. These commands pointed to man's sinfulness and thus caused him shame, but they never had the means of making him truly holy. As we said in Chapter 6, these were given to an unregenerate people and as such reflected the spiritual deficiencies within them. In that sense, they were "dead works."

In the texts from Colossians and Galatians, Paul uses our death in Christ as a basis for imploring the believer not to go back to the *stoicheion*, with their focus on external matters. For instance, in warning the Galatian Christians about departing into religious legalism, Paul says, "through the Law I died to the Law," (2:19) and then explains, "I am crucified with Christ," (v. 20) right before exclaiming in frustration, "You foolish Galatians! Who has hypnotized you, before whose eyes Jesus Christ was vividly portrayed as crucified?" (Gal. 3:1). We see it also in Romans 7, where Paul describes the Christian as having died to the Law, which could never make him holy and only excited his fleshly passions. Instead, the Christian is raised to live according to the leadership of the indwelling Spirit. The new man does not engage in good behavior in order to earn God's love or keep God from pouring out His wrath, but because that is his new identity in Jesus Christ. So he should not go back to the old identity that tried to overcome that inner sinfulness by outward acts. The solid fact that Paul's audience had shared in Jesus' death was the reason for them not to go back to religious thinking.

Now everything is from God, who reconciled us to Himself through Christ and gave us the ministry of reconciliation: That is, in Christ, God was reconciling the world to Himself, not counting their trespasses against them…. Therefore … we plead on Christ's behalf, "Be reconciled to God."

The Prodigal Brother tells us that God could not be reconciled to us without pouring out His wrath on Jesus. But when Paul preached the cross, he said it made the believer a new creation, so that through it Christ enabled the sinner to be reconciled to God. Paul says, "In Christ, God was reconciling the world to Himself." Please do read that again: God was, in Jesus, reconciling *the world* to *Himself*, not *Himself* to *the world.*

The Prodigal Brother says God needed the cross because *He* was alienated from *us* and hostile towards *us,* on account of our inability to do the right things. But in Colossians 1:21-22, Paul says, "You were once alienated and hostile in mind because of your evil actions. But now He has reconciled you by His physical body through His death..." Similarly, Paul tells the Romans, "For the mind-set of the flesh is hostile to God because it does not submit itself to God's law, for it is unable to do so" (Rom. 8:7). Similarly, Peter did not say that our sins made the Shepherd get angry at us and leave the sheep fold. He says that *we*, as sheep, went astray from our Shepherd and needed to be brought back to Him. That is what the cross does for us.

The Father did not have to be convinced to reconcile with us. If that were so, He would not have been working together with the Son to reconcile us to Himself. When Jesus was on earth, we do not find people trying to convince Him to be reconciled to them. Rather, we find Him running all over the countryside of Israel pleading with us to accept His Father's love and grace. It wasn't us who desired reconciliation. It was God Himself who desired it, but *we* would not be reconciled to Him because *we* were "alienated and hostile in mind." Thus, we read the call of reconciliation: "Let us draw near [to God—see v. 19] with a true heart in full assurance of faith, our hearts sprinkled clean from an evil conscience" (Heb. 10:22).

As we said in chapter 3, the problem with man is that, in Eden, he chose to doubt God. He chose instead to live with a conscience that trusted in his own "knowledge of good and evil." He distrusted God's statement regarding the Tree of Knowledge of Good and Evil. From that point forward, man could never really trust that God meant the best for him. Man could never completely accept God's grace. In the new birth, that spirit that lived divorced from God and unable to trust or truly love Him, is replaced with a new spirit that loves and trusts God as the basis of its very nature.

Or, as Paul so tenderly puts it, "For you did not receive a spirit of slavery to fall back into fear, but you received the Spirit of adoption, by whom we cry out, "Abba, Father!" The Spirit Himself testifies together with our spirit that we are God's children" (Rom. 8:15-16). *Abba,* meaning "Daddy" or "Papa", is a name that a small child uses for his father: A spirit of child-like trust and love is given to us, replacing a broken and dead spirit of distrust and fear. Thus, the words of Jesus are fulfilled in the new birth. "I assure you: Unless someone is born again, he cannot see the kingdom of God," (John 3:3), and in a similar nature, "I assure you: Whoever does not welcome the kingdom of God like a little child will never enter it" (Mark 10:15).

The message of the cross and the empty tomb is the message of reconciliation: In His resurrection, Jesus Christ raised us with a new spirit of trust and love. Contrary to what we have often been told, the Gospel is not Christ's plea to God to be reconciled to the world. Rather, the Gospel is Christ's plea to the world: "Be reconciled to God."
He made the One who did not know sin to be sin for us...

To understand this, we need to understand a bit about Isaiah and the Torah. Well-meaning proponents of Penal Substitution will often cite Isaiah 53:5 in their defense:

> But He was pierced because of our transgressions,
> Crushed because of our iniquities;
> Punishment for our peace was on Him,
> And we are healed by His wounds.

The text says, "Punishment for our peace was on Him," and so the thinking is that this is a divine endorsement of

Penal Substitution. But there are two colossal problems with such an interpretation. First, there is no sense in Isaiah that somehow God needed someone to beat to death in order to feel better. As Ladd writes, "Even in the Old Testament, the idea of atonement as the propitiating of an angry deity and transmuting his anger into benevolence is not to be found."[1] Instead, that idea comes to us from pre-Christian paganism.

Second, we must understand the Jewish view of the death penalties in the Torah. Isaiah was written within the context of the Old Covenant, not the New. In order for Isaiah's audience to understand the idea, Isaiah had to interpret the cross in regards to the Law Covenant with which the Jews were familiar. That Covenant indeed formulated punishment for sin, but even that Covenant did not allow an innocent to be punished with death in the place of a guilty man. Rather, in the Torah, the focus of the punishment was on ridding the Israelite community of the spiritual defilement embodied in the guilty person, something much closer to the ideas of the cross that I present here. Moses explains this in multiple places, notably:

- Deuteronomy 17:7: "The witnesses' hands are to be the first in putting him to death, and after that, the hands of all the people. **You must purge the evil from you.**"
- Deuteronomy 21:21: "Then all the men of his city will stone him to death. **You must purge the evil from you.**"
- Deuteronomy 22:21: "The men of her city will stone her to death. For she has committed an outrage in Israel by being promiscuous in her father's house. **You must purge the evil from you.**"
- In Deuteronomy 22:24: "You must take the two of them out to the gate of that city and stone them to death... **You must purge the evil from you.**"

Isaiah's Jewish audience would interpret the death punishment in Isaiah 53:5 in light of the death sentences in the Torah. That was how they thought of death sentences. They were not merely an external punishment for punishment's sake, but a means of purifying the entire community of the defilement of sin. Thus, Isaiah could conclude of it, "We are healed by His wounds."

As we saw, Peter actually quoted from this exact text of Isaiah 53:5, saying, "He Himself bore our sins in His body on the tree, so that, having died to sins, we might live for righteousness; 'by His wounding you have been healed.'" According to Peter, the fact that Jesus "bore our sins in His body" meant that we shared in the crucifixion of Jesus. We died in Him so that we might live for righteousness. Peter interpreted Isaiah 53:5 in exactly the light that an ancient Jew like himself would: If a sinless Messiah was wounded for the transgressions of all, it would mean that the evil in all of them was purged from them by His sacrifice. So "Punishment for our peace was upon Him," and "by His wounding you have been healed," would have meant one in the same in such a mindset. If we shared the Jewish concept of the death penalty, we might call Jesus' death a punishment, but it would be a punishment that heals us, not a means for God to get His anger out of His system by crushing someone.

In such a framework, the one who received the death penalty was actually an embodiment of the evil he or she had done. It was as if the person was infected with a horrible virus and needed to be quarantined completely through death. As Paul said, Christ "became sin for us." In a parallel text in Galatians, Paul says, "Christ has redeemed us from the curse of the law by becoming a curse for us, because it is written: 'Cursed is everyone who is hung on a tree'" (Gal. 3:13). Note that Paul did not interpret that curse in the Law by saying that Jesus *took* a curse for us, but that He *became*

267

a curse for us. By taking our evil cancer into Himself on the cross, Jesus became the embodiment of sin.

This is not at all to say that Jesus became a sinner. The sin, after all, was not His. Rather, it is to say that, as God, He could take the sin into Himself, and yet not be defiled by it. This seems in keeping with Peter's statement that He "bore our sins in His body on the tree." Peter does not say Jesus "bore our sins upon His body," but, "bore our sins *in* His body." He could take sin into Himself, allow Himself to be identified with it in a sense, and allow the Father to purge it from us with His purifying wrath.

When we read the New Testament writers, we cannot help but get the sense that sins are real entities. They are not merely legal violations of arbitrary directives. Rather, somehow they cause the cancer of sin within us to metastasize, hardening us more and more against God. They cause our hostility to God to grow within us, so that Paul can say we were hostile to God "because of [our] evil actions." James explains it like this: "But each person is tempted when he is drawn away and enticed by his own evil desires. Then after desire has conceived, it gives birth to sin, and when sin is fully grown, it gives birth to death" (James 1:14-15).

It is as if these sins wreak havoc upon us, creating scars deep within us until, in the end, we are nothing but a mass of cancerous spiritual scar tissue. Eventually, this brings destruction all on its own. It is no use thinking that God was arbitrary in saying that sinners would die. It was not a mere legal punishment as our human law systems have it. Rather, in Romans 5-7, Paul speaks of it as if it is an absolute fact of how the spiritual world operates. He states, for instance, "What fruit was produced then from the things you are now ashamed of? For the end of those things is death" (Rom. 6:21).

We had to die. Explicit in Paul's discussion of the cross in Romans 5-7 is that sin naturally results in death (Rom.

5:12, 6:23,7:5), just as a rock naturally falls to the ground if you drop it from your hand. He says the only way to be free of sin's dominion is to die the death sin brings: "Our old self was crucified with Him in order that sin's dominion over the body may be abolished, so that we may no longer be enslaved to sin, since a person who has died is freed from sin's claims" (Rom 6:6-7). We needed some way for this death to operate in us by a different mechanism, so that we could die and live to talk about it. And this is what Jesus did for us by allowing us to share in His death. As the texts from Deuteronmy demonstrate, death is not simply a punishment for punishment's sake. It is God's means of purging evil from the created order. Death doesn't merely punish sin. It purges sin.

Jesus said, "Just as Moses lifted up the snake in the wilderness, so the Son of Man must be lifted up…" (John 3:14). Jesus, in a sense, took our scar tissue within Himself, the fallen part of us that believed the Serpent's lie. God consumed that dishonest hostility with His wrath. Jesus allowed our cancer to produce death in Him so that it could not produce death in us. Together, Father and Son destroyed it. To be honest, this is not so much the opposite of Penal Substitution, as it is a sort of "Penal Substitution on steroids," wherein Christ destroys our disease of hostility towards Him. He doesn't merely take a punishment to symbolically appease God's temper.

Our hostile nature—the nature of the Prodigal Brother in us that could not accept grace and instead wanted to live by his own strength—was taken away by Christ on the cross. Thus we did not have to perish in order for it to be purged from us. But because Jesus is both God and man, the sort of purifying destruction could not destroy Him in His divinity. He was above it, so that it could be poured out on our sin *within* Him, but not destroy Him. So He rose again. Wayne Jacobsen explains it this way:

One of my best friends died of melanoma almost two years ago. Doctors tried to destroy the cancer with the most aggressive chemotherapy they could pour into his body. In the end, it wasn't enough. The dose needed to kill his melanoma would have killed him first. That was God's dilemma in wanting to rescue us. The passion He had to cure our sin would overwhelm us before the work was done. Only God Himself could endure the regimen of healing our brokenness demanded.

So He took our place. He embraced our disease by becoming sin itself, and then drank the antidote that would consume sin in His own body. This is substitutionary atonement. He took our place because He was the only one that could endure the cure for our sin. God's purpose in the cross was not to defend His holiness by punishing Jesus instead of us, but to destroy sin in the only vessel that could hold it until—in God's passion—sin was destroyed.[2]

... so that we might become the righteousness of God in Him.

Paul says in Romans that Jesus was "raised for our justification" (Rom. 4:25). This shows one of the biggest problems with Penal Substitution. It teaches that Jesus' sufferings on the cross satiated God's wrath through punishment, and thus His death, not necessarily His resurrection, allowed us to be justified. Really, there is no need for the resurrection in the Penal Substitution framework:

This reductionist approach shrinks or 'down grades' the whole gospel to a single sentence: 'God is no longer angry with us because Jesus died in our place.' Indeed, that is exactly why evangelistic presentations based on penal substitution often don't even bother to

mention the resurrection, because for them it serves
no direct purpose in the story of our salvation.[3]

Paul, in contrast, teaches that it is faith in Jesus' resurrection that causes us to be justified. Right before saying in
Romans that Jesus was "raised for our justification," Paul
showed through the example of Abraham that it had always
been faith in God that justifies a man before Him, not religious works or performances. No one could win justification
by the works of the Law.

Similarly, the Galatian Gentiles thought that they had to
be circumcised to be right with God. In response, Paul told
them too of Abraham's justification by faith. In closing, he
said he had been crucified to the world, and the world to him.
Then he added, "For both circumcision and uncircumcision
mean nothing; what matters instead is a new creation." It is
not simply punishment that causes the Christian to be justified before God. It is that Christ has made the Christian a
new creation. The old man who was in enmity and hostility
towards God, unable to trust God and instead trusting in his
own "knowledge of good and evil," was taken into Jesus
Christ on the cross and destroyed. The Christian, in Christ,
is raised a new man who accepts the call to "be reconciled
to God." We can be justified by faith because we are raised
with Jesus' trust towards the Father.

We lack peace with God because we are always trying
to demonstrate our own intrinsic righteousness via the law
court of Romans 1:18 to 3:20. Such attempts only continually remind us that we are unrighteous, so that they condemn
our consciences. So long as we focus on our own merits, it
is impossible for us to be reconciled to a God of grace and
mercy. We become the Prodigal Brother, refusing to go into
our Father's house because that Father will not honor us for
our own performance-based righteousness.

271

Paul writes that in the cross of Christ, God "condemned sin in the flesh" (Rom. 8:3). God didn't merely punish *sins* (plural), but condemned the *sin* (singular), the disease that causes us to commit *sins*. The result, as Paul says, is that "no condemnation now exists for those in Christ Jesus" (Rom. 8:1). In Christ, we have peace with Him because we admit the unrighteousness our *self*-righteousness, and accept by faith the freely offered gift of the righteousness of God. Thus, our conscience is freed from condemnation, and we are now able to bear being in His presence. We accept, as it were, the robe that the father offered to the poor and naked Prodigal Son.

Thus, we *become* the righteousness of God. Jesus, as God, is the righteousness of God. Because we die in Him and are raised in Him, our new life is inextricably tied up in His. "For you have died, and your life is hidden with the Messiah in God" (Col. 3:3). It has been rightly said that when God looks at a Christian, He does not see the Christian in his sin, but Christ in His righteousness. But why? Because, as Paul has it, we participated in His death, and rose in His resurrection, becoming united with Him. God sees Christ and not us, because through the Spirit we are wrapped up in Jesus, and Jesus is in us. He Himself is our robe of righteousness.

A Participatory Death and Resurrection

You might recall our discussion of Isaiah in Chapter 3. He could not stand in God's presence because of the overwhelming power of guilt and shame. If I were to use the words of Hebrews, I would say that he needed to have his conscience cleansed from guilt. The burning coal came to purify him, and as such it cleansed his conscience of his shame, and thus allowed him to stand in God's presence.

The atonement did not make God willing to accept Isaiah. God had already chosen Isaiah. God provided atonement so

Isaiah could stand being near Him. When the angel brought the burning coal to Isaiah's lips, he didn't say, "Your sins have been punished in someone else." Instead, the Angel said, "Now that this has touched your lips, your wickedness is removed, and your sin is atoned for" (Isa. 6:7). The atonement, as presented to Isaiah, was not someone else receiving his punishment, but his own wickedness being removed by God. It is not merely that his *sins* (plural) were atoned for, but that his *sin* (singular) or wickedness was atoned for. The coal removed the disease that kept Isaiah from desiring God's presence.

The New Testament texts we studied paint a picture of that kind of atonement: Because He was not only man, but also God, Jesus could die a miraculous death that the believer could take part in. How this works, exactly, is a mystery because God's Triune being and Christ's incarnation are mysteries to us. Nevertheless, the Bible demands that it is true.

Jesus on the cross put to death our inherited enmity against God. And in Jesus' resurrection, the Christian also is resurrected spiritually, born again by the impartation of Jesus' resurrection life. Blood, in the Bible, represents life (Gen. 9:4; Lev. 17:11, 14), and His blood—His life—is in us, and our life is wrapped up in His. Thus, we are right with God.

For the Christian, sinning is a matter of identity. The cross is a cure for what ails us, and like any good cure, a change may occur immediately, but it takes time for the full effect to be realized. Thus, remnants of the old way may still exist. In fact, because the physical body was born under sin, the full effect of the cross will not be realized in us until the final resurrection, when our bodies are transformed. So the sins that the Christian may continue to commit are the habitual and physical remains of the cancer that was destroyed. After dying in Jesus and being raised up in Him, Jesus' perfection is wrapped around the sinner. The believer might still commit sinful acts. But because of the believer's new identity through the death and resurrection of Jesus, God says that isn't really the believer doing the sin. "Now if I do what I do not want, I am no longer the one doing it, but it is the sin that lives in me" (Rom. 7:20-21).

That cancer was put to death, so no one can now charge sins against those who are in Christ. Consequently, there is no condemnation on the believer himself anymore. Even if the believer sins, God does not call the believer a sinner anymore. The sins the believer committed and continues to commit, are counted against the old hostile nature. Because of Jesus' resurrection life in the believer, sins no longer produce eternal death. The sinner is raised with Jesus' immunity to the death caused by the cancer. So Paul can thus say (Rom. 7:24-8:3):

> What a wretched man I am! Who will rescue me from this body of death? I thank God through Jesus Christ our Lord! So then, with my mind I myself am a slave to the law of God, but with my flesh, to the law of sin.
>
> Therefore, no condemnation now exists for those in Christ Jesus, because the Spirit's law of life in Christ Jesus has set you free from the law of sin and of death.

Though we may stumble, we are no longer ruled by the hostile, untrusting sinful nature. We fall, but we no longer reject the grace that can pick us up again. Rather, we live by the indwelling of God in the Spirit, as the Spirit pours Jesus' resurrection life into us. Quite literally, we could not enter the Kingdom of God unless we were born again. We could not return to the Father's estate until we were able to trust Him to take care of us. The cross and the empty tomb give us the new birth of trust in His grace. As the power of the Spirit grows in us through our relationship with God, more of the vestiges of the old man are washed away by the blood—the resurrection life—of Jesus Christ.

That washing is what baptism signifies. Both Paul (Rom. 6:3-5, Col. 2:12) and Peter (1 Pet. 3:21-22) affirm that baptism points to our participation in Jesus' death and resurrection. In the first of the two Christian sacraments, we find the cross represented exactly as we find in Scripture: We are plunged under the water to signify sharing in Jesus' death and burial, and we are raised from the water to signify participation in His resurrection.

But Penal Substitution has no such connection to baptism, because it argues that our old cancer was not truly put off through the cross. Baptism completely loses its meaning in a Penal framework. It is as if, for a millennium, we have been baptizing souls with no idea why we were doing so. We have forgotten that Jesus instituted baptism in order to remind us of what He did for us at the cross.

The Judge

As we saw in the previous chapter, Romans 1:18 to 3:20 paints a picture of a court room setting, where man and God are in a legal battle against one another, each claiming there is something wrong with the other. As we move through the court case, God undeniably demonstrates that all humanity, Jew and Gentile, cannot be justified against Him in the court of law. Thus, we have a horrible state of human affairs, and God desires that something else should happen to set the state of affairs right. Something must be done to reconcile the legal combatants and provide for a solution to the havoc wrought by human sin.

And that is where the triumphal language of Romans 3:21-22 comes in: A new righteous solution is given. "But now, apart from the law, God's righteousness has been revealed—attested by the Law and the Prophets—that is, God's righteousness through faith in Jesus Christ, to all who believe, since there is no distinction [between Jew and Gentile]" (Rom 3:21-22). In Jesus Christ, the answer to sin, guilt, and shame—promised in the Old Testament—came, but apart from the Law court that condemned us. The Greek word translated as *judgment* in Romans 3:19 is the word *krisis*. It should be obvious which English term comes from it. In Romans 3:21-22, it is as if God brought us under His *krisis* for one purpose: So that, in Jesus Christ, God may rush into the courtroom and declare an amicable and just solution to the crisis between God and man, a solution not based on courts of law but on something much better. Jesus Christ offered a *hilasterion*, a gift of reconciliation for us, so that God could both be just in the court case, and yet justify those who are in Jesus Christ. The gift causes us to have faith in God and thus be justified before Him by taking His side in the court of this world. Thus, God could both destroy sin, and save the one infected by it. Jesus Christ brought a true win-win solution, something truly and perfectly good and just.

But how did this solution work? The traditional Penal Substitution model simply reads into Romans 3:21-26 the idea that Jesus took the torture that the Law required. But as we saw above, that doesn't reflect the spiritual concept of the death penalty in the Law. To take the death penalty in the Law, and to remove evil from within the believing community, were one in the same in the Old Testament sense. In a prophetic way, the Law testified of what the cross would do for us, but the Law itself never allowed for a guilty person to be truly, eternally justified before God. Thus, the solution came "apart from the Law," meaning a reality greater than the Law had to be at work, a reality the Law merely pointed to in shadow form.

God shows Himself to be righteous by freely offering "the redemption that is in Christ Jesus." God doesn't allow sin to go on causing pain and death and suffering forever. He doesn't merely outlaw sin through the Law. He offers a redemption "apart from the Law" that works on the core problem of alienating sin within each person. The timeless God steps into time and offers to redeem the suffering creation by putting the power of sin away in Himself. In so doing, God shows Himself to be just. Paul said that God's justice *is* the redemption that is in Jesus Christ. It is not that God's "just" solution of punishing Jesus Christ *allowed* for redemption. Karl Barth eloquently explains:

In the Gospel is revealed the great, universal secret of the **righteousness of God** which presses upon every man of every rank. In Christ the consistency of God with Himself—so grievously questioned throughout the whole world, among both Jews and Greeks—is brought to light and honoured. What men on this side resurrection name "God" is most characteristically not God. Their "God" does not redeem his creation, but allows free course to the unrighteousness of men; does not declare himself to be God, but is the complete affirmation of the course of the world and of men as it is. This is intolerable, for, in spite of the highest honours we offer him for his adornment, he is, in fact, "No-God." The cry of revolt against such a god is nearer the truth than is the sophistry with which men attempt to justify him. Only because they have nothing better, only because they lack the courage of despair, do the generality of men on this side resurrection avoid falling into blatant atheism. But in Christ God speaks as He is, and punishes the "No-God" of all these falsehoods. He affirms Himself by denying us as we are and the world as it is.[4]

Paul does not detail exactly *how* the solution works in Romans 3:21-26, just that it exists. It is in Romans 6 and 7 that Paul delineates the mechanics of the solution, and there, as we saw, he uses language identical to that of 2 Corinthians 5:14-21: The old hostile nature in us is put to death on the cross, exposed to God's purifying wrath. The cancer is done away with. Christ died *for* us in the most literal substitutionary sense. He exposed Himself to God's wrath though He had no sin in Him, in order that our sin might be placed in Him and destroyed without us actually having to perish. We die in Him, so that we do not have to die in ourselves. The believer is raised with a new life, as a new creation in Jesus Christ. Thus, the entirety of humanity can be a new creation if we will simply accept the call to "be reconciled to God" (2 Cor. 5:12).

My Angry Father

When Dwight Eisenhower liberated Germany from the Nazis, he saw the concentration camps for the first time, and was filled with a powerful anger. He smelled the foul stench of death in the gas chambers; saw the emaciated, zombie-like bodies of the survivors; and was torn by the piles of shriveled and discarded corpses: Men, women, children, and babies whose only crime was their descent from Jacob.

In his anger, Eisenhower wanted the Germans to clearly see what their devotion to Hitler had wrought. So he ordered the local German civilians to tour the camps, to walk into the foul gas chambers, to see the ovens, to view the piles of corpses and the broken survivors. Footage of that event shows people overcome with horror and disgust, coughing and sobbing, finally realizing the awful results of their hatred and Hitler-worship.

The wrathful anger that the Prodigal Brother foists on God, is not the kind of righteous anger General Eisenhower had at the heart-rending evils of the Holocaust. Rather, the Prodigal Brother sees a god who is angry because we haven't paid him what we owe. He is like an angry mobster, incensed that the little laundromat on the corner didn't pay him their protection money last June.

But the Prodigal Brother's No-God is not angry at what angers us. He isn't truly heart-broken at the suffering, pain, and brokenness within us and our world. He is a god who looks at the Holocaust, and counts up the number of violations of federal regulations 24, 78, and 93. He then tells us the fine for our crimes, and becomes infuriated when we are not able to pay it. Because of his anger, this No-God must beat someone to exact his payment in flesh. This No-God is utterly sick. He has no heart of love and compassion for us.

But the God of Jesus Christ is a true God who is not worried about what we owe. In Paul's theology, the creation of the debt in the Law was merely a tool to convince the sinner that he was doomed and needed a savior. Thus, when Jesus brought our old self to death on the cross, He didn't so much *pay* the debt, as much as he "erased the certificate of debt, with its obligations, that was against us and opposed to us, and has taken it out of the way by nailing it to the cross" (Col 2:14). The debt mechanism had served its purpose—the sinners who owed it died in Jesus Christ—so it could be written off and in its place a surplus of Christ's perfection is counted for us.

In Jesus' parables, God simply writes off the debt when someone could not pay it. But He became angry when cruel men exacted suffering from the innocent. The message of God's anger as displayed in the cross is His righteous desire to destroy the sins that so haunt us. He is angry at the chains of slavery that bind us to our "knowledge of good and evil," and keep us from the healing power of His grace and love. He destroys the shame that plays like a record over and over in our minds, keeping us up at night, torturing our consciences and holding us back from accepting His love in our broken-ness. In place of the shame, He gives us a completely new identity, His child.

God's wrath is against the "godlessness and unrighteous-ness of people," the evil within us that has resulted in every war, every famine, every plague, and every act of genocide. So in the cross, the Father and Son set out to put that horrible suffering to death, and to raise us up a new creation that is surrounded by His love, resting in Him even in our greatest moments of sadness.

God's anger is a righteous anger against the evil that keeps us from Him. It is an anger born of His love for His suffering creatures. It is the just and selfless anger of a broken-hearted Father. His anger is displayed against the powers that torture us with shame and guilt, the powers that lead us into sin by promising some greater glory, only to bring us to greater suffering.

God's wrath is against the Hitler's of the world, to be sure. But in a deeper sense than we realize. His wrath comes against the spiritual powers that caused the Hitler's of our planet. One of the psychological reasons Hitler became such an evil sociopath was that his father would regularly brutalize him for no reason whatsoever. The sin of Hitler's father was transferred to Hitler. And Hitler in his own evil transferred it to countless innocent men and women. While that does not excuse Hitler for the evil that he did, it demonstrates that the power of sin is beyond the control of any of us. We do not control sin. Sin controls us. We are its fearful slaves, laboring to save ourselves from its harsh whip. God's wrath is against the long chain of causality, the chain of slavery that binds us for generation after generation. In Jesus Christ, He set about to put that chain to death, by redeeming one person at a time.

It is the "one person at a time" nature of the atonement that makes the grace of the cross so amazing. When you or I say, "Jesus died for me," we must understand what that means in light of the Bible's description of the cross. It wasn't that Jesus simply died for all of us in a collective sense. He didn't merely die as a symbol of *collective* punishment for humanity's *collective* impiety. The Omniscient Mind does not see collective masses of unidentified faces that blend together into a tableau of human nothingness. That is how we see it because of the weakness of our limited thinking.

When He set about to redeem us by dying for us, He did it individually. He did not say, "I shall die for them." He said, "I shall die for Peter." And He said, "I shall die for Paul." And He said, "I shall die for Moses." And He said, "I shall die for Abraham." And He said, "I shall die for Brent." When He set about to die for *us*, He said all of these things, all at once, saying them for each individual and not simply for a collective. He chose to take within Himself the spirit of slavery that keeps each of us, individually, from accepting His embrace. The mind of God the Son, able to think millions of thoughts at once, was thinking individually of each person who needed the cure of His death in order to be reconciled to His love. And that is the central thing about the cross: It is not the selfish anger of an abusive father, but the curative passion of a perfectly loving God.

The Prodigal Son Revisited[5]

The Prodigal's desire to take his inheritance early was a statement to the father: "I want you dead!" Indeed, that was what Adam and Eve said to God in Eden. But our Father never requited that hatred. He wanted us alive in Him, to know Him and live in His love. And Jesus wanted us to live with Him, to experience the wonderful love of the Father that He has known from eternity.

In Jesus, God called out to us in His tears, "Please! Please! Come home! Just come home!" We were hostile and would not accept God's reconciliatory love. As prodigal children, we thought we could make our own way in the world, apart from our Father's grace. So Father and Son took the hatred and shame and guilt of our internal hostility, and destroyed it together in the cross. The angry, proud, and hostile son in us was taken away. We are left in tatters and rags, bald and broken and crying. God brings us under His *krisis* so that we may be humbled enough to accept His mercy. He brings us to the end of our ropes so that we can become the tax collector crying out for mercy in the corner of the Temple.

Jesus, the Crucified, became the Crucible, voluntarily exposing our cancer to the curing power of His Father's wrath. The Father did not punish the Son. The Father and Son voluntarily worked together to free us from our bondage. It was something they both desired to do, from the deepest core of their one Being.

But it was not easy for them. The Father had to pour His wrath into the One He had loved for Eternity with a love no human being can comprehend. The Son had to experience the wrath of the Father He had cherished from before time had begun. We hear Jesus crying out to His Father, "My God, My God, why have you forsaken me!" But in response, we hear only rumbling earthquakes and explosions of thunder. Perhaps that was the only response the Father could give: The terrible, earth-shattering sound of His breaking heart. No doubt it was heart-rending for Abraham to walk with Isaac up the hills of Moriah, believing he would have to slash the throat of his beloved son and stand there silent while Isaac bled to death on the altar. How much more heart-breaking could it have been for the Father to expose His beloved Son to His wrath to purify the cancer in us?

God desired no prize so great as the prize of the return of His prodigal children. His love for us is a jealous love, a love that will not relent in bringing us back to Him, no matter the cost. It was not Father against Son, or Son against Father.

The Father did not abuse His Son. The Father and Son freely desired to pay whatever cost it took to bring us back home. Through the Spirit, they buried our sin of distrust in the grave and raised us up to take part in their perfect relationship as Father and Son. So we are born again, new and clean little babies, resting in the Father's arms. We died in Jesus Christ so that we would no longer reject the invitation to return to our Father's house. Together, they came running for us, the Father in the Son, the Son in the Father, filled with a compassion that surpasses understanding. In the death and resurrection of Jesus Christ, God fell on our necks and wept, embracing us in His wide arms as His great warm tears of joy rained down to cleanse us and make us whole.

Chapter 11

When We Rise

—⁓—

We live in a wheel
Where everyone steals.
But when we rise,
It's like strawberry fields.

Bush (rock band)| *"Glycerine"*

It doesn't seem like something you would say if you intended to go out and deny it by your actions. In fact, it is such a mysterious statement that most attempts to explain it have fallen terribly short. I am speaking, of course, of what Jesus said at the Wedding of Cana, before He performed His first miracle. His mother asked Him to do something about the embarrassing wine shortage. His reply: "What has this concern of yours to do with Me, woman? My hour has not yet come" (John 2:4).

I have sometimes mused that Jesus' hour must have come only a few minutes thereafter, because He indeed changed the water into wine. But I suspect that is not the real point of His statement. It seems more that He did not want His miracle to be misconstrued as Him doing something that He would instead do much later. But what?

Perhaps this mystery has something to do with the nature of a first century Jewish wedding. They were very celebratory affairs. The couple would be hitched, everyone would rejoice, and the dancing would begin. People would hold hands and spin round, they would move in and out in a timing that seemed to be an almost atavistic habit learned from centuries of wedding celebrations. The bride and groom would be hoisted onto the shoulders of the crowd and paraded around the room like a king and a queen coming into their kingdom. The wine would flow freely, and guests would feast and dance for days on end. Certainly they would have found many of our modern weddings extremely dull. I wouldn't blame them.

All of this was for a very good reason. The Old Testament viewed the Covenant at Sinai as a wedding contract between God and the descendants of Jacob. Each Jewish wedding, in a small way, reflected the joy of Israel's deliverance from bondage in Egypt and their invitation to a free and prosperous home in Canaan, a home flowing with milk and honey. The wedding reminded the guests of their identity as a chosen people, married to Yahweh by the Law contract. It reminded them of their special history, their special place in God's heart. If there was a reason to celebrate, that would be it.

Jesus asked His mother, "What has this concern of yours to do with me? My hour has not yet come." This is not the only place where John records that Jesus' hour had not yet come. When Jesus was preaching in the Temple, His words enraged the worshippers there. "Then they tried to seize Him. Yet no one laid a hand on Him because His **hour had not yet come**" (John 7:30). The next day Jesus returned to the Temple to preach, and He met the Pharisees and the woman caught in adultery. John records again, "But no one seized Him, because **His hour had not come**" (John 8:20).

In contrast, mere days before His death, Jesus said, "**The hour has come** for the Son of Man to be glorified" (John

12:23). Then He said, "Now My soul is troubled. What should I say—Father, save Me from this hour? **But that is why I came to this hour**" (John 12:27). Right before the Last Supper, John records, "Jesus knew that **His hour had come** to depart from this world to the Father" (John 13:1). As Jesus gave His disciples the Upper Room Discourse, explaining what His ministry meant and what He was about to do, He told them, "Look: **An hour is coming, and has come**, when each of you will be scattered to his own home, and you will leave Me alone" (John 16:32). And finally, as Jesus was praying in Gethsemane, sweating drops of blood in spiritual agony, He said, "Father, **the hour has come.** Glorify Your Son so that the Son may glorify You" (John 17:1). Jesus' hour had finally come, the hour when He would give His life for many and pour out His blood as a drink offering for us.

Every Gospel writer includes the story of Jesus breaking the bread and giving the wine in the Lord's Supper. Every Gospel writer except one: John. Recall that when Jesus turned the water into wine, He desecrated special Jewish purification jars to do so. He turned the water of Jewish ceremonial purification into wine, which He would later use to symbolize the blood He shed on the cross. It seems as if, rather than leave the Lord's Supper until right before Jesus' death, John foreshadowed it at the beginning of his Gospel, and inserted it at the end by reference, through the statement, "The hour has come."

Jesus fully intended to turn the water into wine in Cana. No one knows a son like his mother. Mary must have known that Jesus' statement was not a refusal to do the miracle, but a means of explaining what He was about to do. That is why she immediately told the servants, "Do whatever He tells you" (John 2:5). Jesus wanted to be clear that He was not coming to protect the Old Covenant symbolized by the wedding celebration. He was not coming to move people towards religious obligation, towards empty ceremonies like ritual purification that could only clean the outside of a person. This was not *His* wedding to *His* bride. In turning the religious water into celebratory wine, He wanted us to realize He was foreshadowing what He would do on the cross and in the resurrection. When the chief servant tasted the wine, He told the groom, "Everybody sets out the fine wine first, then, after people have drunk freely, the inferior. But you have kept the fine wine until now" (John 2:10). The servant was speaking, not only toward the groom of Cana, but to the Groom who had come to lay down His life and take it up again.

When His Hour Had Come

I find all of this interesting because of what Paul told the Roman Christians. In describing the death and resurrection of Jesus, Paul said we had died in Him to the Law and been raised to be married to Jesus Christ (Rom. 7:1-4):

> Since I am speaking to those who understand law, brothers, are you unaware that the law has authority over someone as long as he lives? For example, a married woman is legally bound to her husband while he lives. But if her husband dies, she is released from the law regarding the husband. So then, if she gives herself to another man while her husband is living, she will be called an adulteress. But if her husband dies, she is free from that law. Then, if she gives herself to another man, she is not an adulteress.
>
> Therefore, my brothers, you also were put to death in relation to the law through the crucified body of the Messiah, so that you may belong to another—to Him who was raised from the dead—that we may bear fruit for God.

When Jesus' hour had come to die and rise from the grave, He would divorce us from the laws of religious obligation and the *stoicheion*, and marry us to Himself. Having died to the religious categories of Sinai — to righteousness by works and holiness by human effort, to fear of punishment and slavery to religious thinking — the church is bound up in Jesus Christ, bought by the Son to be His bride, to relate to Him as a loving wife relates to her loving husband, in intimacy, love, and joy. The Wedding at Cana was not Jesus' time to be bound to His bride. That time came when He rose from the grave.

When Jesus stayed with Mary and Martha and Lazarus, we find Martha playing the part of the dutiful hausfrau, no doubt preparing the meal, washing the dishes, keeping the house clean, and so forth. By the measure of the duties that human society required of her, she was being a perfect hostess.

But in contrast, her sister Mary was in the living room with the men, sitting at Jesus' feet as He taught. Martha was incensed by this. In Jewish society, only the men were allowed to sit around. Women had to busy themselves with domestic work. So Martha, perhaps mistaking herself for Jesus' nagging wife, came to Him and said, "Lord, don't You care that my sister has left me to serve alone? So tell her to give me a hand" (Luke 10:40).

Jesus had little use for the social conventions of his time. In fact, He flouted them with abandon. Rather than upbraid Mary for not working to feed and care for Him, Jesus gently rebuked her sister Martha: "Martha, Martha, you are worried and upset about many things, but one thing is necessary. Mary has made the right choice, and it will not be taken away from her" (Luke 10:41-42).

In this we might find a metaphor of what Jesus wanted in His bride, the Church. Jesus didn't fancy women who labored as the busy housewife, constantly eyeing their many religious tasks to ensure they are pleasing to Him. The one thing that is required of His bride, is to sit at His feet as *He* serves *her*. It is to sit and listen to Him teach, to look on Him with the gaze of awe and affection that can only come from the truest of true loves. Jesus does not seek the dutiful, staid domestic life of religion, but the passionate romance of spiritual intimacy.

Losing Our Religious Life

Jesus once said, "The one who loves his life will lose it, and the one who hates his life in this world will keep it for eternal life" (John 12:25). The Prodigal Brother tells us that Jesus means we must perform all sorts of religious works to gain acceptance by God. In other words, the Prodigal Brother interprets this to mean to commit ourselves to a sort of dreary asceticism. But when we view Jesus' statement in its context, we find something altogether different (John 12:23-26):

The hour has come for the Son of Man to be glorified. I assure you: Unless a grain of wheat falls into the ground and dies, it remains by itself. But if it dies, it produces a large crop. The one who loves his life will lose it, and the one who hates his life in this world will keep it for eternal life. If anyone serves Me, he must follow Me. Where I am, there My servant also will be. If anyone serves Me, the Father will honor him.

In light of a Biblical view of the cross, this statement takes on an entirely new meaning. Jesus said this right before His death, speaking of what He would do on the cross and in the resurrection. He was preparing a means for them to come to the Father in Him, to die in Him and rise again in Him.

Only those who hate the life of trusting in their own efforts and powers and merits, will be able to accept the call to lay down and die in His death, and rise in a newness of life. John Lynch, Bill Thrall, and Bruce McNichol put it this way:

> Grace is a gift only the non-religious can accept. They're the only ones who can get it. They're the only ones who can use it. Religious folks see grace as *soft*. So they keep trying to manage their junk with their own willpower and tenacity. Nothing defines religion quite as well as a bunch of people trying to do impossible tasks with limited power while bluffing to themselves that it's working.[1]

Jesus was not saying that we must work harder to "manage our junk" in order to be His disciple. He was saying that we must die entirely to the illusion that we can fix our greatest problems, overcome our greatest shortcomings, or soothe the greatest pangs of loneliness in the depths of our hearts. Jesus was saying that we must follow Him to Calvary, lose our life in His death, and gain a greater life of grace in His resurrection. The cross didn't come so that we could continue to live in bondage to our religious mindset here, and only someday be freed from it in Heaven. The cross came to free us from the slavery of self-improvement, so that we would live in the transforming power of the Father's love. Read what Paul famously wrote in Ephesians 2:4-7:

> But God, who is abundant in mercy, because of His great love that He had for us, made us alive with the Messiah even though we were dead in trespasses. By grace you are saved! He also raised us up with Him and seated us with Him in the heavens, in Christ Jesus, so that in the coming ages He might display

the immeasurable riches of His grace in His kindness
to us in Christ Jesus.

In the Spirit, we who are in Jesus Christ have died with
Him, and we have been raised with Him to be seated in the
very presence of God. That is what Jesus meant when He
said, "Where I am, there My servant also will be." We do not
merely hope to someday be seated next to God in Heaven,
but in Jesus Christ we are surrounded by His loving presence even now. When Jesus said we must hate our life on
this earth in order to receive eternal life, He did not mean
that we are forbidden from joy and peace, but that we must
hate the very thing we are without Him, shameful, self-righteous, proud, and self-dependent. We are broken people
who cover up our emptiness with the fig leaves of religious
works and ethical merits and wealth and pleasure and status.
But eventually, it all comes unraveled. Without Him we are
wolves that live by the power of our own acumen and vora-
cious appetite. But when we live as that beast, we divorce
ourselves from the only thing that can make us joyful, holy,
and at peace: The Father's loving presence. But the resurrection brings us to Him, seating us next to the Father, in Jesus
Christ. The life we lose in the cross is the life lived to the
world's graceless performance-oriented principles. The life
we gain in the resurrection is the life lived in the grace of
God's transforming presence.

That is why, in Christ, we are raised a new creation, a
child in the Father's arms. Only in His arms can we know life
as He means it. Only in His arms can we be freed from our
self-dependence, so that He can remove that grasping spirit
that tries and fails, tries and fails to achieve greatness by the
"knowledge of good and evil." Only when we are hidden in
a God of grace can His tender hand touch the deepest places
of our brokenness.

A Case of Mistaken Identity

Because they have fallen under the Prodigal Brother's teachings, many innocent and dedicated Christians suffer from a case of mistaken self-identity that flows from a faulty view of the atonement. They think Jesus died to bind them to religious obligation, not to free them from it. When the Bible teaches the resurrection, it declares that we were raised in Jesus Christ. We were born again into a new way of relating to God. This way of life is not based on religious performance, but on the authentic relational intimacy the Son has had with the Father for eternity. Recall the passage of Colossians 2:20-3:4 that we read in the last chapter:

> If you died with Christ to the *stoicheion* of this world, why do you live as if you still belonged to the world? Why do you submit to regulations: "Don't handle, don't taste, don't touch"? All these regulations refer to what is destroyed by being used up; they are human commands and doctrines. Although these have a reputation of wisdom by promoting ascetic practices, humility, and severe treatment of the body, they are not of any value against fleshly indulgence. So if you have been raised with the Messiah, seek what is above, where the Messiah is, seated at the right hand of God. Set your minds on what is above, not on what is on the earth. For you have died, and your life is hidden with the Messiah in God.

Everything in this world runs, in some way, by the *stoicheion* that entered into human nature at the fall. Even the Law, because it was given to an unregenerate people, could not reflect the completely other-worldly reality of grace and truth that came to us in Jesus Christ. These *stoicheion* can only ever deal with what is, in some sense, external to us.

Whether through pleasure, politics, wealth, status, or religious observances, the *stoicheion* attempt to use the powers of the material world to purify the spiritual man. This is madness. The *stoicheion* is our disease. It cannot serve as our cure.

When we share in Christ's death, we put to death the man that operates by the trust in the *stoicheion* of religion, law, and human abilities. And we are raised in Jesus Christ to something infinitely better: We are "hidden with Christ in God." We have been delivered by Him into what is above, into the true heavenly reality of love and trust in God. We have been invited to be "partakers of the divine nature" (2 Pet. 1:4). Jesus' resurrection becomes, for us, the Fruit of the Tree of Life that Adam and Eve rejected. He becomes an integral component of who we are. In a manner of speaking, the old spiritual DNA of the fruit of the Tree of Knowledge, is replaced by the spiritual DNA of Jesus Christ. Because we rise in Him, we are surrounded by Jesus and welcomed as sons and daughters through His relationship of Divine Sonship with the Father. The book of Hebrews masterfully describes what this means for us (Heb. 2:10-13):

> For it was fitting, in bringing many sons to glory, that He, for whom and through whom all things exist, should make the source of their salvation perfect through sufferings. For the One who sanctifies and those who are sanctified all have one Father. That is why He is not ashamed to call them brothers, saying:
> "I will proclaim Your name to My brothers;
> I will sing hymns to You in the congregation."
> Again, "I will trust in Him." And again, "Here I am with the children God gave Me."

By suffering for us as a man, Jesus Christ brought us into sonship with the Father, brought us back to the Father's estate and declared to the Father that we are home. The One who makes us holy shares His glorious sonship with us, so that the Father wraps His arms around us by wrapping them around His ascended Son Jesus Christ. Thus, by rising from the grave and ascending on high, Jesus not only made the Father known to us, but He made us known—known in intimacy—by the Father. He rose again, ascended, and declared to the Father, "Here I am with the children God gave me."

Broken Chains

The Christians in Galatia were struggling with the reality of their adoption by God. After Paul had planted the churches there, false apostles had come in and told them that Paul did not have full apostolic credentials. They told the Galatians that Paul did not really understand the complete Gospel. He was leaving out the most important part: Circumcision and observance of the Law. They were told they could not be saved until they put themselves under the Law's jurisdiction by becoming circumcised. Paul's epistle to the Galatians is by far his angriest work, full of a righteous indignation at both the false apostles, and the Galatian Christians who allowed themselves to be deceived. He told them "You who are trying to be justified by the law are alienated from Christ; you have fallen from grace!" (Gal. 5:4). To explain the difference between the Old and New Covenants, Paul used the metaphor of the difference between a slave and a son:

> Now I say that as long as the heir is a child, he differs in no way from a slave, though he is the owner of everything. Instead, he is under guardians and stewards until the time set by his father. In the same way we also, when we were children, were in slavery under

the *stoicheion* of the world. But when the completion of the time came, God sent His Son, born of a
woman, born under the law, to redeem those under
the law, so that we might receive adoption as sons.
And because you are sons, God has sent the Spirit of
His Son into our hearts, crying, "Abba, Father!" So
you are no longer a slave, but a son; and if a son, then
an heir through God.

When Jesus died, we also died to the world's basic principles. Our slavery in the pig-pens of religion had ended, and
we instead were raised in Him, given His Spirit of Sonship,
so that we relate to God as His children. But what does that
mean for us? How does our relationship to God change when
we are given that Spirit?

Consider the difference between a slave and a son. A
slave lives by fear: He is always afraid of punishment for
not doing his duties, and he must always toil to ingratiate
himself with the master of the household by his performance.
He is constantly on a sort of probation. So long as he keeps
working, he can be taken care of and not beaten. He can
continue living his life of meager subsistence. But if he fails
to work, he might be punished, or thrown out of the house,
or even killed.

We might think that being thrown out would mean
freedom for the slave, but in the first century Roman Empire,
slaves who were rejected by their masters would lose their
only hope of support. They had no real rights, were often
terribly uneducated, and generally had no marketable skills
to offer except to be a slave again. There was no hope at that
time—as there was in the antebellum American South—of
escaping north into a land of freedom with full legal rights
and charitable people who would get them on their feet.

But a son has no such worries. His place in the house is
not based on how hard he works for the master of the house-

hold. Rather, the master is his father, so he shares in the fruits of the household. His place in the household is assured, not because he renders to his father the labors his father requires, but because of his identity as the father's son. He cannot be thrown out of the house for not working hard enough. Nor will his father kill him. To be sure, his father might have to sometimes correct him for misbehavior, to teach him as a loving father always does, but the father will not whip and beat him as one would a slave, and the father will not reject him or kill him. His status as a son means that he does not labor to gain profits for his father, but instead he shares with his father in the profits of the entire estate.

When I was growing up, I never had to fear that my father would kick me out of his house. I knew that, no matter what happened, my father would always provide for my needs. I could rest in the assurance that he would take care of me and that he always sought what was best for me.

I was secure in the absolute, undeniable fact that my dad would always love me. Always. Forever. Though he might praise me for bringing home good grades, or he might reprove me for using vulgar language, my place in his heart was never based on my performance: My place in his heart was always assured simply because of *who* I was, his son. Even before I was able to do anything but lay in his arms and suck my thumb, my father loved me because of who he was as my father, and who I was as his son. His love was never earned.

It was mind-boggling for me when I first realized how the Prodigal Brother in me had so deceived me. For my entire life, I had thought my heavenly Father was a worse father than my earthly one. I had always thought I had to do just the right things to stay on His good side. If I didn't do the right things, He would become infuriated and throw me out of His house. But my earthly father would have never done such a thing. Just like the Prodigal Son, the only way I could have gotten out of my earthly father's house is if I had left of my own free will. If my earthly dad would not kick me out of his house because I messed up, why would my heavenly Father do something so unloving?

Like the Galatians, some Christians see their heavenly Father as the worst sort of father imaginable. They perhaps imagine a god who is a drunk. He stumbles home from the bar one night, completely sauced. As he arrives at the driveway, he finds that his younger son has forgotten once more to mow the lawn like he was told. Because of his intoxication, the drunken father becomes irrationally angry. He kicks down the door, growling and yelling, his screams slurred by alcohol. He runs into the younger son's bedroom, ready to beat the kid to death, when suddenly his older son shows up, jumps between him and the younger son, and suffers blow after terrible blow from the mighty fists of his drunken father, until the father exercises the rage out of his system. The older son lies dead on the floor, and the father feels better and callously goes to sleep.

But that is not the Father we have been raised to know. If we who believe are indeed "hidden with Christ in God" through Jesus' resurrection, then we know that God will always love us as He loves His Son Jesus. We are the apple of His eye because Jesus Christ was first. We are His beloved children, in whom He takes pleasure, because Jesus Christ is His Beloved Son in whom He is well pleased. Because Christ holds us in the palm of His steady hand, the Father holds us in His heart for eternity. As Jesus said, "My sheep hear My voice, I know them, and they follow Me. I give them eternal life, and they will never perish—ever! No one will snatch them out of My hand" (John 10:27-28).

The New and Living Way

The true cross and the empty tomb tell us a very different story than religion has ever offered. The Biblical basis for Christian holiness is totally at odds with fear-based religious thinking. Fear motivated the unregenerate man who lived in hostility towards grace. But that man was put to death on the cross. Fear cannot motivate someone who trusts in the new identity given to him or her by the resurrection of Jesus Christ. Fear fails to motivate because the child of God loves and trusts His Father. Growing up, no one could ever have convinced me that if I messed up or did not do enough good deeds, my earthly father would douse me with gasoline and start throwing matches at me. I knew my father. I trusted him completely with my very life. The Christian, because he has been adopted as a child of God, need not fear such things from his heavenly Father either. Only those who reject the adoption of grace are afraid of judgment. As John says (1 John 4:17-19):

> In this, love is perfected with us so that we may have confidence in the day of judgment; for we are as He is in this world. There is no fear in love; instead, perfect love drives out fear, because fear involves punishment. So the one who fears has not reached perfection in love. We love because He first loved us.

"We are as He is in this world," John says. Christians are Abba's children, and thus they need not fear that their Father will destroy them. The love that He has for us drives fear from us, and we begin to know Him and love Him, seeing Him as the safest place for us to be, even when we have messed up. To become mature—fully grown in faith—we must be near the Father, and fear of punishment makes that impossible. Only grace can serve as an antidote to sin, and it is the intimacy He gives us that can transform us into His image. Fear of punishment only brings judgment. It can never make one holy. But the Father's perfect love perfects us. His love transforms with a gentle hand and a quiet whisper and a warm embrace.

When Paul exhorted the immoral Corinthian Christians to put away their former pagan sexual practices, he did not use the argument that God would kick them from His household if they did not do so. He did not tell them that God was horribly angry and could no longer stand the sight of them. Paul knew who they were in Jesus Christ. He said they were "sanctified in Christ Jesus and called as saints" (1 Cor. 1:2).

Paul told the Corinthians, "Do you not know that the unjust will not inherit God's kingdom? Do not be deceived: no sexually immoral people, idolaters, adulterers, male prostitutes, homosexuals, thieves, greedy people, drunkards, revilers, or swindlers will inherit God's kingdom. Some of you were like this; but you were washed, you were sanctified, you were justified in the name of the Lord Jesus Christ and by the Spirit of our God" (1 Cor. 6:9-11). As we said before, when the Prodigal Brother reads this, he only reads the first part, about sinners not inheriting the kingdom. He doesn't read the second part, about how the Corinthian church was filled with people who had been like that. To be "justified in the name of the Lord Jesus Christ" means that God does not call a Christian a sinner. He does not attach to the Christian any of the descriptions Paul gives in this passage, and that is precisely Paul's point: Paul's appeal was not based on the threat of damnation for the saved Christian, but the fact that the Corinthians were contradicting the new and holy identity they had been granted by the purifying blood of Jesus Christ. They weren't living in the enjoyment of the greatest gift that had ever been given to them. Having been delivered from a world they had come to despise, they were contradicting their freedom by letting that world ensnare them all over again. Continuing his line of thought, Paul explains his meaning this way (1 Cor. 6:12-20):

> "Everything is permissible for me," but not everything is helpful. "Everything is permissible for me," but I will not be brought under the control of anything. "Foods for the stomach and the stomach for foods," but God will do away with both of them. The body is not for sexual immorality but for the Lord, and the Lord for the body. God raised up the Lord and will also raise us up by His power. Do you not know that your bodies are the members of Christ? So should I take the members of Christ and make them members of a prostitute? Absolutely not! Do you not know that anyone joined to a prostitute is one body with her? For it says, "The two will become one flesh." But anyone joined to the Lord is one spirit with Him.
>
> Flee from sexual immorality! "Every sin a person can commit is outside the body," but the person who is sexually immoral sins against his own body. Do you not know that your body is a sanctuary of the Holy Spirit who is in you, whom you have from God? You are not your own, for you were bought at a price; therefore glorify God in your body.

Paul's exhortation did not come from the threat of hell-fire, but from an appeal to the church's identity as the bride of Jesus Christ and the Temple of His indwelling. In their letter to him, they had said, "Everything is permissible for me." This is partially true: Because the Christian is saved by grace, he does not live under the threat of "everlasting destruction" for his sins (2 Thess. 1:9). But their statement does not at all reflect the identity of one who has been adopted as a child of God. Recall our discussion in Chapter 4 about how God sees good and evil, versus how fallen man sees good and evil. Religion, reflecting the fallen nature, sees things through categories of "allowed" or "not allowed." It sees everything in terms of rules. But the resurrected man is one that looks at things as good in the original sense: Helpful, beneficial, joyful, and most of all, loving. Or, the resurrected man will see things as evil in the original sense: Twisted, corrupted, and destructive. The Corinthians were still stuck in their religious categories, so they could only see good and evil in terms of what is or isn't allowed. But as Paul countered, the resurrected man knows that not everything is helpful in walking out his life with the Father. The resurrected man has been saved by Jesus Christ in order to be under the gentle leading of the Holy Spirit, not in slavery to his baser passions and addictions.

The Corinthian Christians thought their sexual immorality was acceptable because it reflected the principle of "food for the stomach, and the stomach for food." The implied parallel was, "Sex for the body, and the body for sex." They argued that sexual immorality was only an external matter of no consequence: "Every sin a person can commit is outside the body." But Paul knew that sexual debauchery was much deeper than mere eating. It brought a sort of unity with the other party that was not consistent with the unity of spirit that the believer has with Christ Jesus. Paul did not urge the believers to fear the Father's anger as demonstrated in the cross. Rather, he urged them to understand the moral implications of the resurrection they had shared in. Our spiritual new-birth is God's down-payment on the final resurrection, when our physical bodies are redeemed as well. As such, both our souls and our bodies belong to our compassionate master, Jesus of Nazareth.

Similarly, Paul also used the truth of the resurrection to give the Galatians a New Covenant ethical foundation, apart from the Old Covenant Law to which they had become entangled (Gal. 5:22-26):

But the fruit of the Spirit is love, joy, peace, patience, kindness, goodness, faith, gentleness, self-control. Against such things there is no law. Now those who belong to Christ Jesus have crucified the flesh with its passions and desires. If we live by the Spirit, we must also follow the Spirit. We must not become conceited, provoking one another, envying one another.

Because the Christian has been raised to life by the Spirit, he belongs to God's Spirit. The identity of the Christian, purchased for him by the blood of Jesus Christ, is the most precious gift any human being has ever received. To trust in that identity is to realize that there is a God who desires to free us from the pain and shame that come from sin. The Christian should cherish his identity, not go back to the old ways that were a product of the old identity of sin. To live out of the old identity is to pull the rug out from under himself. It is to live in poverty and chains when the eternal riches and freedom of divine love have been handed to us free of charge.

Thus, the basis of Christian obedience is not the fear embodied in rule-based ways of approaching God, but in a child-like trust through which His Spirit gently guides and instructs and transforms us as a father would shape and guide his beloved children. The fruits of the Spirit are not rules. They are gifts of sublime joy and freedom given us by a loving Father. The reason for Christian holiness is not fear that God will condemn us, nor the shame of not measuring up to a religious standard. The reason for Christian holiness is that holiness is who we are raised to be in Jesus Christ: The Father's children and the Son's bride. Holiness is simply being the new creation Christ made us in His resurrection.

Papa and Abba

When I was young, I would always look forward to time with my maternal grandfather. Papa, we call him. Papa is the sort of unique person who can make everyone he is around think they are each the center of his universe. Papa is the son of a German immigrant, and he inherited the German love of tinkering and mechanics and engineering. When I went to see Papa, or he came to see me, he would involve me in whatever fix-it jobs or mechanical work he was doing.

As he worked, he would describe to me what he was doing, and ask me to help with this or that. He might ask me to fetch him this hammer or hand him that wrench or hold this screw in place. I would of course comply. But why? To be sure, I was being obedient, but I never thought of it this way. I simply thought of it as Papa involving me in his life, and me just taking part in whatever he was doing. I never saw it as a chore I had to do or as a command or obligation I had to achieve in order for Papa to love me. I knew Papa loved me. Everyone who is around Papa knows he loves them. Rather, my obedience was just me being who I am, Papa's grandson. And I was really no *actual* help to Papa. Not in the strictest sense of the word. He could have completed his tasks without me, but Papa included me simply because of who he is, my loving grandfather.

I suspect that our adoption as the sons of our heavenly Father—"Abba," as Jesus and Paul called Him—is meant to bring the same sort of obedience. He doesn't strictly need us to complete whatever thing He might be doing, but He involves us because He loves us. He wants us in His life, and He wants to be involved in ours. Our obedience is one of Him inviting us into His doing, bringing us along to live in the holiness of His life. Obedience comes because we are invited to live along-side Him, not because we are trying to earn the right to be in His presence. The Son, of course, always had the right to be in the Father's presence, and through the resurrection He brought us into that right. So ours is an obedience born of the Spirit of adoption that raised us from the grave. This obedience is simply God being who He is—our Abba—and us being who we are—His kids. Anything else means trying to go back to the slavery of the Prodigal Brother.

Bearing Fruit

When Jesus spoke of the obedience born of His resurrection life, He used the metaphor of a vine with many branches (John 15:1-6):

> I am the true vine, and My Father is the vineyard keeper. Every branch in Me that does not produce fruit He removes, and He prunes every branch that produces fruit so that it will produce more fruit. You are already clean because of the word I have spoken to you. Remain in Me, and I in you. Just as a branch is unable to produce fruit by itself unless it remains on the vine, so neither can you unless you remain in Me. I am the vine; you are the branches. The one who remains in Me and I in him produces much fruit, because you can do nothing without Me. If anyone does not remain in Me, he is thrown aside like a branch and he withers. They gather them, throw them into the fire, and they are burned.

When the Prodigal Brother reads this, he reads it this way: "You are vines meant to bear fruit. If you do not work hard to bear fruit to God, you will be thrown into hell. So work to produce fruit to God, or else." But Jesus did not say it that way. He did not make our justification before God contingent on our fruit-bearing. Rather, He told His disciples, "You are already clean." Jesus did not say we ourselves are vines. He said we are branches connected to the One True Vine. He did not say that we would be thrown into hell if we did not bear fruit. He said we would wither and die if we did not remain in Him, and thus we would be burned as dead yard waste much as one might burn fallen leaves in late autumn.

The source of our life is the life of the Vine to which we are connected. We are alive to the Father because we are recipients of Jesus' life. When you remove a broken branch, you don't do so because it is otherwise perfectly good, but has merely failed to give you enough fruit. Quite the opposite: It doesn't give you enough fruit *because* its internal connections to the vine have withered. It is a dead branch, held on to the vine only by its external skin and bark, and not by its internal veins. The only logical thing to do is cut it off, because it is already essentially dead. So when Jesus says that His Father removes branches that do not bear fruit, it is not His anger resulting in punishment, but the recognition that it is a dead branch that refused to be connected to the Vine's life.

One of the things you will *never* find in a vineyard, are a bunch of branches trying quite hard to bear healthy grapes. You will *not* hear them grunting, *not* see their muscles straining, *not* watch them shake as they work to pop grapes out of their buds. The branches simply bear fruit because of who they are: It is in their DNA. As long as they have a healthy internal connection to the source of life—the vine—they will bear fruit simply because of *who* they are, not because of *what* they do.

Similarly, Jesus did not give us a recipe for fruit-bearing that was based on our ability to figure out the right evangelistic methods or our ability to conquer bad habits through willpower. He did not give us a recipe for fruit-bearing that was motivated by fear of failure, or shame, or earning the

Father's love. In fact, He did not give us a recipe for fruit-bearing at all. Rather, He told us simply to stay in Him. We have died in Him. We have been resurrected in Him. He is our life, as Paul says (Col. 3:4). He is our Vine, the one who gives us the water and nutrients we need to thrive and grow. His resurrection life in us, not our own human power, causes us to produce fruit. We bear fruit only by His power in us, by His guidance and love and joy. And this we only receive if we stay at His side and allow Him to hold on to us. Nouwen explains the difference between remaining in His love, and living to the religious expectations of ourselves and others:

> The farther I run away from the place where God dwells, the less I am able to hear the voice that calls me the Beloved, and the less I hear that voice, the more entangled I become in the manipulations and power games of the world.[2]

But what is this fruit of which Jesus speaks? Is it indeed great feats of evangelism or great religious works or miracles or driving out demons or prophesying? Actually, no, not at all. Jesus explains in Matthew 7:15-23 (NRSV):

> Beware of false prophets, who come to you in sheep's clothing but inwardly are ravenous wolves. You will know them by their fruits. Are grapes gathered from thorns, or figs from thistles? In the same way, every good tree bears good fruit, but the bad tree bears bad fruit. A good tree cannot bear bad fruit, nor can a bad tree bear good fruit. Every tree that does not bear good fruit is cut down and thrown into the fire. Thus you will know them by their fruits.
>
> Not everyone who says to me, "Lord, Lord," will enter the kingdom of heaven, but only the one who does the will of my Father in heaven. On that

day many will say to me, "Lord, Lord, did we not prophesy in your name, and cast out demons in your name, and do many deeds of power in your name?" Then I will declare to them, "I never knew you; go away from me, you evildoers."

Jesus first says we will know false prophets by their fruit. If they are true prophets, they produce good fruit. If they are false prophets, bad fruit. Then, He points to works like miracles, casting out demons, and even prophesying as works that *do not* constitute good fruit in His eyes. People who claimed to be His instruments may have done these things, but that wasn't the fruit He was looking for. It isn't that those things constitute bad fruit, necessarily, but they don't truly constitute fruit at all.

So what is this fruit? It is doing the will of the Father. What is the will of the Father? In the Gospel of John, Jesus says, first, "This is the work of God: that you believe in the One He has sent" (John 6:29), and then, "For this is the will of My Father: that everyone who sees the Son and believes in Him may have eternal life, and I will raise him up on the last day" (John 6:40). The will of God is that we trust in His Son. Only if we trust in His Son do we place our trust in the new identity He has given us. Only when we come to Him as His adopted children can we know the power of His grace in our lives. The only way for us to be at our very best, is to let Him love us even at our very worst.

But lest we find that too ambiguous, Paul actually tells us exactly what fruit Jesus is referring to when He said we bear fruit by staying connected to Him: "The fruit of the Spirit is love, joy, peace, patience, kindness, goodness, faith, gentleness, self-control" (Gal. 5:22-23). In fact, as Paul says, that one towards the end—faith—is the one on which all of the others hinge. The only way for us to bear those fruits, is to trust Him to do so in us, to surrender to His leading in the trust that He knows how to do for us what religion has always taught us we can only do for ourselves. We do not bring about the fruit of the Spirit by substituting our external performance and effort for true internal transformation. Thus, Paul says famously (Eph. 2:8-10):

> For by grace you have been saved through faith—and that not of yourselves; it is the gift of God—not of works, lest anyone should boast. For we are His workmanship, created in Christ Jesus for good works, which God prepared beforehand that we should walk in them.

You might recall that earlier in this chapter we dealt with the preceding verses, Ephesians 2:4-7. Paul is speaking in the context of what the resurrection means for us. The resurrection means living by the Spirit. It means letting the Spirit work in us. It means living out a new life that recognizes that transformation only comes by trusting the Father. Paul says the resurrected life means giving up our trust in our own works—our own performance-oriented attempts to make ourselves good—and instead trusting in God's workmanship in us.

The fruits of the Spirit—love, joy peace, patience, kindness, goodness, gentleness, self-control, and especially faith—are the fruits that Jesus is speaking of. They are fruits internal to us, created in us by the Spirit as He lives in us. It is no wonder that we can only bear these fruits if we remain in His love (John 15:9): These fruits can only be brought out of us if He Himself makes them real within us.

When Jesus spoke of those false prophets who claimed to have performed miracles and prophesied and done all sorts of things in His name, He condemned them because they did not give Him the fruit He truly wanted. He told them, "I never knew you." What if that is what Jesus wants? What if the fruit He truly wants is to know us? Not merely know facts about us, but to know us in the intimacy of relationship?

The fruit Jesus is looking for is not a bunch of religious works to serve an institution or outwardly keep a list of rules. The fruit Jesus is looking for is a fruit that grows from our intimacy with Him. What if that is what the resurrection is all about, raising us up in Him so that we can be His—truly *His*? What if that, above all else, is what He truly wants—*us*? Not *us* as a means for something else, but *us* ourselves. If we shared in Jesus' resurrection in order to become the Father's children, then we are not saved in order to be mere tools God uses for some other purpose. A slave is used for some other purpose. But a father's children *are* his purpose. The fruit the Father brings about in us is meant to be enjoyed by Him, *and* by us. We are made alive by the Spirit through the resurrection, so that we may bear fruit to God. But there is nothing more wonderful for us than this, because it is the joy of being whom God always desired us to be, from before the foundation of the world: His children and the bride of His Son. The fruit of the Spirit lets us be the care-free child and the romantic bride. The fruit frees us from our own agendas and ideas and strivings and performance-based self-valuation.

The Story of the Newspaper Salesman

A few weeks ago, a nice young man appeared on my doorstep. He was representing a local charity that provides fun activities and helpful care for orphans and other disadvantaged children. The man told me outright that he was not asking for donations. Too bad for him. His group sounded like exactly the kind of folks I would like to help. Instead, he said they were giving free delivery of Chicago's *The Daily Herald* newspaper for six weeks. If I signed up for the newspaper, then the *Herald* would give a certain sum of money to the man's organization.

I have no need for a newspaper. I do not read physical print newspapers, and if I did, I certainly would not read *The Daily Herald*, which is the worst of Chicago's three abysmal papers. When people deliver papers to me, I often forget to pick them up, so I end up with multiple papers on my driveway, water-soaked and moldy eyesores. The last thing I need is another worthless paper delivered to my house.

So I told the man I wasn't interested. But the thing is, if he had simply *asked* for my money, I would have gladly given him probably $20, far more than he would have gotten from the *Herald* if I signed up to receive the paper. But he was so insistent on me receiving the paper that I didn't want, that I was offended enough to not offer him anything.

What if that's the way it is with God? What if we come offering Him something He has no desire for, in exchange for His blessings, when really He just desires to bless us whether or not we give Him our own fruit? What if, instead of us giving Him a piece of dry moldy bread, what He desires from us is to live in His love? What if that, and only that, will produce enough delicious fruit for Him *and* us?

That is indeed the message of the resurrection: In Christ, we have died to, and been raised from, that old way of trying to please God through giving Him dry moldy bread. Instead, we have His Life in us, and His greatest desire is simply for us to remain in His love, to stay at His side on His estate, to have Him hold us in our brokenness and whisper to us, "You are my beloved child." We do not have to come before Him as fearful slaves, but as His trusting little children. God knows us, and hears us, because He knows and hears His Son, with whom we are hidden *in* God (Col. 3:3).

"Here there is not Greek and Jew, circumcision and uncircumcision, barbarian, Scythian, slave and free; but Christ is all and *in all*" (Col. 3:11). We have been raised in Jesus to be wrapped up within His perfect relationship with His Father. God will do exceedingly more for us than we can ever expect, because He will never stop loving His Eternal Son, in Whom we abide. We do not slave away trying to give the Father what we think He might want. We have been raised into the life of the Vine. His life will give us every-thing we need, even the fruit of obedience itself. "He who did not spare His own Son, but delivered Him over for us all, how will He not also with Him freely give us all things?" (Rom. 8:32).

Chapter 12

Coming Home

—⁓—

In Christ He demonstrated at Calvary the deep desire
of His heart to have men come under His benevolent
care.

Phillip Keller\A Shepherd Looks at the 23rd Psalm

One night, I flipped on Moody Radio in Chicago on
my drive home from class. I heard a sermon in which
the pastor said our good deeds and rule-keeping were like
deposits into a grace checking account. When we pray, God
examines the balance of grace-cash in our account that we
have accumulated by our religious performance, and if there
is enough, He draws from it to answer our prayers. In other
words, we earn God's provision by our own efforts, a concept
completely at odds with a God Who "is gracious to the
ungrateful and evil" (Luke 6:35) and Who "causes His sun
to rise on the evil and the good, and sends rain on the righteous and the unrighteous" (Matt. 5:45). I had to marvel at
not only what I was hearing, but whom I was hearing it from.
Moody Radio is *the* evangelical radio-station extraordinaire,
highly respected in the national Christian community. Yet
they were broadcasting a sermon that was a complete denial
of the Gospel itself. Perhaps all of us in Christianity should

meditate for a time on Paul's very serious warning: To teach a gospel contrary to his masterful explanation of grace, is to subject oneself to God's curse (Gal. 1:8, 9). This is not merely true for mortal pastors. Paul even said it is true for angels from heaven.

That curse is not simply another religious rule. It is a natural and unalterable fact about spiritual life, both for humans *and* angels. In fact, for any created being. The rejection of grace is the rejection of life. In fact, the first sin was a rejection of the grace of God as symbolized by the Tree of Life. This is not because God arbitrarily demands we accept grace. It is because life is intrinsic only to Him. We cannot earn life by serving Him: In order to serve Him, we must *first* be truly, spiritually alive. The only way to be spiritually alive to Him, is to receive the impartation of His divine life. Life simply cannot be earned. It can only be received, and thus grace is the only means of attaining an everlasting intimacy with God.

So if that is true, why would we ever downplay the importance of grace? Why would a pastor, who has no doubt repeatedly studied Paul's descriptions of grace, ever preach a sermon about earning answers to prayer? That is, in a sense, the question we asked at the beginning of this journey: Why is it that God's grace is so difficult for us to accept? This entire book has aimed to find an answer to that one question, and with it the answer to a greater question: What does God do about it?

The importance of these questions must not be underestimated. As we said, grace is the only means by which we can receive an intimate knowledge of God. As such, grace alone constitutes both the gate and the key to eternal life and the divine joy of authentic holiness (Titus 2:11-14). Despite the central importance of grace in our lives, we see resistance to grace all around us, even in the church, and even in ourselves. We hear it in the aforementioned sermon. We see it when popular Christian authors write books with such subtitles as "How to Attract God's Favor and Blessing." The Gospel's answer to the graceless sermon and the misguided book: Grace is *unmerited* favor. We cannot attract it. We can only receive it.

Rejecting grace is not something that only *other* people are guilty of. It is not simply the sin of non-Christians. We Christians find it even in ourselves. I find it in myself daily, even hourly. I find it when I allow shame and guilt to cloud my vision of the Father's love for me, pushing myself into the darkness of despair and self-torment when my heavenly Father desires instead to cradle me in His arms.

We see it also in our pseudo-Christian clichés. For instance, we repeat to ourselves the mistaken dictum that Christianity can be defined as a commitment to certain moral standards. No, that is not Christianity. Even an atheist can try to live by moral standards. The Pharisees were obsessed with moral rectitude, but they were still heading for destruction. The Christian life is not lived by trying to do things for God. The Christian life is lived by resting on the solid foundation of what God has already done for us. Jesus did not tell us to focus on bearing fruit. He told us that if we focus on remaining in His love, the fruit would take care of itself.

Often we fall prey to the lie that the distinguishing mark of Christianity is moralism, rather than intimacy with a loving God (John 17:3). When confronted with the immorality of an adulterous woman, Jesus Christ told her, "Neither do I condemn you." Jesus tells us it would be better to forgive the most promiscuous homosexual on earth 490 times, than it would be for us to reject him even once. But too many times we Christians focus on condemning the immoral, rather than forgiving them. And because of that, we have made our hearts increasingly unreceptive to God's forgiving grace, a grace that is both for "them" and for us.

On both sides of the political aisle, we Christians portray the destructive lie of the *stoicheion*: If we could just pass the right laws, it would solve the majority of our nation's problems and we would all live happily ever after. But the Gospel says the only real solution to human ills is not politics, but a person, Jesus Christ. Even worse, we find Christians trying desperately to place copies of the Ten Commandments in public buildings. Funny, the New Testament calls the Decalogue the "ministry of death," (2 Cor. 3:7) and says that it had no lasting power to bring holiness or righteousness or life. Instead, Paul said the Decalogue served as a veil over the faces of those who focus on it, keeping them from seeing the life-changing glory of Jesus Christ (2 Cor. 3:7-18). It is possible—nay, *probable*—that posting the Ten Commandments in courthouses can serve to keep others, and even ourselves, from the very One who alone is humanity's cure. If we want to solve America's problems, perhaps we should stop trying to post "the ministry of condemnation" in courthouses, and start turning the hearts of men and women towards "the ministry of righteousness," the loving grace of the Lord Jesus Christ.

Our obsession with politics—on both the Christian right *and* the less numerous Christian left—demonstrates that we have forgotten the point of the Gospel: Laws—even *the* Law given by God at Sinai—are incapable of solving humanity's true problems. In fact, laws, especially religious ones, have the power to keep us from the true solution, the grace of Jesus of Nazareth. Rules only re-arrange the deckchairs of sin on the Titanic of our fleshly lives. Only the cross and resurrection of Jesus Christ have the power to eternally transform the human heart.

Oh, That's Easy

In his book *What's So Amazing About Grace*, Philip
Yancey tells a story that demonstrates the uncanny insight of
the British apologist C.S. Lewis:

> During a British conference on comparative reli-
> gions, experts from around the world debated what,
> if any, belief was unique to the Christian faith. They
> began eliminating possibilities. Incarnation? Other
> religions had different versions of gods appearing in
> human form. Resurrection? Again, other religions had
> accounts of return from death. The debate went on for
> some time until C.S. Lewis wandered into the room.
> "What's the rumpus about?" he asked, and heard in
> reply that his colleagues were discussing Christianity's
> unique contribution among world religions. Lewis
> responded, "Oh, that's easy. It's grace."[1]

Easy, indeed. But so very difficult. The world we see
around us proves that grace is not as easy to fathom, receive,
or live in as we would like to think. If even ourselves—the
adherents of the only grace-centered faith in the world—have
such a difficult time developing world-views that reflect
grace, then we must admit that truly living in the space of
grace is perhaps the hardest thing for a human to do. It may
just be that one of our greatest needs is to discover an answer
to the question, "Why is God's grace so difficult for us to
accept?"

Grace is difficult to accept because of our excuses for
rejecting it. We tell ourselves that if people don't think they
are required to perform to some standard, then they will
sin with abandon. Is this the proper perspective for those
who have been adopted as Abba's little children? After all,
grace is God's act of adopting us as His children even after

we have spat in His face. And moreover, is fear of punishment, or a desire to earn love, a legitimate reason that any child should respect his parents? Would anyone want their own children to obey them simply out of fear of their anger? Would anyone want their own children to think their parents' love had to be earned? Would a child grow up to be a whole and well-functioning adult if he was raised by parents who only accepted him if he did enough good deeds, and who kicked him out of the house whenever he goofed up?

The answer to all of these questions is of course, "No." It is "No" because authentic holy obedience naturally springs from a healthy, intimate love between father and child. It is an obedience and *mutual* respect borne of deep and instinctive relational bonds. How much more powerful would that loving obedience be if the father lived *within* the child, and the child *within* the father? On the other hand, if something would be sick and twisted within an earthly father-child relationship, why do we assume it would be good and healthy — even holy — in a heavenly Father-child relationship? God is better than the best human father, not worse than the worst.

Implicit in our rejection of grace is our own fear that *we* will somehow become rampant sinners if we let go of our fear of punishment and instead seek to live within the grace of God. The very fact that we say something like this shows that we are motivated only by the fear of sinning, rather than love for our Father. More to the point, this statement should testify to us that, if we have any problem, it is in the opposite direction: Legalism.

The unrighteousness of the Pharisees did not result from trusting in grace, but from their unwavering belief that righteousness could be earned through religious and ethical performance. Even with all of their attempts to perfectly keep every one of the 613 commands in the Torah, Jesus still accused them of lawlessness (Matt. 23:28). The Bible tells us it is grace, not the law of religious obligation, that trains us in holiness. God's love living within us is the only way to avoid true lawlessness, whether it be the lawlessness of moral license, or the lawlessness of religious performance.

In my own experience, I have found that the more focused on rules I become, the more I sin. But the more I meditate on the truth that I have a Father in heaven who loves me and gently cares for me, the less desire I have for what is evil, and the more I find within me an overwhelming desire to extend grace and love even to those who do not extend them to me. God's love displaces sin in our lives by giving us the enjoyment of something infinitely greater. But if we do not find perfect love to be more desirable than religious obligation, we will instead desire self-righteousness more than the God Who *is* perfect love itself.

The Gospel does not advocate fear of punishment or religious obligation as a motivation for holiness. Right in the middle of a passage exhorting Christians to live in holiness, Paul explains why he offers his moral instruction: "For the grace of God has appeared, with salvation for all people, instructing us to deny godlessness and worldly lusts and to live in a sensible, righteous, and godly way in the present age" (Titus 2:11-12). Paul also wrote, "The law came along to multiply the trespass. But where sin multiplied, grace multiplied even more, so that, just as sin reigned in death, so also grace will reign through righteousness, resulting in eternal life through Jesus Christ our Lord" (Rom 5:20-21). The laws of religious obligation not only fail to control sin, they multiply it. Paul offers grace, not commandment-keeping, as the opposite of sin. In fact, he offers it as the antidote to sin, because only grace can "reign through righteousness." Only grace has the power to cure us of sin, because only grace relies on omnipotent divine love-power instead of impotent human will-power. Only grace wraps us up in Jesus' life and thus guides and trains us as we follow Him in what He is doing. Therefore, Paul tells us that sin's power over us is broken *because* we are not ruled by obligation, but by grace (Rom. 6:14).

The fact is that fear-based motivation has never produced true holiness. All it can produce is rote rule-keeping. Fear does not bring one to reflect the tender holiness of a loving heart. The entire history of Israel demonstrates that fear of condemnation is not a permanent solution to sin. Instead, God offers the cross and the resurrection as the only cure for the hostility and distrust within us that result in harmful and unloving behaviors.

Another common objection: Isn't all this grace-talk just the same as saying a Christian can just sit on his couch all day gazing at his navel? Obviously, if I put forth the effort to write an entire book about God's grace, that would disqualify me as someone who believes in navel-gazing Christianity. The truth is that grace results in a powerful obedience of authentic relational intimacy, not a faked obedience of religious slavery. Grace brings obedience to us because God's grace invites us to take part in His life, to find our identity in Him, to share in His love for others, and to focus on His love for us. All of these things result, not in our attempt to control our life by religious principles, but in an unavoidable participation in God's life in this world.

A young child who loves to spend time in his father's presence will naturally be brought into whatever act his father is doing. For instance, when I was a child, I would accompany my dad on Friday evening trips to the grocery store. He would often suggest that we go pick out some flowers for my mom. By bringing me into his life of love for my mother, he naturally caused me to fulfill the commandment to honor my mother. But the fact is, I was not seeking to keep the commandment. I was simply seeking to share life with my father. I acted in an authentic holiness simply by being my father's son. In regards to my mother, I was not a couch-potato.

Further, Abraham's life demonstrates that grace does not result in couch-potato spirituality. Abraham is the father of the faithful because he trusted in a God of grace, and that foundational trust, by its nature, brought about a holy obedience, even to the point of offering Isaac. As we discussed in Chapter 5, Abraham could not have obeyed God's order to sacrifice Isaac if he did not completely trust that God would make good on His promises of grace. And the only times Abraham was disobedient came because he was not living out of a trust in God's gracious provision.

The Brother, the Son, or the Loving Father?

Really, all of our human objections to grace stem from an innate human way of thinking that sees our relationship with God as one of slave to taskmaster. Ancient pagan creation myths had the gods create man as slaves because that is how fallen humanity thinks about divinity. But where on earth did we ever get the idea that God's purpose for us is merely keeping rules and doing religious deeds? Where on earth? Apparently, from a serpent, on a tree, in a garden.

The Prodigal Brother thought his assiduous rule-keeping and hard work would gain him something better. In fact, that sounds a good bit like his belief that he could gain a better life by his own "knowledge of good and evil." It wasn't that he wanted to ingratiate himself to the father because he loved the father. Like the monk and the businessman in Chapter 4, he only did good in order to get some greater reward, not because he loved good in itself, or Goodness in Himself. In contrast, faithful Abraham sought God Himself as the exceedingly great reward to be prized above all else.

When the father gave the wayward sibling a celebration, the Prodigal Brother was incensed. He had always thought the way to earn a grand feast was by his hard work and diligent obedience, but the father gave the feast freely to someone who had done nothing to merit such blessings. In that moment, the Prodigal Brother realized all his good works were not worth a dime, and his entire world came crumbling down. He was no better off than his immoral sibling, and in fact was in many ways poorer for his efforts.

The Prodigal Brother's objection wasn't that he missed out on eating the choice steak. After all, the father invited him to eat the fattened calf alongside his returning brother. His problem was that the father did not throw the celebration in honor of *his* hard work, loyalty, and moral performance. In short, he could not accept grace because *he* wanted *his* performance to be the center of the universe.

That's the way it is with grace. The reason we do not accept grace is that it makes God the center of the universe, instead of us. Somehow, that defies everything in our flesh that wants credit for doing good. We so much wanted our abilities to be the most lauded thing in the universe that we created religion just to convince ourselves that such blatant idolatry is actually holy. To put it bluntly, we reject grace because it defies our fleshly desire to make ourselves like gods by our own knowledge of good and evil.

The father's grace for the Prodigal Son made *the father* the center of the estate: It was his love that bound the estate together. It was his love that reconciled the lost son. It was his love that chose to celebrate because celebrating reconciliation is what love does. The father did not give the party to glorify his dishonorable child's dishonorableness. The father chose to give the bash to honor the Prodigal Son precisely because the father's love was the point of the matter. He gave a bash for no other reason than that *he* loved the son.

The Prodigal Brother wanted to boast in his own ability, not in his father's love and grace for him. That is the one common factor in all our excuses for rejecting grace. We have some idea that the point of this entire life is to do enough good things, and avoid enough bad things, so that

God praises us for the excellence of our own moral and religious achievements. We seem to think that is the way things are meant to be: In the end, we boast about what dutiful sons and daughters we were, staying on the estate and toiling like slaves, unlike our younger siblings who gave themselves over to self-indulgence. And then, the father is meant to give *us* a mere young goat because *we* performed so well. But in reality the father has always desired to give us the fattened calf simply because *he* loved us even before we could do anything to earn it.

But to believe this is to cease trusting in ourselves. It is to lose the false illusion of control over our spiritual life that religion gives us. To accept the Father's invitation to the party means trusting that the Father in heaven has something much better to give to us than we could ever give ourselves, and that He will be faithful to give it to us by His free grace, even though we have not been faithful enough to earn it. Such a scenario is deathly frightening to the unredeemed Prodigal Brother within us, because he is governed by the fruit of the Tree of Knowledge of Good and Evil. He simply cannot see life as anything other than an attempt to gain something greater by his own efforts. If God's love comes free of charge, then no slave can receive it. Receiving the greatest thing of all requires giving up our slavish efforts altogether. Since we are by nature slaves, it means we must die and be born again as sons.

Grace is the only basis for human existence and joy. The very nature of a creation's relationship to its Creator can only be one of dependence and trust. That is why Jesus protected the woman caught in adultery. That is why He honored Mary Magdalene when she washed His feet. That is why He honored a tax-collector over a Pharisee. They all knew they depended on His love.

And that is why the father celebrated the return of the Prodigal Son: Unlike his older brother, the younger son had finally learned that his only hope in life was to trust his father to take care of him. The older brother wasn't unlike the younger, really. Both thought they could make it by their own efforts, apart from the father's grace. The only difference is that one tried to make it away from the estate, while the other tried to make it within the estate. The older brother's heart was always distant from the father, even while he was at home on the estate. But the younger brother eventually found his heart yearning for the father, even though he was away. It reminds me of what Paul wrote about the Corinthian church (1 Cor. 1:28-31):

> God has chosen the world's insignificant and despised things—the things viewed as nothing—so He might bring to nothing the things that are viewed as something, so that no one can boast in His presence. But from Him you are in Christ Jesus, who for us became wisdom from God, as well as righteousness, sanctification, and redemption, in order that, as it is written: "The one who boasts must boast in the Lord."

God rejoices over the Prodigal Sons instead of the Prodigal Brothers in order to demonstrate to us the incontrovertible fact that He alone is the source of love, life, and happiness. The only place to find true rest is in God's "My Rest"—to rest in the fact that He is good and gracious and entirely trustworthy. All other ways lead to destruction because they eventually try to make us the creators, creating goodness out of our abilities, rather than receiving goodness from His omnipotent grace. All other paths are attempts to become "like God, knowing good and evil," to replace His gracious provision with the feeble power of our own flesh.

But it is more than that, really. God does not rejoice over the Prodigal Brothers because they will not truly accept His rejoicing. They want a relationship in which they control

Him: They like to remind him that they have done this, that, and the other, and consequently He is obligated to give them something. They don't want Him. They want the things He might give. So they will not accept Him for who He is. God is worthy to have as a Father on the basis of His own loving goodness, not just on the basis of the punishment we fear, or on the goodies we expect Him to give to us. But the Prodigal Brother within us can only accept a false god of religious obligation and performance, because only then can we control him and use him—and the rules we assume he is obsessed with—to get the things we want. That, in a nutshell, is another answer to our question. Why is it so hard for us to accept God's grace? Grace is terrifying to the Prodigal Brother because it means that God is beyond his control. The Prodigal Brother is "hostile in mind" (Col. 1:21) to God. Because he does not believe that God is truly good, he cannot trust God to do good by him.

A World of Hurt

Where does that leave us? One of my favorite places is the Art Institute of Chicago, one of the finest art museums in North America. At the entrance to their European art exhibit, the patron is greeted by a 7 foot by 9 foot master-piece, Caillebotte's *Paris Street*. The painting shows a broad cobble-stoned avenue in the suburbs of 19th century Paris. Finely dressed middle- and upper-class denizens walk the streets on a rainy day, each covered by a large black umbrella. The umbrellas serve to cordon off each pedestrian from the others. Everyone is dreary. Some are walking with their heads down. The clothes are all black or grey, the colors of mourning. All of this, typified by the covering umbrellas, is meant to illustrate humanity's disconnection and alienation from one another, resulting in dreary joylessness.

Caillebotte masterfully demonstrates the sad state of fallen humanity. We are a race of beings who are each alone, isolated from true relationship because we do not accept the only One who can love us in the way we truly and deeply need. We are spiritual orphans, trying to please a cruel master of the orphanage by slaving away and always keeping the orphanage rules. All our fine external trappings and all the umbrella-like coverings of religion, do not so much solve our problems, as they instead make our joylessness and disconnection more pronounced. Religion keeps us joyless because it makes us think that if we do this or that, we will someday convince someone to adopt us—in fact, convince Him to adopt us. It leaves adoption far off, as something we will never truly have but will always yearn for. And because of this, we know only the power of rules—the Law—and not the power of love—God's adoptive grace.

We are people who live under the rule of Law, not the rule of Grace, so we have no grace for each other. Our umbrellas push us away from each other, just like the people passing the street in Caillebotte's masterpiece must give each other a wide berth so as not to knock umbrellas. The Prodigal Brother had no grace for his returning sibling because he believed that dutifully doing the right things, and dutifully avoiding the wrong ones, is the only reasonable basis for dispensing rewards. He had to avoid his younger brother so that the grace given to the Prodigal Son would not tip over the older brother's religious covering. The basis of grace was entirely foreign to the Prodigal Brother, something that invaded his religious world. He could not conceive of a father who gave simply because he loved even the unlovable, rather than because the unlovable made themselves lovable.

So that is how we all feel, somehow unloved and unlovable, but also believing that we—and others—have some ability to make ourselves lovable. Thus, we value others just like we expect that God values us: We only value them in proportion to their efforts to make themselves lovable to us. In the final analysis, we end up valuing neither ourselves nor others. We all end up valueless because we do not accept a gracious God who attaches an infinite value to us for no other reason than that is just who He is. By rejecting love apart from merit, we have made ourselves an unloved species, and thus we do not love. Our umbrellas of religion and human effort do not keep out the cold rain of sin and suffering. They keep out the warm sunshine of the Father's love. We are a broken people inhabiting a broken planet of pain and alien-ation and shame. Despite all our fine external decoration and material excess, we are quite literally in a world of hurt.

A Light Shines in the Darkness

Because God truly loves us apart from any ability on our part to earn it, He chose to redeem our brokenness even though we don't deserve it. As we saw in earlier chapters, when Jesus came to live among us, He spent three and a half years confronting and dismantling our religious thinking. He didn't do it because He had a rebellious heart. He did it because religion is itself a form of rebellion cloaked in the fine silk of moralism. Or, as Barth said, the religious life is nothing but "romantic unbelief."[2] Religion is the Prodigal Brother, living as a slave instead of a son, and demanding his slavery be recognized when God wants to offer instead the freedom of His love. Religion, by its very nature, is indeed unbelief: It cannot believe in a God who truly loves and favors us apart from our efforts to earn it. So the Prodigal Brother in us keeps us from the only thing that can piece together our brokenness: The tender love of our gracious Father. That is why Jesus confronted our religious thinking. He wanted to heal our hurting hearts by confronting the darkness of our false reality with the light of divine love.

But what of our own graceless hearts? To come talking about grace will not do. Our problem isn't that God never exhibited grace before Jesus of Nazareth. He, in fact, offered grace in Eden itself. Our problem is that we by nature will always reject grace. We reject grace because grace is counter to our fallen nature. What if God were to simply throw grace at us when we were still controlled by the Prodigal Brother within us? The result is that we would interpret it as His celebration of our own merits, rather than a celebration of His love. We would be back where we began, thinking that the way to the promised land of glory is through human religious performance. It isn't possible for someone ruled by the fallen slave-nature to approach God in any other way but by religious merit, no matter what we may try to tell him. We would have never actually accepted grace as grace, but misconstrued grace as something we had earned.

In fact, we do the very thing all the time. As Jesus said, God is gracious to the ungrateful and evil, and blesses both the righteous and evil alike. But our own lives confirm to us how often we misinterpret His loving provision as a reward for our good behavior. We enjoy the benefits of grace while retaining the misconception that we are God's slaves.

What we need to truly accept our Father's grace is some radical change deep within our spiritual nature. We need a cure for the spiritual disease of religion. But what's more, we have to be brought to a place where we actually *realize* we need a cure in the first place. No one accepts a cure when he thinks he is well. Jesus, after all, said only the sick need a physician, not the healthy.

That is why, as Paul says, God saves us by bringing us under His *krisis* (Rom. 3:19-21), a crisis of judgment in which we see the brokenness of the Prodigal Brother within us, and then find in contrast the loving goodness of a God of grace. Truly, God uses religious obligation to bring us to the end of religious obligation. In other words, God shows us that righteousness cannot be achieved by trying to do good things, no matter how "righteous" those things might be in themselves. In the end, religious obligation doesn't so much bring us directly to repentance, as it brings us into a crisis in which we see ourselves as the wolves we are. But it is God's grace that brings us to repentance, because it is God's grace that gives us a safe place in which to admit our faults. It is grace that takes us into the celebration of the Prodigal's return.

The Prodigal Son did not repent of his sins against the father until *after* the father had embraced him and fell on his neck in tears. So often, we want to keep up the Prodigal Brother's religious veneer, because we are terrified of what will happen if we are unmasked. But when God brings us under His *krisis*, He does it so that He can demonstrate Himself as a God of grace who is willing to take all of our shame and guilt and spiritual nakedness. He shows Himself as One Who can unmask us gently and safely, so that He can cure our brokenness by covering us in the fine royal robes of His estate. He gives us the hunger pains in the pig pens of human religion in order that we accept His embrace when He comes running for us.

By bringing the Prodigal Brother within us under His judgment, God demonstrates to us our complete self-condemnation. He shows us that under the fine clothing of religiosity, moral rectitude, business acumen, or whatever else, we are sickly, diseased, scabby, and pale. To rid us of this disease of performance-based thinking, He takes our hostility to His grace and nails it to the cross. In the person of the Son, He took our death, the natural result of a self-dependent spirit. He allowed our death to outwork itself within Himself, and He suffered under the pain and alienation that our grace-hating spirit produces. He endured a pain no human has ever known, in order to effect a cure for our disease.

In His blood He delivers that cure to us, removing the Prodigal Brother-ness in us that would not allow us to accept the invitation to return to the Father's house. "In Christ, God was reconciling the world to Himself" on the cross (2 Cor. 5:19). We were hostile in mind, but in Christ our hostility may be put to death so that we may accept Jesus' plea, "Be reconciled to God" (2 Cor. 5:20).

Having put the Prodigal Brother in us to death, He raises us in His resurrection, uniting us forever with Himself by grace. He wraps us in the royal robe of His estate, the resurrection life of Jesus Christ. God invites us to partake in the Son's loving intimacy with the Father. We are adopted from the orphanage of religion into the estate of the Father's grace.

From Slavery to Sonship

The problem with humanity is simply that we are slaves. We want to be free, but only free to live in more slavishness. We want our slavishness to triumph over the slavishness of others, and in the end we desperately want our slavishness to triumph over freedom. The reason is quite simple: We have come to identify with our chains, to believe that our chains are good and holy, and to fear that if our chains are removed, we will be destroyed. We are so afraid of getting it wrong, and thus inciting God's anger, that we think fear is the only proper way to relate to God. Because of this, we fear that living in His grace will somehow mislead us into angering Him.

To remove our shackles, God puts to death the Prodigal Brother within us who can only think of himself and God in the terms of slavery. The Prodigal Brother within us isn't just in chains. He *is* our chains. We fear freedom because the Prodigal Brother within us is has cowed us into believing that toiling as a slave is the only means to avoid eternal hellfire.

The Prodigal Brother chose to starve outside his father's house rather than go into the feast and thus admit that grace was greater than his own efforts. To enter the party would have been to feel the shame of the realization that his entire life was built on a false understanding of who his father was. Similarly, we fear any attempt to destroy our chains because if our chains are destroyed, so is our self-righteous identity as a dutiful and perfect slave on the estate. We cannot deal with the way grace strips us naked, taking off the fine adornment of human effort in order to bring us to God in our vulnerability.

Thus, we need a new identity. We need an identity that is not bound by the shackles of our own abilities and efforts. We need our chains, the spirit of the Prodigal Brother, broken for us. At Calvary, Jesus took our manacles within Himself. He became the blast furnace in which our steel shackles were melted away. He endured the pain of the intense heat needed to melt our bonds, and died from the molten metal within Him. But His life triumphed over the death of our slavery, and His blood cleanses us of the Prodigal Brother within us.

When He rose, He brought us up with Him, giving us a new identity as the Father's little children. He removed our fear of grace by giving us a spirit of sonship. A son naturally receives his father's grace. Living by his father's grace is what a son does, even before he is born. It is part of a son's sonly nature. Likewise, when we are born-again as sons and daughters of God, we become able to receive His grace in our lives. We stop pushing Him away with our arms, and we allow Him to draw us close with His.

Just the Way You Are

I am reminded of a pastor I once knew. Often, in the middle of a service, he would remind us of one simple and beautiful truth: "God loves you just the way you are, and He loves you so much that He isn't going to let you stay that way." God loves each and every broken little lamb, each and every starving little Prodigal Son and Daughter, each and every lash-worn slave of the *stoicheion* of this world. And He loves us so much, that He refuses to let us stay that way.

That it is the message of the cross of Jesus Christ. In a sense, Jesus became a Prodigal Son Himself, but a Prodigal Son of obedience, not dissipation. He and His Father desired to bring us back to the estate. He left His Father's estate and came after us while we were still away in "a distant country" (Luke 15:13). He lived next to us on the pig farms of human religion so that He could free us from that life and bring us back to our Father. That is why we needed the cross, so that He could bring us home. Jesus died and rose again, so that we could be born again, at home with our Father. The cross happened so that we would be willing to accept the adoption as Prodigal Sons. Jesus put to death the Prodigal Brother in us who desired to be a slave instead of receiving the adoption as a son.

> And He re-ascended to heaven. Then in the silence, looking at His Son and all His children, since His Son had become all in all, the Father said to His servants, "Quick! Bring out the best robe and put it on Him; put a ring on His finger and sandals on His feet; let us eat and celebrate! Because my children who, as you know, were dead and have returned to life; they were lost and have been found again! My prodigal Son has brought them all back." They all began to have a feast dressed in their long robes, washed white in the blood of the Lamb.[3]

Why is it so hard for us to accept grace? Why is it so difficult for you and I to accept the Father's unconditional and unmerited love? Why do we have such trouble trusting that He really does desire the best for us? Because thousands of years ago a disease entered us, wrapped in a piece of fruit, offered by a sly little snake. It was a disease of human effort, a spirit that desired to earn what was given, to build for itself a home while rejecting the mansion that was already constructed for us. We reject God's grace today because we did so at the very beginning, and plunged ourselves into the depths of darkness. We became the Prodigal Brother, slaving away on the estate, hoping to earn what was always offered freely, hoping we could merit a meal of a young goat, when our Father has always wanted us to feast on the fattened calf, free of charge. It is hard for us to accept grace for one very simple reason: We think we are slaves, when God wants us to be His kids.

To set us free, Jesus Christ put our disease to death in His cross and raised us up in His life. God did not need the cross to love us. God did not need the cross so He could feel okay about us. God did not need the cross to get His anger out of His system with a great cosmic temper tantrum. *We* needed the cross in order to be reconciled to Him, to be freed from our self-reliant religious works in order to return to His "My Rest." *We* needed the cross to transfer us from the slavery of the Old Jerusalem, to the freedom of the New. *We* needed the cross in order to be rescued from the pig pens of the world's religious principles. *We* needed the cross in order for the Prodigal Brother in us—our chains of slavery—to lay down and die, so that he could no longer keep the Prodigal Son in us from falling into the Father's arms. That is the message of the cross of Jesus Christ: God loves us—the ragged, dirty, and malnourished Prodigal Sons and Daughters of this world—just the way we are, and He loves us so much that He isn't going to let us stay that way.

Endnotes

—✺✺✺—

Introduction: A Difficult Grace

1. Hufford, D. "The Works Addiction" (Blog Post). *The Free Believers' Network*. http://www.freebelievers.com.
2. Tertullian, *Apology*, Chapter XXX.

Chapter 1: In Vino, Veritas

1. Latin: "In wine, there is truth."
2. Banks, R. *Paul's Idea of Community*, p. 15
3. Note Paul's use of *stoicheion*, or the "basic principles of the world," (NIV) in Gal. 4 and Col. 4. Cavey, B. *The End of Religion*, p. 34.
5. Yancey, P. *What's So Amazing About Grace?*

Chapter 2: The Genesis of Grace

1. Lewis, C.S. *Mere Christianity*, p. 50.
2. There is a theory, called the Documentary Hypothesis, that says the first five books of the Bible were written in separate forms by multiple authors over hundreds of years, and then sown together by a redactor in the four or five hundreds BC. An archaeological discovery by Israeli archaeologist Gabriel Barkay revealed major

problems with that interpretation, because parts that weren't supposed to exist together before 600 BC were found wrapped around each other in an abode from about 200 years before then. Further, parts of the text that are supposedly written by different authors are found together essentially mid-sentence or mid-thought, indicating a seamless authorship. Ultimately, I suspect the hypothesis is merely western man foisting his ideas of how to write literature over onto the ancient near-eastern Jews.

3. Viola, F. *From Eternity to Here*, pp. 18-19.
4. Barth, K. *The Epistle to the Romans*, Rom. 1:4-7.

Chapter 3: Leaving Home

1. God sometimes He refers to Himself in the metaphor of a mother (Is. 66:13, Matt. 23:37).
2. Lewis. C.S. *The Magician's Nephew.*

Chapter 4: God Flushes the Toilet

1. Yeats, W.B. "The Second Coming."
2. Strong's Greek/Hebrew Definitions, OT:7451
3. *Ibid.*
4. Strong's Greek/Hebrew Definitions, OT:7489

Chapter 5: The Faithful, of the Father

1. *Bible Knowledge Commentary*, Gen. 15:6.
2. Luther, M. *Commentary on Galatians*, Gal. 1:1. Trans. by Timothy Graebner.
3. Jacobsen, W. *He Loves Me!* pp. 169-170.
4. Quoted in *The End of Religion* by Bruxy Cavey.
5. Nouwen, H. *The Return of the Prodigal Son*, p. 39.

Chapter 6: The Ministry of Condemnation

1. I used the NRSV here, rather than the HCSB, because its translation as "disciplinarian" is closer to the Greek meaning than the HCSB's "guardian."
2. Brinsmead, R. "Sabbatarianism Re-examined," p. 13.
3. Galatians 5:2, especially, shows that Paul's audience were not yet circumcised, meaning they were not Jews. But they were considering becoming Jews by going through the rite of circumcision.
4. See also Rom. 7:1-6, where Paul equates being under the Law to being "in the flesh."
5. DeLashmutt, G. "Paul's Usage of *ta stoicheia tou kosmou*." Xenos Christian Fellowship, http://www.xenos.org/essays/stoich.htm
6. Luther, M. *Commentary on Galatians*, Gal. 4:3. Trans. by Timothy Graebner.

Chapter 7: Anno Domini

1. Lev. 4:2, 22, 27; 5:15, 18; Num. 15:22, 24 – 28; 35:11, 15.
2. Strobel, L. *The Case for Christ*, p. 106.

Chapter 8: Broken and Beloved

1. Strange, J. "Nazareth." *Anchor Bible Dictionary*. Quote taken from Wikipedia.
2. Yancey, P. *The Jesus I Never Knew*, p. 32.
3. *Ibid*, p. 32.
4. Cole, N. *Organic Church: Growing Faith Where Life Happens*, p. 156.
5. Yancey, P. *Ibid.*, p. 258.
6. Pritchard, Ray. *Credo: Believing in Something to Die For*, p. 57

7. Yancey, P. *Ibid.*, p. 33
8. Jamieson, R., A.R. Fausset, and D. Brown. *A Commentary Critical, Experimental, and Practical, on the Old and New Testaments*. Luke 15:20.

Chapter 9: The Prodigal Son's Punishment

1. Full title: "A Participatory Model of the Atonement."
2. Jacobsen, W. "Easter and My Struggle with the Brutality of God's Plan." Crosswalk.com. http://www.crosswalk.com/spirituallife/11601827/
3. Bayne, T. and G. Restall. "A Participatory Model of Atonement." In *New Waves in Philosophy of Religion*, p. 152. Edited by Yujin Nagasawa and Erik J. Wielenberg.
4. *Ibid.*, p. 153.
5. Spurgeon, C. *Spurgeon's Morning & Evening,* Day 8.
6. I use the KJV here because it still retains a more literal sense of the Hebrew wording regarding judgment. Because this concept of judgment is so foreign to the modern reader, more recent translations deal with the words more idiomatically, merely giving a sense to the reader of what the word implies.
7. *Theogeek: Hilasterion in Romans 3:25.* (http://theo-geek.blogspot.com/2007/07/hilasterion-in-romans-325.html)

Chapter 10: If One Died for All

1. Ladd, G.E. *A Theology of the New Testament.* Quoted in "Redeeming the Cross" by Steve Chalke.
2. Jacobsen, W. "Easter and My Struggle with the Brutality of God's Plan." *Crosswalk.com.* http://www.crosswalk.com/spirituallife/11601827/
3. Chalke, S. "Redeeming the Cross," p. 3.

4. Barth, K. *The Epistle to the Romans*, Rom. 1:17. Emphasis in the original. (This, above all others, is my favorite quote outside of Scripture).

5. A special gratitude goes to Wayne Jacobsen, whose writings served in many ways as the inspiration for this section.

Chapter 11: When We Rise

1. Lynch, J., Bill Thrall and Bruce McNichol. *Bo's Café*, p. 89.

2. Nouwen, H. *The Return of the Prodigal Son*, p. 47.

Chapter 12: Coming Home

1. Yancey, P. *What's So Amazing About Grace?*

2. Barth, K. *The Epistle to the Romans*, Rom. 2:5-6.

3. Marie, Pierre. Quoted in Nouwen, H. *The Return of the Prodigal Son, p. 573*

CPSIA information can be obtained at www.ICGtesting.com
Printed in the USA
LVOW090208050312

271587LV00001B/59/P